Brilliancy

Books by A. H. Almaas

Essence with *The Elixir of Enlightenment:*
The Diamond Approach to Inner Realization

Facets of Unity: The Enneagram of Holy Ideas

The Inner Journey Home: Soul's Realization of the Unity of Reality

Luminous Night's Journey: An Autobiographical Fragment

DIAMOND MIND SERIES

Volume 1. *The Void:*
Inner Spaciousness and Ego Structure

Volume 2. *The Pearl Beyond Price: Integration of Personality*
into Being: An Object Relations Approach

Volume 3. *The Point of Existence:*
Transformations of Narcissism in Self-Realization

DIAMOND HEART SERIES

Book One. *Elements of the Real in Man*

Book Two. *The Freedom to Be*

Book Three. *Being and the Meaning of Life*

Book Four. *Indestructible Innocence*

DIAMOND BODY SERIES

Spacecruiser Inquiry:
True Guidance for the Inner Journey

Brilliancy: The Essence of Intelligence

For more information on A. H. Almaas and
all of his publications, please go to:
www.ahalmaas.com

Brilliancy

THE ESSENCE
OF INTELLIGENCE

☙

A. H. Almaas

Diamond Body Series: II

Shambhala
Boston & London
2006

Shambhala Publications, Inc.
Horticultural Hall
300 Massachusetts Avenue
Boston, Massachusetts 02115
www.shambhala.com

©2006 by A-Hameed Ali

All rights reserved. No part of this book may be reproduced in any form or by any means, electronic or mechanical, including photocopying, recording, or by any information storage and retrieval system, without permission in writing from the publisher.

9 8 7 6 5 4 3 2 1

First Edition
Printed in the United States of America

♾ This edition is printed on acid-free paper that meets the American National Standards Institute Z39.48 Standard. Distributed in the United States by Random House, Inc., and in Canada by Random House of Canada Ltd

Designed by Jeff Baker

Library of Congress Cataloging-in-Publication Data
Almaas, A. H.
Brilliancy: the essence of intelligence / A. H. Almaas
p. cm.—(Diamond body series; 2)
Includes index.
ISBN-13: 978-1-59030-335-1 (alk. paper)
ISBN-10: 1-59030-335-0
1. Intellect. 2. Wisdom. 3. Intellect—Religious aspects. I. Title
BF431.A554 2006
153.9—dc22
2006000547

Contents

The Diamond Body Series vii

Editor's Preface xi

Introduction 1

Part One 5

  1. Brilliancy and Intelligence 9
  2. Synthesis 25
  3. Presence and Time 41
  4. Completeness 53

Part Two 61

  5. Brilliant Inquiry 63

Part Three 89

  6. Meeting One 93
  7. Meeting Two 115

8. Meeting Three 139

9. Meeting Four 173

10. Meeting Five 201

11. Meeting Six 235

12. Meeting Seven 255

13. Meeting Eight 273

About the Diamond Approach 303

Index 305

The Diamond Body Series

This series of books is an attempt to outline the methodology of the Diamond Approach, a contemporary spiritual teaching with its own direct understanding and view of reality. The Diamond Body series refers to the practice and embodiment of the Diamond Approach, as a complement to the Diamond Heart series, which pertains to the direct experience of true nature on this path, and the Diamond Mind series, which relates to the objective knowledge and conceptual understanding of this teaching.

The series ranges from direct discussion of methodology, to the illustration of various applications within different contexts, to the integration of some of the classical methods of spiritual work into this teaching. Some of the volumes in this series illustrate the methodology through actual work on elements of the body of knowledge that is unique to the Diamond Approach teaching, such as the aspects of spiritual essence, the dimensions of reality, and the facets of mind.

To appreciate the place and function of the methodology in any approach to spiritual work, we need to understand how the methodology relates to the view of reality on which it is based and to the teaching that arises from that view. This understanding will help clarify the role of this series of books in the revelation of the Diamond Approach.

Throughout history, human beings have felt the need for intentional, focused work and guidance, to be able to advance beyond the average human development known in most societies. Much of our human potential lies in realms not accessible or even visible to normal consciousness. This is specifically the case for humanity's spiritual potential, which is the ground of human consciousness and the source of true and lasting fulfillment, peace, and liberation.

This situation has led to the arising and development of many teaching schools throughout the ages, inner work schools that specialize in the development of the total human being—particularly the actualization of the depth of human potential. Such a spiritual school is usually built on a teaching that emerges from a specific logos—a direct understanding of reality and the situation of human beings within that reality. Through the teaching, the logos reveals a path toward the actualization of our human potential. The methodology of the path also reflects the wisdom arising from this direct understanding. It is not just a haphazard collection of techniques aimed at helping students to arrive at certain inner states. The methodology will be successful in unfolding the path when it is a faithful expression of the particular logos of that teaching. You could say that practicing the methodology of a teaching is the specific key needed to open the door of this teaching's logos of experience and wisdom.

This understanding of the relationship between logos, teaching, method, and reality has another important implication. As a methodology is practiced within the logos of a particular teaching, objective reality will reveal itself in forms relevant for the journey of self-realization undertaken through that teaching. In other words, a profound and fundamental manifestation of reality characteristic of one teaching may never arise for followers of a different teaching, because each teaching orients to reality through a different logos.

One way of understanding this is that because each teaching traverses different terrain in its unfolding journey, the same underlying reality will be revealed in different forms along the way. Consider, for example, that the Inuit people of the Arctic Circle recognize more than twenty forms of snow and ice. These are true forms of physical reality never recognized by someone living in temperate latitudes, because the climate and the demands of the environment are different. In a similar way, followers of a spiritual teaching will encounter distinct experiences of objective reality that are appropriate to the journey of the soul addressed by that teaching.

This awareness is especially important in understanding descriptions of essential reality in the books that come out of the Diamond Approach. The methodology of the Diamond Approach prepares the soul to experience, perceive, and appreciate that Being appears not only as needed at any given point in her journey, but also in specific forms—which we call essential aspects—that arise in response to the constantly changing needs of the individual soul. However, though these states and qualities are referred to as universal and fundamental to all human souls and to reality itself, this does not mean that people engaged in deep spiritual work based on another logos will encounter reality in the form of essential aspects. Other teachings align the soul for traversing other paths of realization, and so essential reality may appear differently.

The central thread of wisdom informing the methodology of the Diamond Approach is that our normal human consciousness does not possess the knowledge or skill necessary for traversing the inner path of realization. However, the intelligence of our underlying spiritual ground tends to spontaneously guide our consciousness and experience toward liberation. This spiritual ground, which is the ultimate nature of reality, is unconditionally loving and compassionate in revealing its treasures of wisdom to whoever is willing to open to it. We simply need to recognize the truth about our present experience and learn the attitudes and skills that will invite the true nature of reality to reveal itself. Toward that end, this methodology brings together classical spiritual techniques and new practices that can help us be open and vulnerable to our true nature.

The task of communicating the teaching and logos for this method is the central function of the Ridhwan School, its teachers, and all the literature of the Diamond Approach. Like any genuine spiritual teaching, the degree to which this logos reveals itself depends on how faithfully the method is applied. And the skill in applying the methodology develops over time as the experience and understanding of the teaching matures.

However, since this method arises from a true logos of reality, and therefore is inherent to objective reality, it is available for anyone to learn regardless of whether they are in contact with the Ridhwan School—if they are able to recognize the truth of this view for themselves. This means that it is possible to connect to this logos and practice its particular method by seriously studying the teaching on one's own. To do so, however, requires an unusual degree of sincerity, devotion, and intelligence. Such is the limitation of the printed word, in contrast to the direct transmission that can occur when one is in contact with an exemplar of the teaching. Hence, we can only hope for limited benefits when the method is practiced apart from the active guidance of the teaching and the teacher.

Still, we believe there is value in providing some understanding of the methodology of the Diamond Approach. This is for the benefit of not only the students directly engaged in this work, but also the readers who would like to learn and practice some of the elements of the method on their own. In addition, we hope this series will be useful in appreciating the contribution of this approach to an overall understanding of reality, human nature, and what it means to actualize humanity's full potential.

Because the heart of this methodology is a disciplined invitation to reality to reveal its secrets, the Diamond Body series offers the unique benefit of supporting both the pursuit of the inner path of realization and the exploration of the deeper principles of investigation and study that are relevant in any research discipline. Using elements of the Diamond Approach methodology can lead not only to a quickening and an openness to aspects of our inner potential, but also to the development of skills that can be useful for study in other fields within the sciences and humanities.

This is the universal message of the Diamond Approach: When we learn how to invite our true nature to reveal itself, it will guide us toward realizing our spiritual ground and, at the same time, actualize our potential in all walks of life.

Editor's Preface

What if you could experience intelligence directly? Not just experience having a smart thought or making a wise choice, but actually experience the feeling of intelligence itself. What if you could sense the element in your consciousness that, when it is present and active, imbues you with intelligence?

Intelligence is generally considered to be a characteristic of our mind that some people have more of and others less of, leading some of us to feel smart, others not so smart, and some stupid. But what if intelligence is not just an attribute, not just a description of how we perceive ourselves when certain conditions are met? What if it is an actual quality in our experience that we can sense, in the same way that we sense joy, for example? We know that if we pay attention at the times when we are feeling joy, we can describe the actual sensation of joy. What if we could do the same thing with intelligence?

In *Brilliancy*, A. H. Almaas does just that. He describes in detail and with precision the very source of intelligence as a brilliant presence in our consciousness. He invites us into our own experience of this source, what he calls the essential quality of Brilliancy.

Most books and studies about intelligence are oriented toward its practical application—what it can do for you and how to acquire more of it. The more technical or scientific books tend to focus on analyzing the source of intelligence in the functioning of the human brain. In hospitals, labs, and research centers, scientists are attempting to explain how the mind works, by studying our mental capacities and functions and correlating the data with our current understanding of our biochemistry and the physiology of our nervous system. The question is intriguing, but the answer has always been elusive: How is it that we are able to be intelligent creatures?

The various current approaches to answering that question explore intelligence through types of awareness, capacities, or behaviors that are believed to result from the functioning of intelligence in the individual. Tests such as IQ measurements are based on the assumption that if you can do a particular thing or if you respond in a certain way, then you have intelligence—or at least a particular intelligence related to those actions. The assumption underlying these tests is that the greater one's intelligence, the greater one's success. And though it has become clear that intellectual know-how is not a guarantee of success in life, we now have the additional complexity of considering emotional and moral intelligence—not to mention spiritual intelligence—in our search for a more productive and rewarding life.

What is unique about *Brilliancy* is that it explores the *direct experience* of intelligence. It does not attempt to provide alternatives to scientific methods of measuring it or offer practical advice on how to get smart quick. Almaas is looking at the actual nature of our consciousness itself: What is it in us that results in intelligent thinking, behavior, and action? To answer this question, he does not engage in intellectual exercises, academic research, or conceptual arguments, but instead he guides us through direct and intimate contact with intelligence as it appears in our own consciousness.

Almaas shows us that intelligence is a gift inherent in human nature that we can learn to contact and appreciate. He challenges the view that we become intelligent through practice or by increasing our knowledge, our skill, or our cleverness. Our essential intelligence becomes more available through a process of understanding what prevents it from spontaneously operating. Our inquiry, then, is actually a matter of exploring how the natural and effective movement of our true nature in our mind, our behavior, and our actions has been blocked as we have grown up.

Almaas's work evidences its own brilliancy in its capacity to guide us in that inquiry and help us to contact the subtlety and power of intelligence as a presence in our experience. With great depth of insight, he articulates both the psychodynamic and the phenomenological barriers to this aspect of our true nature. In addition to the talks in which Almaas shares this understanding, *Brilliancy* offers a unique glimpse of the power of the method of inquiry that he has developed. Transcripts of the author's work with his students make up the latter half of this book. And it is here that we witness his students discovering the blocks to their own essential intelligence. Through Almaas's open curiosity and the guidance of his questions, they confront their conditioning and in that process begin to experience intelligence directly.

We are all familiar with the strong association of certain aspects of human nature with masculinity or femininity. Warmth, softness, receptivity, and love tend to be associated with the feminine, while strength, independence, will, and reason are linked with the masculine. Intellectual achievement is also often believed to be more outstanding in males. Men are valued for their brains and women for their beauty, a cultural stereotype that has not been fully eradicated even though it has long been discredited. Though women have excelled in all areas where intelligence is a major standard, the biases still run deep in our conditioning.

Almaas does not directly address in this book the societal aspects of human intelligence, but he does reveal a fundamental factor that may well play a part in these broader social issues. Through his extensive work on himself and with students of the Diamond Approach, he has discovered what seems to be a basic element in every person's development that shapes our access to and experience of our essential Brilliancy: our unresolved relationship with our father. Essential intelligence is projected on the father, or the primary father figure, by the young soul, who then unconsciously believes that the source of intelligence *is* that person. As a result, the child's emotional and physical relationship with the father will profoundly affect how intelligence comes to be unconsciously perceived and understood as the child develops.

As Almaas's students explore their relationships to their fathers in this book, we get to see the complexity and challenge of this veil over our own personal brilliance. And as we observe the students in process, we can also appreciate how understanding our history experientially can immediately open us to the presence of this quality. In witnessing one breakthrough after another, we are inspired by the discovery that although Brilliancy may be fundamentally linked to our issues with our father, once freed it is purely our own. It is a quality of our presence, inseparable from us as a living consciousness, and is in no way dependent on our father, his love, his attention, or his support.

Almaas shows us that Brilliancy is a basic expression of our true nature because it is inherent in the nature of reality itself. It is directly linked to the underlying intelligence of the universe, the exquisite and luminous nature of the patterning and functioning of all of creation. Since Brilliancy is an inherent quality of the fundamental spiritual ground of reality, then the development of the universe, on all levels, animate and inanimate, would have to express this intelligence. Recent developments in the study of evolution, and findings about cosmic constants, may indicate the functioning of this intelligence. They clearly show that random mutations alone cannot account for the complexity of life's development in the relatively short time since it appeared on Earth, and that randomness can hardly explain the reality of cosmic constants.

These recent discoveries about the development of the universe and of life on our planet have spawned many theories. Those circles that believe that these phenomena indicate intelligence have developed the view called Intelligent Design. Though Almaas does not take a stand on the formulations of Intelligent Design, he experiences intelligence implicit in the form and unfoldment of the universe. And he strongly believes that a deeper understanding of what intelligence is can help the ongoing discussion of this subject in the culture at large.

The understanding of Brilliancy as the essential intelligence in the universe finds no conflict between a fundamental intelligence and the evolutionary process, whether of the universe or the life within it. In fact, we can see this intelligence operating in the universe in a way that directly supports the scientific observations of evolutionary theory and the new understanding of cosmic constants.

In this book, by exploring essential intelligence as it appears in our personal lives, Almaas reveals how this quality directly impacts our experience of time and presence, our recognition of meaning in the various threads of our experience, and the sense of completeness in our own souls. It is Almaas's revelation of this spiritual nature of Brilliancy as the ground of our individual intelligence that truly sets this work apart from others on the subject. As he has done in all of his books, Almaas takes us into the heart of the matter by reminding us of how that spiritual ground is inseparable from a full human life. *Brilliancy* leaves no doubt that the more we recognize and appreciate that ground of Beingness, the more intelligently our life will unfold and grow.

Byron Brown

Brilliancy

Introduction

What is intelligence? Is it simply one element in the functioning of the brain? If so, how much of it is determined by heredity and how much by one's upbringing? If not, is it a quality or mode of consciousness? And if it is an expression of consciousness, what then is its relationship to the physical body, and to the brain in particular? And what influences its development? Looking at intelligence as an expression of consciousness, we can see it in one of two ways, depending on the theory—either as an epiphenomenon of brain development or as a phenomenon that emerges only when brain complexity reaches a certain level.

These questions point to how controversial the nature of intelligence is, especially in light of contemporary scientific theories. And if we are familiar with spiritual teachings, the situation may appear even more complex. In those contexts, spirit or spiritual nature is frequently described as intelligence or the intelligence in all things, and we also hear that the universe has intelligence underlying or governing it.

In this book, it is not my primary interest to address these questions, nor do I intend to challenge the various positions except in limited ways. Clearly there is evidence that intelligence is related to brain functioning and that it is partly related to hereditary factors and partly to environmental ones. And it is obviously related to the functioning of consciousness.

My attempt in this book is simply to point out another element related to intelligence, another dimension of it that can be directly experienced and ascertained. In understanding this dimension of intelligence, we will see how it is related to consciousness, without challenging the evidence that correlates it to brain functioning or heredity and environment. Yet we will also see how our spiritual nature is the deepest source of intelligence and, therefore, why spirit is frequently referred to as intelligence.

The understanding reflected in this book is a result of a particular spiritual transformation that reveals the ground and nature of consciousness. This ground turns out to be the underlying nature of everything, even the physical universe—and hence the body and its brain. This spiritual ground, what we call Essence—the essence of consciousness and all of reality—reveals itself through many qualities, which are primordially inherent to it.

These qualities may manifest undifferentiated from each other—as the presence of spiritual nature beyond mind and normal experience—or as differentiated and discriminated experiences of ontological presence. In the latter case, spiritual nature manifests itself through differentiated qualities, which we refer to as essential aspects. These essential aspects are intimately related to our various mental, emotional, physical, and spiritual faculties.

One thing we discover in this revelation of the nature of spirit is that it is characterized not only by qualities such as Power, Love, and Truth, but also by a particular luminosity that appears to our mind to be intelligence. In other words, we realize that we can actually experience intelligence directly—not through an activity, as we normally do, but as a palpable presence, as a presence of pure consciousness characterized by intelligence.

We find out that intelligence is an inherent quality of our spiritual nature, fundamentally inseparable from it. Yet in functional activities, it flows through our consciousness, and through its physiological supports—the brain and the nervous system—to give these functions a kind of efficiency and completeness we usually associate with intelligence.

We discover our spirit as intelligence, intelligence that manifests in what we call intelligent functioning, yet is experienceable directly and apart from its functioning.

We experience ourselves, then, not as *having* intelligence but present *as* intelligence. In this experience, we find out what the essence of intelligence is, the source of this capacity. In our study in this book, I discuss not only the characteristics of this essential presence of intelligence, but also how it is determined and influenced by environmental factors. I look at some of these specific factors, our relationship to them, and how that relationship deeply influences our experience and realization of intelligence. And although I do not discuss the influence of heredity or the role of the brain in relation to intelligence, it is part of my understanding that aspects of Essence function through the physical organism, including the brain. Therefore, our realization of the aspect of intelligence will also be influenced by our heredity.

In Part One of *Brilliancy,* the teaching on the aspect of Brilliancy takes the form of four individual talks. These talks were presented as part of a retreat on this aspect that took place in California. The exercises referred to at the end of the talks were followed up with discussion; however, those questions and comments are not included in this part. The intention in Part One is to provide a concentrated presentation of the phenomenological dimension of the Brilliancy aspect, the essence of intelligence.

In Part Two, a talk from a different retreat is presented on Brilliancy as it pertains to the practice of inquiry. In Part Three, the reader will have the chance to witness the unfoldment of personal inquiries by students as they explore Brilliancy in relation to their own experience. These inquiries occurred over the course of several meetings in a smaller group retreat in Colorado.

Though it is clearly not an exhaustive study, I hope that *Brilliancy* will contribute to the understanding of intelligence from the perspective of deep spiritual perception. This book also presents this investigation of intelligence within the specific context of the teaching of the Diamond Approach, in order to demonstrate how that particular method appears in actual application. Therefore, this book is both a study of the question of intelligence and its development and liberation, and an illustration—using the aspect of intelligence—of the methodology of the Diamond Approach in the work of realizing Essence in its various aspects.

Part One

༼༽

The teaching of the Diamond Approach takes place in different contexts: Students can work individually with a teacher or can participate in a group with one or more teachers, and often they do both. Each format is designed to support a different aspect of the spiritual journey.

The most basic and personal form of the teaching occurs in individual sessions between a student and her teacher. Here the student learns through guidance and example the ongoing practice of open and open-ended inquiry. (Inquiry as the primary practice of the Diamond Approach is explored in depth in *Spacecruiser Inquiry: True Guidance for the Inner Journey*.) The teacher guides the student in exploring her present experience in an embodied way that supports intimate contact with that experience through awareness of physical sensation, emotional feeling, and mental attitudes and beliefs. This investigation is continuous with the practice of presence, which is the dedicated attention to sensing and operating from one's immediate felt experience.

The Large-Group Format

Two other teaching formats take place in a group setting. *Brilliancy* has been written to give the reader some sense of these formats and how the group work unfolds. Part One demonstrates the central component of the large-group format: communicating the perspective and understanding of the Diamond Approach through giving talks.

Students are usually exposed to the conceptual orientation of this teaching in groups ranging in size from twenty-five to two hundred and fifty students (with all-school retreats sometimes as large as seven hundred). Each large group has a consistent membership that meets together over a period of many years. The group teaching occurs during intensive weekends or retreats of various lengths, and the meetings take place twice a day for two to ten days. In each meeting, the teacher presents a talk on a particular element of the material being investigated. The talk is followed by one or more exercises in which the students explore their own experience in relation to what was presented. After the exercise, students generally have an opportunity to ask questions or discuss their experience with the teacher.

Presence and the Teaching

Often a weekend or short retreat is devoted to exploring one aspect or dimension of true nature. Fundamental to the presentation of the material is the presence of the essential aspect in the consciousness of the teacher. The teacher's effectiveness in bringing the quality into the experience of the group is largely based on his capacity to embody the particular aspect and transmit it through his words, gestures, and tone. In other words, his ability to be a clear channel for the teaching depends on his personal realization—the degree to which he has worked through his own barriers to that quality of Being.

This essential presence in the teacher will inform and guide the talks and simultaneously be deepened and expanded by what those talks evoke in the students. The talks may explore any or all of the following: the situations that bring up the need for the aspect, what it feels like when the aspect is missing, what strategies are commonly used to mask the absence of the aspect or what substitutes are sought in its place, the universal barriers to experiencing the aspect and the ways those barriers may arise in one's personal history, the experiential characteristics of the aspect, common misconceptions about it, and the impact of the aspect in one's experience when it is present. The choice of topics and the sequence of presentation vary according to the needs of the situation.

Contact with the teacher's presence as it infuses the talk will evoke the particular psychological and experiential constellation related to that aspect in the student's consciousness. This constellation will be enhanced and made more accessible to cognitive perception by the teacher's description of the elements of that constellation (need, absence, substitute, barrier, history, qualities, impact, and so on). These are universal elements of each essential aspect, which means that they are part of everybody's inner psychic reality, whether one is aware of them or not.

Thus the teaching is designed not to indoctrinate or just provide information but to bring to consciousness previously unrecognized elements of the student's experience. As this happens, the student will have the opportunity to explore what comes forth and to gradually learn more of the truth of her inner life. This in turn allows the student to become aware of the unconscious attitudes and beliefs she has held that have prevented direct access to the particular aspect of true nature being explored. Those beliefs begin to dissolve the more they are exposed and explored, allowing greater contact with the essential presence.

The Unfolding of the Teaching

As you read the Part One talks in succession, it is possible to appreciate how the teachings of the Diamond Approach unfold to reveal deeper and more subtle understandings of human nature in a way that parallels the unfolding of individual experience. The teaching is not a linear progression of deductive reasoning such as one might make in a rational argument; nor is it a statement of information with examples and discussion. The Diamond Approach embodies the same principle in both its teaching and its practice: inquiry into experience in a way that allows the truth of that experience to reveal itself.

So the subject of the talk unfolds as one recognition leads to a certain implication, which in turn leads to further understanding, resulting in new recognition, and so on. Thus, the teaching and the embodied presence of the teacher evoke a revelational process in the room. Through this process, the particular aspect being discussed often arises in the group's experience. This generally occurs if the overall development of the group members allows them to open to the presence of the aspect.

Invoking Presence

If the aspect does not arise in the group, the presentation has most likely evoked the issues or barriers that are blocking contact with it. In some cases, this is the intention of the talk: to bring forth the many beliefs and ideas about an aspect that prevent its arising. Either result is appropriate because both the aspect and its barriers must be experienced as essential steps in the unfolding of the true nature of the soul. It is also quite possible that both the aspect and its issues will arise at the same time in the group, in different individuals. The teacher's ability to recognize and address the level of development of the group as a whole is one of the important factors that determine the predominant response in the group field.

The "group field" refers to the collective state of consciousness in the room. It is an expression of many factors, including the energy level, focus of attention, emotional response, and quality of openness in the members of the group. The group field, which is experienced directly and immediately as a felt sense, both impacts and reflects the way the teaching is received. The palpable quality in response to the teacher cannot be translated through words on a page; hence the transcripts do not do justice to the fullness and immediacy of what took place in the room. However, we hope the unfolding of the talk itself will give the reader some flavor of what the students received in the teacher's presence.

1

Brilliancy and Intelligence

☙

Being is such a wondrous reality. It manifests to our perception as the universe we find ourselves in, and it also manifests its pure qualities in our experience of ourselves, as the deep treasures within our souls. We call these pure qualities of Being the aspects of Essence. Each is a perfect manifestation of Being.

Our universe, in its totality, is the way Being presents itself to our experience. In this retreat, we will be working with and exploring an essential aspect that is one of the wonderful possibilities that human beings can experience and be. We will investigate a particular manifestation of this universe, which also is a particular manifestation of ourselves, of who we are. In itself, this aspect is a wonder, with its own beauty; but when it is realized, it also adds beauty and radiance to everything in our world.

For me, talking about and working with this aspect feels like the universe having fun. This quality of Being is an amazing thing to talk about and delve into. So for us to work hard to get enlightened or get free as we move into this exploration would be laborious and miss the point. What we will be doing instead is participating with the universe in the universe enjoying its own beauty. Why not?

When the manifestations of the universe are seen as essential aspects, each one is perceived on its own as magnificent. Each is also seen to have both profound and practical value. Being beautiful and being useful go together. And part of the beauty is the recognition of the practical functioning of the universe. We can see that the universe functions in a way that is precise and aesthetically appealing.

In our work here, we will try to penetrate the veils of our usual beliefs and fixations about what we know, veils that make everything appear old, stale, and boring. "Oh, yes, I know this. This is the world; this is how things work," we smugly think. We all grow up believing that we see the universe as it actually is; we do not suspect that our perception is largely determined by our accumulated beliefs, feelings, past knowledge, and conditioning. How the universe actually is and how it really functions is hidden from our perception. We need to penetrate our familiar knowingness and open ourselves to the unknown, to the mystery. Then, when we see the mystery of the universe in a fresh way, it is possible to see that the way it functions is exquisite.

Learning about Being—studying it, exploring it, realizing it, or connecting with it—is not a matter of trying to get rid of problems or trying to get somewhere because you desperately need to. Rather, if we recognize that the universe is truly a wonder to explore, this exploration can become the most enjoyable activity possible. It is enjoyable and fulfilling because we are doing nothing but perceiving, experiencing, and learning about what we are, and about reality and the truth of the universe. Seeing how things really are is seeing the beauty and magnificence of existence.

Each aspect of Essence has many characteristics and qualities. When I refer to an aspect by a certain name, I do not mean to restrict its meaning only to the quality described by that particular label. For example, the aspect of Loving-kindness has in it the qualities of warmth, gentleness, softness, sorrow for the presence of suffering, a natural inclination to help, empathy, sympathy, and so on. Some aspects, such as the one we will study now—Brilliancy—have more primary characteristics than others, which means that there are many ways to recognize these aspects. We will begin today with the quality most central to this aspect: intelligence.

Usually we think of intelligence as something useful, something handy, something that helps. While that is true, it is also true that intelligence is the exquisiteness of Being and its beauty. It is the exquisiteness of our Being that makes us intelligent. When you perceive how Being manifests in its various dimensions, you realize that intelligence is always part of its manifestation. The exquisiteness of its appearance points to the majesty of intelligence, a complete and awesome presence.

The quality of intelligence is intrinsic to all of Being, to all of Essence, to all of the universe; it is not limited to this particular aspect. The aspect of intelligence is like a distillation or focusing of a general quality of the universe in one specific, precise, exact, very clearly delineated presence. You feel it as the pure presence of intelligence. It is absolutely that quality; the intelligence is in clear relief. Other aspects of Essence have intelligence; for example, the aspect of Love has intelligence in it—but that is not one of its dominant qualities, which are sweetness and softness. That is why I think of each aspect as a Platonic form, the prototype of a specific quality. Each aspect is the essence of that quality.

Usually we think that some people are intelligent, some are not so intelligent, some are more intelligent than others, and so on. We are aware that there are grades and variations of intelligence that can be measured and that may relate to the development of the physical brain. However, I'm not talking about intelligence as a capacity of the brain. I see the aspect of intelligence as the living consciousness that accounts for intelligent functioning, any kind of functioning. Most likely, the more a person actualizes this essential aspect and the more it affects the brain, the more gray matter is activated. I don't know the exact relationship between the essential aspect and the gray matter. But what I want to emphasize is that there is something more intrinsic about intelligence than the presence of gray matter, the cells themselves, or our mental faculties.

What is intelligence? When we recognize that someone is intelligent, what does that mean? Does it mean that her mind is bright and transparent? Does it mean that she can think clearly? Does it mean that she makes good decisions? Does it mean that her perceptions are precise and accurate? Does it mean that she functions efficiently? Does it mean that she has a high IQ? Each of these characteristics is a manifestation of intelligence, or a functioning that reflects intelligence. But what is intelligence itself? As we continue we will see that intelligence is in fact a specific quality of essential experience. It is not a by-product of the brain's functioning but a manifestation of Being itself.

When we focus on intelligence experientially—that is, as a psychological process, we find it impossible to describe. We don't really know what intelligence is. We normally think only of its products—a good idea, a good insight, clear perception, an intelligent action. We know what an intelligent action is, what an intelligent solution is—but what is intelligence itself? What is it that makes the solution an intelligent solution or the action an intelligent action? We say, "Well, it's effective." That is true; there is effectiveness and economy in intelligence. But even more significant than those is the presence of elegance.

It is well known in scientific research that even though efficiency and accuracy are significant measurements of the usefulness of a solution or theory, what establishes the presence of intelligence in the idea is beauty. You see the presence of intelligence in an action when there is grace—an elegance that gives the action an exquisite quality. Yes, the action is clear and specific and does the job; but more than that, it is an action that reveals beauty and elegance, like a flash of lightning brilliantly illuminating a landscape.

This element comes into play when there are several possible scientific theories about a certain subject, each of which could be true. In the absence of experimental verification, one way to decide which theory is more likely to be correct is to consider elegance. It is assumed that the more elegant the theory is and the more beautiful its formulations, the closer it is to the truth.

But elegance is a characteristic of intelligence, which means that we have not yet described exactly what intelligence itself is. We supposedly measure it with intelligence quotients; but what is actually measured is not intelligence itself but its capacities, the products of intelligence. What is measured is how fast you think or how good you are at making connections. What we want to study is the specific element that is common to intelligent action, intelligent thinking, intelligent communication, intelligent research. What is it that makes all of these intelligent?

As I said, intelligence is a basic quality of the universe, and a fundamental quality of Being and of the human soul. While intelligence exists in every aspect, it is very specifically, very precisely revealed in the aspect we are working with. You wouldn't call this aspect the Love aspect. There is love in it, but referring to it as the aspect of intelligence is more accurate. Yes, there is clarity in it, but intelligence describes the quality better. And there is discrimination in it, but the primary flavor here is intelligence. You see, you can have clarity without the quality of intelligence, you can have discrimination without intelligence, and you can have sound, logical thinking without intelligence.

Question?

How can you have discrimination without intelligence?

You can discriminate without your discrimination being an intelligent discrimination.

Oh, I see, it can be habitual.

It does not even have to be habitual. For instance, you could have a regular insight or you could have a brilliant insight, right? What differentiates a regular insight from a brilliant one? The brilliant insight has more intelligence involved in it.

And you are saying that the difference has to do with whether an essential aspect is present?

Yes. An additional element is required for there to be intelligence: You have to be real—in touch with your essence, or true nature—to be truly intelligent.

There is one particular aspect that is specifically and purely the presence and functioning of intelligence. And yet the question remains: What is intelligence? During this retreat, we want to taste it, feel it, experience it, be it; we want to be intimately in contact with it; we want the atoms of our mind, of our soul, to be 100 percent merged with intelligence so that we really know it directly.

Even if we cannot describe our experience precisely, we will probably say all kinds of intelligent things about it. This is because the more you taste intelligence, the more you can't help but say intelligent things. Your tongue becomes intelligent. And if intelligence actually goes into your mind, your thoughts can't help but be intelligent thoughts; if intelligence flows through your limbs, your actions can't help but be intelligent.

Thus far I have introduced intelligence in a very general way—activating our interest and curiosity about it and attempting to penetrate our belief that we know what intelligence is. I have been questioning the customary convictions and accepted knowledge about intelligence. I have also introduced the idea that intelligence is an essential aspect, which means it is a certain quality of consciousness, a living presence with the flavor of intelligence.

Now, intelligence is also something very organic. I was thinking about this word "organic" last night, and I realized that it is not a precise enough term for what we mean when we say that Essence or intelligence is organic. This is because we usually associate "organic" with biological functioning, and that is not what I mean when I say that intelligence is organic. I see it as organic in the sense that intelligence is alive; it is conscious, and it functions in a purposeful way. To say that it is organic means to me that it is part of your soul, an intrinsic part of your makeup, inherent in your consciousness. Intelligence is not added to you as a characteristic or as something learned.

So intelligence is not a characteristic of some part of you in the way, for example, that seeing is a characteristic of the eye. Seeing is something that the eye alone does. So when I say that intelligence is organic, I mean that it is fundamental to who you are—it's not a quality or a function of a part of you, or some capacity you have—it is truly essential to you. It is inherent in the entire body, and in fact, inherent in your very existence.

Are you actually saying it is organ-like?

Not exactly. That's the issue I'm trying to clarify.

We think of organs in terms of biological organs. Essence functions purposefully; it has a function, but it is not really like a physical organ. Physical organs are the closest analogue to an essential aspect that we know in physical life. That is one reason why I use the word "organic." In contrast to physical life, however, essential life is more real, more alive, more energetic. There is more excitation, more of a living quality to an essential aspect than to a physical organ functioning in the body. And in the aspect of intelligence, the quality of being organic is even more striking.

The aspect of intelligence is a constant explosion or illumination. The illumination that is always and continuously illuminating is the presence of the aspect itself. The presence and the illumination are one and the same, like the sun and its light. This constant illumination, or exploding, is the functioning of intelligence. But it is not illuminating or exploding in a haphazard way. It is very intelligent, and it is organic intelligence in the sense that it is different than a computer kind of intelligence—it's not simply associating this with this, that with that, and then putting all these things together and arriving at an outcome. Essential intelligence is more innate, more intuitive. Connecting things the way the computer does is similar to what we call reasoning or thinking—which can be intelligent or not. I don't think it is accurate to call the functioning of computers artificial intelligence, because it is not really intelligence. You could perhaps say "artificial logic" or "artificial thinking." But intelligence is something else. A computer does not have the quality of consciousness I am calling intelligence.

Intelligence is also organic because it is creative. The computer cannot create something original; its creations are already implied in its programming, no matter how complex and adaptive the programming may be. The computer's creations are nothing but the elaborations and combinations of what is already in its memory. A computer can never be original. But intelligence has the characteristic of being creative in a completely original way.

Intelligence always has the capacity of shedding more light. It is always capable of being more intelligent; it is always capable of taking a more intelligent direction, of making a more intelligent observation. This is because real intelligence is alive, and that's what differentiates it from a nonliving thing like a computer. Natural intelligence doesn't have any limit; the maximization of functioning can go on and on infinitely because it comes from a living, organic place that is constantly creating, emerging, flowing. It is the flow itself that is the functioning of intelligence. I hope this explains what I mean when I say that intelligence has an organic characteristic.

Now I want to consider intelligence in terms of how we actually experience it as an essential aspect. How do we perceive and recognize it directly? What is its experiential flavor? To answer these questions, we will begin with the name I give to the aspect of intelligence: Brilliancy.

There is a reason why I call it Brilliancy and not brilliance. Brilliance is a quality of something. It is a characteristic that qualifies something else. We say that something is brilliant red, or a brilliant idea. If you look at any color, you see that it can be dull or brilliant. White can be brilliant white or not. A diamond can either be a brilliant diamond or not. Therefore, while brilliance doesn't exist as a color on its own, it can be a quality of any color. So brilliance is basically a characteristic of color, a characteristic of light.

I call the aspect of intelligence Brilliancy because it is the presence of brilliance that is not the brilliance *of* something. The experience of the aspect of intelligence is what you would perceive if you took the brilliance of any color and made it an independent quality, a presence on its own that is purely brilliance and is not the brilliance of anything else. This pure brilliance, existing on its own, is the very consciousness and substance of intelligence. What you observe is brilliance in itself, not something that is brilliant. So I call the quality itself Brilliancy in order to differentiate it from the characteristic of brilliance.

Physical perception of the natural world reveals no thing, no color, that is just brilliance. Brilliance is always a quality of something. On the essential level, however, brilliance exists independently; it exists as a pure Platonic form, as pure presence, as the actual substance of intelligence. It is like a medium, or a liquid, that is made out of brilliance. If you can imagine taking a mirror and holding it in the sun until you see the brilliance of the reflection, and then taking that brilliant reflection and liquefying it, you would have some idea of what the flow of the presence of Brilliancy looks like. It is like a liquid mirror.

I've always taken the brilliance of any color to be an attribute of that color. When I analyzed what made that particular color brilliant, it seemed to come down to the fact that there is a purity of reflection or a purity of color—a non-muddying, as it were.

That's true.

... at that particular wavelength and for that particular light.

Right.

Is that what you are talking about when you are referring to Brilliancy?

No, that is what I am referring to as the quality of brilliance.

Well, I understand, but that is the reflection in the physical world of the state of Brilliancy—this purity of light. And it is the handle that allows us to relate to Brilliancy.

Right, it's the handle that we have in the physical world; that's what we know about brilliance.

When we see a color, it may be a brilliant color or not. If it is brilliant, that means it is pure, it is undefiled, it is uncontaminated color. That's why one of the ways of experiencing the aspect of Brilliancy is the perception of purity. Intelligence is another way of experiencing it. Innocence is another way—in the sense of existing in the Platonic form of absolute and total purity, before any contamination.

This quality is truly amazing. In fact, I used to call Brilliancy the amazing-amazing because I was amazed whenever it revealed itself. When I said earlier that we will be exploring one of the beauties in our universe, I was referring to this amazing reality of Brilliancy. How can such a thing be? How can brilliance exist as something on its own? According to physical laws, there is no such thing; it is impossible. You can't just have brilliance flowing there by itself, not qualifying anything but itself. But one of the miraculous beauties in the essential realm is that there are manifestations that defy physical laws, that are far beyond our normal experience and even our imagination.

Brilliancy is a pure presence, an ontological presence. It is a beingness, a thereness, a conscious substance, a consciousness. Essence is presence in the most real sense of what presence means. It is not a product of your mind or imagination, or your past knowledge or experience. It is as fundamentally present as the chair you are sitting on, even more fundamentally so. Many people believe they know what presence is when in fact they don't, and so they miss the chance to really find out. Brilliancy is presence just like any other essential aspect, except that it is the presence not of love, not of compassion, not of will, not of clarity, but of brilliance.

Question?

Is Brilliancy the same as intelligence?

Yes, it's the same. Brilliancy can be experienced as intelligence, which is the main quality of the aspect of Brilliancy. But it can be experienced in other ways. As I mentioned before, one way of experiencing it is purity, another is innocence, and yet another is exquisiteness.

When we experience the pure intelligence of Brilliancy, it gives a sense of utmost preciousness to our consciousness, to the soul, and also to the totality of the universe. Brilliancy is really the essence of intelligence. I don't know how to say it better. Intelligence has an essence, has a true intrinsic existence that can be experienced as part of us. It is not an activity of the mind; it is part of the essence of who we are, of our innate nature.

One consequence of this truth is that experientially I can *be* intelligence. When I am Brilliancy, it is not that I am intelligent; rather, I am *intelligence*. When you are being Brilliancy, your functioning is intelligent; but you are also, and more importantly, existing *as* intelligence. This is a new concept of intelligence. But the fact that there is such a thing is part of its beauty. And if you have been thinking all this time that your IQ is low or high, it turns out that the true situation is that there is a certain substance you are more or less of.

When you see someone who is really brilliant, really intelligent—such as one of the great synthesizers of science—your subtle perception might notice that it is the presence of the substance of Brilliancy in his mind that makes the person brilliant. When we say that someone is brilliant, it is more literally true than we usually think. So to be brilliant is not just to have brilliant thought patterns. There is also luminescence—a radiance or brightness in that person's functioning that you can actually perceive directly. It is this perceivable brilliance that imparts the qualities of beauty, grace, and elegance.

Brilliancy gives intelligence to any functioning in which it is present. What we ordinarily recognize as brilliance in the functioning of some individuals is the expression of the presence of Brilliancy in their psyche. We see its influence in their functioning and we say they are brilliant. If we were able to look with our inner eye into their psyches, we would perceive the aspect of Brilliancy present in their consciousness, like a luminous fluid lighting up their functioning from inside.

Brilliancy can also be experienced as the utmost refinement. In experiencing the presence of Brilliancy, it is as if one were experiencing the smallest possible atoms in existence. I am not implying that this aspect exists as atoms or is experienced as atoms. I am using the analogy of atoms to illustrate refinement because Brilliancy is so fine, so delicate, that its refinement is almost complete. The only thing more refined is the presence of the Absolute itself.

The presence of Brilliancy is so fine, so exquisite, and so delicate, that it operates in an amazingly penetrating way. It can penetrate anywhere. There is no place in the body or in the psyche that Brilliancy cannot easily penetrate; it just flows smoothly, as if there were no hole too small for it. That is why brilliant minds are also penetrating minds. Penetration is part of the exquisiteness of the functioning of intelligence, one of the elements that makes intelligence not only brilliant but also beautiful, delicate, and refined. Experiencing intelligence is knowing yourself as the most delicate, the most refined, the most exquisite presence, and at the same time as organically intelligent in a purely brilliant way.

The presence of an essential aspect manifests as a substance, as subtle matter, only through the direct and immediate experience of that aspect. This direct experience of each aspect has characteristics of color, texture, taste, and so on. In terms of color, Brilliancy is brilliant, which is not one of the known colors. One can say it is brilliant white, or brilliant silver white, but that is not completely accurate. The color is pure brilliance, like the shimmering reflection of the sun on the surface of an ocean or lake. What you see are pools of liquid brilliance. This is the closest thing in nature to the way Brilliancy is seen in inner vision. In our consciousness, the texture of this light is total smoothness—absolutely delicate, exquisitely fine and refined. Its flow is so smooth and easy that it moves with amazing speed. Even mercury is dull and slow compared to the flow of Brilliancy.

Brilliancy usually flows in the body through the cerebrospinal fluid in the spinal column. As such, it is directly involved with the nervous system and the brain, so it affects the functioning of thought. Imagine Brilliancy flowing through your synapses; imagine feeling it in your nerves. Imagine the sensation of exquisite smoothness and purity coursing through your nervous system, lighting it up, setting it ablaze with the brilliance of intelligence. Like a lubricant or a conducting substance of complete smoothness in your nervous system, Brilliancy dissolves any resistance in the nerves with its smoothness and flow, with its incredible ease, speed, and penetrating power.

Brilliancy makes the inner sensation of your consciousness so delicate, so subtle, so exquisite, that you truly know what the refinement of consciousness means. Although its presence can be quite full and immense, Brilliancy makes you feel as if your senses have been cleansed with some kind of divine shower, so that your very sensations are exquisiteness itself. Even clarity is seen as an external reflection of that pure radiance. Brilliancy is the explosion of illumination from which clarity comes.

Associating intelligence with brilliance is a common practice; when we say people are bright, we mean that they are intelligent. And if they are even smarter, we say they are brilliant. It is becoming obvious from this discussion that "brilliant" is a very apt description because the person can literally become brilliant. When Brilliancy is fully present, your very existence is brilliant, in the sense of intelligence as well as appearance. So the brilliance of light, of radiance, and the brilliance of intelligence are the same thing on the essential level. Our language reflects this essential truth: Brilliancy actually is intelligence. More exactly, Brilliancy is the essence of intelligence.

Also, we see here a kind of beauty that is different from the usual sense of beauty. The miraculous beauty of Brilliancy is that there is no distinction among how it looks, how it feels, how it tastes, and how it functions. Its aesthetic sense and its usefulness are inseparable—they are one and the same. Presence and functioning, quality and the effect of the quality, coincide here. They are all one thing, and that is exquisiteness.

Aren't the nature of exquisiteness and Brilliancy itself kind of identical? The description of exquisiteness is Brilliancy. The quality that makes a thing exquisite and the quality that makes a thing brilliant is Brilliancy.

Some people use the term "exquisiteness" in reference to other things, but I think it is most obvious in the experience of Brilliancy. Brilliancy makes everything exquisite—both the external perception and the inner sensation of your consciousness.

What does "exquisite" mean? It means fineness, delicacy, beauty, exactness, precision. The precision is the beauty, and the beauty is the precision. The precision is the intelligence, the intelligence is the functioning, and the functioning is inseparable from the smoothness of how it feels. All of these are one thing. It is Brilliancy that gives our actions intelligence; and because of that, it is a very handy thing in addition to being beautiful to behold. It is beneficial in our daily actions and transactions. It is also very useful when it comes to doing the Work.

One of the ways Brilliancy is useful for the Work of essential realization relates to intensity, or amplitude. When essential presence has the aspect of Brilliancy, you experience that the voltage is suddenly raised in all the processes going on inside you. Brilliancy gives a radiance to all manifestations, including your mind and body. Your processes become more radiant, more brilliant, which means that they become purer and more themselves. When Brilliancy is experienced and realized, one's process accelerates. It has a magnifying effect, an empowering effect, on everything within your field. It is as if your essence were getting a shot in the arm. It makes everything more alive, more luminous, and in a sense, more itself. Everything functions better, more efficiently, more accurately, more to the point. Brilliancy exists on its own—it independently functions as intelligence—but it also magnifies the functioning of everything else.

And yet what characterizes the actual nature of Brilliancy is its direct presence in the soul, which then manifests in the thoughts and actions of that person in the world. In the experience of the presence of Brilliancy, I experience myself not as a body with thoughts and feelings but as a palpable presence, as the very presence of some brilliantly luminous fluid. I am usually in touch with the body and its feelings and thoughts, but I am aware of myself as a sensitive fluid that pervades the body, and which feels deeper and more fundamental than the muscles and bones. And this palpable fluid, which is not really physical—even though it has texture and density like physical matter—feels like the presence of inner luminosity, like condensed brilliant light. This fluid light is so pristine, so immaculate, so true and absolutely uncreated or contaminated by mind or memory, that it has the distinct sense of being totally pure.

The palpable fluid feels like the presence of purity itself. Brilliance and purity are two characteristics of the same fluid, just as pure water is both transparent and wet. We cannot separate the transparency and wetness in water, just as we cannot separate brilliance and purity in Brilliancy.

The presence of purity affects the mind and the totality of consciousness by cleansing them of past experience, of all memory and past knowing. So I feel myself not only as presence that is purity, but also as presence that is virginal, open, and totally sensitive. I recognize this experience to be the prototype of innocence. I am innocence present as pure brilliance, where the purity is the same as innocence. It is like the innocence of an infant—totally open and present, with no mental baggage or premeditation. But this innocence is the presence itself, just as an infant is too innocent to know that she is innocence itself. It is so innocent that it is pure innocence.

The same with exquisiteness: The presence is so fine in its texture, so shiny in its radiance, so delicate and smooth in its flow, so absolutely light and happy in a completely open and unrestrained way, that the sense of one's presence is exquisite and indescribably astonishing in its beauty and refinement, both in feeling and texture.

As you can tell, I am not giving you an intellectual or systematic exposition of what intelligence is. I've been trying to give you a feeling, some kind of a taste or glimpse of the essence of intelligence. One taste of intelligence is worth many books about it.

What is the relationship between this luminous fluid of Brilliancy and the cerebrospinal fluid?

As I said, it flows in the cerebrospinal fluid, but that does not mean that it is always present there. A person could live her entire life and not have Brilliancy in her system. But when it flows through the cerebrospinal fluid, through the spine, it gives brilliance, it gives intelligence to the various capacities.

Brilliancy has other functions when it flows in the spinal column. One of these is balance. It gives an innate sense of balance. Then you know you are balanced in your consciousness, that you are not in one extreme or another.

Could you say that a person is born with a certain level of intelligence, a possible IQ, that could be enhanced or enlarged through having Brilliancy activated?

I don't know. It seems that different people have different capacities in terms of intelligence. Now whether that's innate in the sense of being physiologically determined so that the person can't go beyond that, or whether it has more to do with the realization of that part of themselves, is difficult to say at the present time. I don't think our capacity for intelligence is completely determined by our physical inheritance. Because Brilliancy is an essential aspect, it is part of the potential of every human being. It is an inherent potential of the soul, regardless of the makeup of the physical body.

How about studies of twins, where they are separated in infancy and raised in different environments, and yet the same level of intelligence seems to be present later on?

Yes, it does seem that to some extent it is physiologically determined.

The way I see it is that different people have different capacities to tolerate and embody Brilliancy, and that affects their degree of intelligence. Some people seem able to tolerate, contain, and develop it; others cannot tolerate it when it starts to manifest in their consciousness and so never have a chance to embody it. Somehow their psyche resists it. That is what I call a kind of soul deficiency.

"Soul deficiency" refers to the situation in which part of the soul is not sufficiently developed to allow some aspect of its potential to manifest. There are many possible reasons for this condition. Perhaps a physiological challenge or limitation in early childhood resulted in an insufficient opportunity to develop a certain dimension of the soul. Other reasons such as emotional abuse or lack of support in the family environment might also have blocked growth in certain areas of the soul. People with such a background may not be able to tolerate one or more essential aspects very well. Thus the experience of some qualities of Essence may be disintegrative for them.

In the case of Brilliancy, its presence in the psyche may be felt as too much radiance, too much brightness, and too much intensity. This means that the soul is not developed enough to tolerate that much refinement; it is experienced as jarring. But I don't know whether you can say that the person who feels disturbed by Brilliancy cannot develop the capacity to tolerate it. I think that most people could, but it would probably take a person with developmental deficiencies a long time.

However, for most people, Brilliancy is not available to the consciousness because psychodynamic issues specifically block this aspect. As you know, the Diamond Approach not only presents the knowledge of each of the essential aspects, it also has an understanding of the specific psychological constellations in the mind and personality that act as barriers to each aspect. You'll be surprised, as we get into it, what kind of psychological issues stop people from being smart. We will explore how the capacity for intelligence can be historically determined in the sense that it is blocked or limited by psychodynamic issues. In time, then, working through those issues can allow your Brilliancy to shine through.

I'd like to understand what you mean when you say that you can go through your whole life without experiencing a drop of Brilliancy.

As I said, intelligence is a quality of all life, of all aspects, right? But Brilliancy is the presence of that quality in a complete, distilled form. It is this distilled form—the Platonic form of intelligence—that I call Brilliancy. And it is rare for someone to embody it. That is what I meant by that statement. Also, most people do not know Brilliancy from their direct experience. Even though it is present in their consciousness, on the rare occasion when they are functioning in a brilliant way, few people will be aware of or recognize at those times the presence of Brilliancy itself.

But isn't Brilliancy essential to ordinary existence?

No, it isn't. I don't think it is essential for survival, especially the way human society is set up now. You don't have to be brilliant to survive.

Usually there are only a few brilliant people around, and the rest of us are brilliant only occasionally. And the people whom we consider brilliant have only a drop or two of Brilliancy in their heads. Imagine if we could take such a person and work with him or her and activate the Brilliancy to the extent that the whole body and the whole psyche is immersed in the ocean of Brilliancy. Do you have any idea what kind of being this individual would be?

Do you know what kind of intelligence this person would have? This would be a person who is intelligent, who is brilliant, in all of the human capacities, in all areas of functioning. Brilliancy would not only be a quality of the mind, but this person would *be* Brilliancy, the embodiment of intelligence. This kind of experience can happen only to a realized being, for it is a spiritual experience. It is the experience of the brilliance of Being, the radiance of the Absolute Truth.

2

Synthesis

☙

We will continue with the exploration of what intelligence is by exploring some of its functions.

The central characteristic of Brilliancy that makes it the essence of intelligence is that it is the prototype for synthesis. The quality of innate and self-existing synthesis gives our soul the capacity to synthesize the elements in our experience. But what is synthesis?

Synthesis is the recognition of the underlying unity that is already present in the various elements of a situation. Sometimes synthesizing means seeing the common factor that brings apparently unrelated elements together; it is seeing a factor that is already present in the situation but not perceived at the outset. For instance, if you are considering several experiences or impressions, to try to connect them in some logical fashion is not synthesis. Synthesis refers to the way that you might suddenly, in a flash, see how they fit together. That flash occurs by you perceiving the unifying factor that is common to all of the elements.

Synthesis is the opposite of analysis, which is the process of dividing things up. Synthesis does not come by simply putting things together. You can never take two things, relate them in a linear way, and then come up with a synthesis. You can call that organization, you can call it combination—but it is not synthesis, at least not from the perspective of Brilliancy.

Putting things together by connecting them would be more like integration. Synthesis is something more fundamental than that.

The synthetic quality of Brilliancy gives our mind and consciousness the capacity to perceive the self-existing unity that is already present in the situation, the common factor in the various elements or objects under consideration.

Take, for example, the Diamond Approach, the teaching we are using here for our work of spiritual realization. Most people describe it as the result of synthesizing the psychological and the spiritual. That is true, but not in the way they imagine it happened. Many people believe that I knew something about both the spiritual and the psychological realms and then somehow put them together. However, I could never have created this Work in that way. In fact, I didn't even think of the process as synthesis until after the fact. The synthesis of the psychological and the spiritual happened by my seeing from the beginning that they are one. I looked at my experience and knew with certainty that psychological processes and spiritual perceptions are inextricably linked as parts of the same experiential domain. I actually cannot separate them in my thinking and contemplation, even if I want to; such a separation would not make sense to my understanding.

Synthesis is a matter of seeing the oneness, the unity, in the two. If you see their unity, you also see the underlying ground that unifies them, that makes them two expressions of the same thing. This capacity for synthesis is an important part of the functioning of intelligence. When we say we have had an intelligent discussion, insight, idea, or action, an important part of the intelligence we are referring to is the functioning of synthesis, which is active, direct, and transcends linear thinking.

Let us take an example of synthesis, here referred to as arriving at an insight. As you look at your current experience, you are in touch with various impressions, observations, and facts. For instance, you feel hurt in relation to a female colleague you spend a great deal of time with at work. But you do not know exactly why, and when you try to find out, the only thing you can see is that you feel somewhat defensive and resentful toward the boss you have in common.

Without a sense of it being connected to these feelings, you are aware that you have been recently interested in the color pink, and seem to see it in many places. Also, you notice that you have been interested in going to the rose garden and spending time there enjoying the sights and smells and the sense of openness and freshness of the outdoors. You tend to feel alive and invigorated while in the park, but you also notice the same feeling sometimes at work, especially recently.

Looking at all these elements, you do not know whether they are connected. But you are aware, you are observing, you are in touch with certain situations and experiencing one thing after another. You are curious and interested in understanding the situation, especially why you are hurt in relation to your friend, even though you know you feel good about her and appreciate both her and your boss.

You are open to whatever understanding might arise—and at some point it happens in a flash: You are watching a movie with a couple of friends, and during a particular scene, you notice that you are starting to get teary and vulnerable, which reminds you of your hurt. The scene is of a man buying a bouquet of flowers for his girlfriend to express his love. Suddenly you see the factor that ties all these elements together—the underlying unity or synthesis. You see it when you recognize that the flowers are all pink roses.

As you notice that, the vulnerability in your heart suddenly becomes a delicate feeling of sweetness, and your heart feels full of a fluffy texture, similar to rose petals, and you begin to see that there is actually a beautiful pink color filling your heart. The insight that leaps out makes you understand why you have been feeling so alive: You are in love with your female colleague but have not allowed yourself to feel it because you believed she was partial to your boss. The love here, which turns out to be the essential Pink Love aspect, is like a thread that suddenly flashes through all the different elements and shows how they are connected. That flash—a flash of light with a sharp brilliance to it—is experienced as the synthetic insight that unifies what was previously disparate. You feel certainty with the insight, and your heart is full and sweet.

I am discussing synthesis because it is a very important element in understanding. Understanding is fundamentally the integration of analysis and synthesis; the capacity to simultaneously analyze and synthesize is what ultimately brings understanding. If you only know how to analyze, your understanding will most likely not be real; you will achieve only a mechanical, computer-like kind of understanding. For understanding to be alive and useful, synthesis has to occur as the apprehension of an underlying unity and harmony that is intrinsic to the situation. In the absence of synthesis, there will only be logical deduction, which by itself is insufficient for real transformation.

We may be able to program a computer to perform some functions of synthesis, but these will not be the living, organic, and global synthesis that is required for the kind of understanding necessary in our Work. Living understanding and real insight into the nature of truth depend on a synthesis that is in touch with the elements of the situation in a living and feeling way, a synthesis that is in contact with the fundamental ground of what is being explored. We need a synthetic capacity that can directly access fundamental truths that are not part of our acquired knowledge and cannot be deduced from it. This true synthetic capacity can come only from a consciousness that has these truths as part of its very nature. In other words, this synthetic capacity must come from our soul, which has this capacity as one of its innate and living functions.

The capacity for a synthesis that is alive and real comes only from Brilliancy. When Brilliancy is present to some degree in our consciousness, real and fundamental syntheses, true insight, and a living understanding become possible—a felt recognition of deeper truth that transforms us. Real synthetic capacity is necessary for study or research to result in new and original insights and knowledge. This is true not just in the study of our inner experience but in any field, including the physical sciences.

Because it gives our consciousness this capacity for synthesis, we are able to recognize that Brilliancy is the essence of intelligence. When Brilliancy touches the psyche, synthesis arises in a felt, directly experienced, perceptual way. Underlying unity becomes apparent. This synthesis is not thought, although thought might arise from it. It can be experienced in a thought but is not the thought itself. Synthesis is an experience, a felt experience that lights up our thinking. And it is this insightful experience of direct contact with an exquisite presence that we recognize as the source and true nature of intelligence.

Does Brilliancy have a feeling associated with it when it is present?
The feeling of Brilliancy is pure bliss.
That's what I wanted to know. [Laughter]
It is a kind of pleasure that you can't call love, you can't call joy. The best

way to describe it is as an intense kind of blissfulness. It's an intensity that in its nature has a pleasurable quality to it.

I feel a blockage around that experience, that being with it can bring anxiety. My sense is that I almost know the bliss is arising because I'm feeling anxious in a certain way. Probably I'm anxious about experiencing that pleasure.

That is quite possible. We will come back to that in due time. Now I want to go back to discussing the synthesis that we are working on in this meeting.

The capacity for synthesis as an integral part of the functioning of understanding has a great deal to do with your own maturity and development. This is because your growth is largely a process of the synthesis or inner unification of your consciousness, of your presence. The greater the inner unification—that is, the greater the maturity of the soul—the greater the capacity for synthesis, for this inner unification is itself the result of synthesis.

Other essential aspects besides Brilliancy are related to unification. For instance, another kind of unification—integration—is a capacity that comes from the Personal Essence, the pearl beyond price.* In this book, however, we are focused on the synthesis, or unification through insight, that comes from Brilliancy.

You seem to be talking about Brilliancy as a catalyst, like the flame in a chemical reaction.

It is like a catalyst; that is why I call it the elixir. The elixir has the specific capacity to act as a transformative agent that synthesizes the elements of the situation.

I am trying to show that synthesis is not like putting a jigsaw puzzle together. Nobody would call that synthesis—that is more like an arrangement or organization. Similarly, if different parts of you become lost or disconnected and you are able to put them all back together and feel whole again, that is not synthesis but integration. Synthesis is recognizing a unity that is already present but that your mind hasn't seen because it has cut things up or perceived and thought of things in a piecemeal way. Your ordinary mind is not able to see the underlying unity because that unity is

---

* See *The Pearl Beyond Price* (1988), Part 3.

currently beyond your awareness. Brilliancy provides the capacity for you to see the underlying unity that was hidden from you. It intensifies your awareness and gives it the penetrating power to see through the mental veils that prevent you from perceiving the unity that already exists.

This is an important factor in the functioning of intelligence. So an intelligent person, an entrepreneur for instance, is a person who can make that synthesis, can see all these various situations, and by a leap of insight can see . . . MONEY! Right? [*Laughter*] That is a practical example, but it shows that synthesis can reveal insights in psychology, finance, communication, or whatever.

But it could also be purely mental, such as figuring out a theoretical problem.

There could be synthesis in the mental sphere, but synthesis itself does not happen through a mental process—that's what I'm saying. Synthesis itself is an essential experience that can happen in any area of functioning. The functioning can be of the intellect, of the heart, or of the totality of the soul, which is the totality of your consciousness.

Are there precursors to synthesis, such as the willingness to let go of certain analytical perspectives in order for synthesis to happen? Don't you have to be willing to loosen the strings of analysis?

It is true that in synthesis you have to be able to let go of the analytical mind, but analysis is not necessarily antithetical to synthesis. Analysis is also the functioning of an essential quality; thus it is not exclusively a mental activity. As we said, the integration of analysis with synthesis is in fact necessary for any true understanding.

Analysis could be considered an aspect of discrimination.

Yes. The discriminating capacity has to do with the Red or Strength aspect. This essential aspect gives the psyche the capacity for real discrimination, and hence for analysis. If you add the Brilliant aspect, you will have analysis and synthesis together—you can simultaneously analyze and synthesize. They are just two different functions of the psyche. The Brilliancy has to do with the synthetic function.

Now the question arises: What gives Brilliancy its synthetic capacity? What makes Brilliancy responsible for synthesis? There is something about Brilliancy that differentiates it from other essential aspects, that accounts for it being the prototype for synthesis. Can we understand what that is? If so, then we will have a greater and more detailed understanding of Brilliancy, which will help us realize more of our synthetic capacity.

Is it because of the intensity of its energy, which is like an electrical charge?

Well, it does have that intensity. What I have in mind, however, is something more specific that we haven't mentioned.

Brilliancy is different from all other essential aspects in that it is a self-existing, unified synthesis of all essential aspects. When you experience Brilliancy, you feel complete in the sense that all essential aspects are present but not differentiated. So Brilliancy is the nondifferentiated essential aspect. We can say that it is the source out of which all essential aspects differentiate. That is why in the past I used to call Brilliancy the Essence-of-the-Essence. Its very presence has all the qualities of Essence implicit in it: Strength, Compassion, Love, Clarity, and so on. All of them are there, but they are completely synthesized as one presence.

We know that Essence manifests in differentiated aspects that are the clearly delineated, pure qualities of Being. There are many of these qualities: Love, Compassion, Joy, Acceptance, Strength, Will, Truth, Existence, Space, Clarity, Consciousness, Peace, Fulfillment, and so on. Each one of these qualities is explicitly differentiated as a Platonic form. Brilliancy is one of these aspects, delineated as intelligence. However, there is something additional about Brilliancy that sets it apart from all other aspects: Brilliancy has all of the other qualities implicit in it in a very organic and complete way. When experiencing it, one can feel all the other aspects in it as if they were actually present in one's awareness; however, one is experiencing only the presence of Brilliancy. Brilliancy is a complete synthesis of all qualities of Being, all aspects of Essence, in one distinct presence.

Remember, this synthesis is not a matter of putting things together. Brilliancy is a pure quality with no parts. It has in it all of the essential aspects—not side by side, not related to each other, not organized in some kind of pattern, but completely synthesized. Thus, it is already a fundamental synthesis of all the qualities that can exist in our consciousness. And because of that, the functioning of Brilliancy is synthetic; for it is itself the epitome, or the prototype, of synthesis. It is the already self-existing synthesis of all the pure qualities inherent in our soul as part of its natural potential. The presence of Brilliancy in any functional sphere of the soul gives the soul the capacity of synthesis in that particular sphere. So if it is present in the mind, for example, it imbues it with the capacity to synthesize on the mental level.

This prototypical functioning always occurs with any essential aspect, for each is the Platonic form, the pure idea, of a particular quality. When present, each aspect provides the soul with the prototype of that quality. It can affect the soul in any of its spheres of experience and functioning by providing the prototype for such experience or functioning. Let's take, for example, the aspect of Strength. The presence of this aspect initiates questions and issues of strength in whatever sphere we are considering. It can affect the physical sphere, so we can feel strong physically or see and experience our physical weaknesses and their associated issues and conflicts. It can affect our mind by putting us directly in touch with our mental strength and capacity or by bringing to awareness our mental weaknesses and their related issues and questions. And it will operate similarly in other spheres of experience and functioning.

By contrast, the Personal Essence is the prototype for integration. It provides the soul with the capacity to integrate various elements of its reality into a unified whole. It brings the capacity for integration to whatever sphere of functioning we are considering—physical, mental, emotional, spiritual, and so on. This is because the Personal Essence is the integration of all essential aspects. Similarly, Brilliancy gives the capacity for synthesis because it is the synthesis of all essential aspects. It is the underlying unity.

Brilliancy is in some sense the source of all aspects and qualities. It is the presence of the aspects before differentiation. Its synthesis is primal and not created, spontaneously existing as the complete synthesis and unity of all aspects and qualities of Being. It is similar to white light, in the sense that all the aspects are like the differentiated colors that we see when we pass white light through a prism.

In some fundamental sense, Brilliancy is related to the Absolute directly, to the ultimate condition of Being. The Absolute is actually the only other dimension of Being that feels complete in the way that Brilliancy does, that feels like it includes all the aspects implicitly. The Absolute feels as if it has everything in it, just as Brilliancy does. But there is a very subtle difference: The Absolute has everything in it virtually, implicitly, in potential. The qualities do not exist yet, but one feels no absence of any of them. The sense of completeness of the Absolute is *implicit*; it is not an explicit feeling or state of consciousness as it is with Brilliancy. There is completeness without the conceptualization of completeness. The essential aspects are still nonmanifest. You feel like everything is there when you experience the Absolute, but you don't know what "everything" is. You can't separate this from that—in some sense they are not there to be separated—because the Absolute is not a presence the way an essential aspect is.

We can say that the Absolute is the unmanifest completeness and Brilliancy is the manifest completeness. Hence the Absolute is the unmanifest synthesis and Brilliancy is the manifest synthesis. Thus, Brilliancy is like the manifest Absolute. And it *is* in fact the radiance, or the brilliance, of the Absolute. If we go to the Absolute dimension, we see that radiance is the way the Absolute manifests its perfections. Its first manifestation is its pure radiance, its completeness, its intelligence. This, then, is the manifest presence of Brilliancy.

So the Absolute is the synthesis of all essential aspects before manifestation. Brilliancy is the synthesis of all essential aspects after manifestation. Both of them are complete: One of them is absolutely dark, one of them is absolutely bright. The Absolute is complete fecundity, complete darkness, complete blackness, while Brilliancy is complete brilliance, complete light, complete whiteness. This is really the difference between the unmanifest and the manifest.

I am just connecting Brilliancy with the Absolute so you can more fully understand completeness and synthesis. Remember, synthesis means that you don't have different parts. Brilliancy is one complete unity. You can't take it apart; you can't analyze it. Thus, it gives the psyche the capacity for synthesis in all of our spheres of functioning.

What do you call—or what is the combination of—the Absolute and the manifest? It must have everything in it.

Why do you want to know what it's called?

I guess I feel like synthesizing.

I don't know. [*Giggles*] My brilliance hasn't reached that far. [*General laughter*] Really, it will take us far afield, to the quintessential dimension, which is too difficult for us to understand at this juncture.

Could you say that part again about not being able to differentiate the parts of its presence?

When I say that Brilliancy is the synthesis of all aspects, that doesn't mean they are put together. The presence of Brilliancy is Love, but at the same time it is Compassion; and at the same time it is Strength; and at the same time it is Clarity; and at the same time it is Will; and so forth. When you put all these together completely and undifferentiated from one another, the experience is of Brilliancy.

Okay, I see in retrospect that I was trying to pull it apart. I had some kind of block, but at that point it wasn't really necessary to do that.

No, you can't pull it apart.

Oh, good. [Laughter]

[Question from another student] Can you put Brilliancy through a prism and see a rainbow?

Well, you could say that the essential aspects are differentiations out of this undifferentiated state.

So Brilliancy gives everything light, in a certain way. I don't know, but I seem to be seeing everything in another dimension.

I see. Yes, that is how things appear when Brilliancy is present. Your perception gets brighter, as if everything had light to it. Brilliancy gives light, both in terms of perceptual brightness and in terms of the brightness of intelligence; but it gives more than light. It is also the source of all manifestation. It is the manifest source of all the aspects.

It's more than the source that is manifest. It's all.

It is *the* manifest Essence. Right. But all essential aspects are manifest, and Brilliancy is the source of them all.

You said that Brilliancy is the only other experience of Being, outside of the Absolute, that has all the qualities in it. How about the Diamond Guidance? I thought it had all the aspects too.

The Diamond Guidance, which is the dimension of Essence related to guidance and understanding, is a specific integration of all the essential aspects. All essential aspects exist in the Diamond Guidance, but differentiated. It is a structure of consciousness that I call a Diamond Vehicle. It holds all the essential aspects, and each one is present in a differentiated and delineated way. So there is Strength, Joy, Compassion, Brilliancy, and so on, all present as themselves. They are, however, organized and integrated in a certain configuration and constitute a complete vehicle. They are all there functioning in unison, in harmony with one another. It is like a group of individuals who function in a harmonious way doing a specific work. One of the aspects can dominate and function while the others recede. Sometimes two of them are functioning while the rest have receded. But when Brilliancy functions, it functions in unity. It is one aspect.

Could you describe the Personal Essence in the same way?

No, it is different. These are all different kinds of unifications—Brilliancy, the Diamond Guidance, the Pearl, and others I have not mentioned. The value of discussing these other manifestations in our present exploration is only to show by contrast what synthesis is. I do not want to do more of that now; things can become too complicated for us. It is really quite enough to deal with Brilliancy in the time we have for this short retreat.

You said that Brilliancy feels good, feels blissful, even though it is not differentiated. This means that it is visible if it is pleasurable.

Yes. The presence does feel blissful. And it is in some sense visible, although not differentiated. This is because it is a manifest presence. Nondifferentiation is not the same as nonmanifestation.

Brilliancy definitely has a positive affect; in fact, it is pure positive affect. That is why I call it a kind of bliss. It isn't exactly bliss—it is more ecstatic. We call it ecstatic bliss when it overtakes you. It could be quite overwhelming.

I'm having trouble with some of the discussion this morning. How about the scientist who has brilliance that manifests in his work but who still has holes in his development, in his inner unification? It would seem that if he is able to work in a brilliant way, then he must have everything, because Brilliancy has everything. Yet it seems that there are holes in his inner unification.

That's true.

That confuses me. He could have everything and yet a hole could be there.

Yes, all that is possible.

Most people believe—and this is an indication of a lack of spiritual maturity—that if you have achieved a certain state, then that state is completely integrated and realized. They believe that it must be everywhere in your consciousness, fully integrated in all spheres and domains of experience and functioning. That is the way most spiritual books and teachings characterize it. They give the impression that realization is always complete and absolute. The fact is that things are not like that most of the time. Realization can be partial. In fact, realization is partial in most instances for most people, which means that a person can have Brilliancy in a certain area but not in others. So a scientist can be brilliant in his field and not be brilliant when it comes to his or her emotional makeup.

This is an important fact, and it implies that spiritual realization has no end. The same thing is true about Love, and in fact about any aspect. You know, you could love your dog to death but still hate everybody else. It is possible.

Okay, I get it.

I am having a difficult time understanding something. It seems that all other essential aspects have a false version—for example, false love that is associated with an object relationship, rather than true Love, which is basically love for yourself and true Being. Today I'm comparing false brilliancy—that is, intellectual brilliancy, computers, and that kind of thing—with true Brilliancy, which is just a state of presence and clarity that has nothing to do with the computer.

Yes, there is a fake brilliancy. That's what is sometimes called being smart or clever, which is being intelligent in an intellectual way—always having the right answer, the right response, being right. That is the appearance of intelligence without the substance. And that obviously becomes a filler for the hole of Brilliancy, for the lack of true intelligence; it takes its place.

That is one reason why I'm discussing Brilliancy in more detail and, specifically, the synthetic capacity that Brilliancy gives. Of course, we keep relating Brilliancy to other things, to its other qualities, which gives us a more complete taste of what it is, which can help differentiate it not only from other aspects but also from false brilliancy. The synthetic capacity has to be a real thing. I don't see how somebody could synthesize in a fake way. Synthesis exposes the false kind of intelligence.

There are cases in engineering or computer programming when someone has an insight that allows him to solve a particular problem. Then, in order to incorporate that insight, he adds in more and more subsets of that problem; and that is called brilliant because out of that, a conglomeration of things can be constructed. But the real synthesis happens when the complete set is seen at its very root and it doesn't need additional pieces added in. The false is when they meticulously construct all the problem sets and attack each one and try to expand it and add more things into it. Synthesis is typically seen in engineering or programming, or even in life, when the complete set is seen as one small, simple, easily defined solution, and the rest of the stuff falls in place because it's all part of this small solution.

That is a very good example. That differentiates the genius in the brilliant discovery from the purely mechanical work that can then expand it or put it into application. We must not think, however, that the brilliance of synthesis cannot happen in applying discovery; for one can have a brilliant insight about how a discovery can be applied or expanded. The point is, there are two kinds, or levels, of functioning.

Another thing about the action of Brilliancy is that when synthesis happens, something new and fresh and original that wasn't there to start with appears. Synthesis creates new knowledge. Whereas if you just put things together, you don't get new knowledge; you just get extensions of the old knowledge. If you want really fresh knowledge, something that is not already there in the information that you already have, a true intelligence has to be operating. That is when Brilliancy is indispensable.

If I opened up a dictionary right now and looked up the word "synthesis," would I see it defined in the way you are talking about?

You might. I do not know for sure. I didn't look in the dictionary, but there might be a description of synthesis in terms of seeing an underlying unity.

How about thesis and antithesis equaling synthesis? That's what I always thought it was.

[Another student interjects.] Yeah, that was going to be my question—because in philosophy, you hear about thesis, antithesis, synthesis, and then the synthesis becoming another thesis, creating something new. The Hegel style, I think. Is this what you are talking about?

Well, I don't exactly know about the logic of Hegel; I have never used it much or studied it sufficiently to say. I do think, however, that his is a way of conceptualizing processes; it is not something close to our lived experience.

What I am talking about is something much more experiential. You can't go about it in some kind of intentional, systematic way. It's not as though you decide: "Let's synthesize this." You can't do that with Brilliancy.

Rather, it's when you're really involved in studying something because you are truly, honestly, organically, innately interested; and if you're really involved, really into it, you will not be looking for synthesis; you might not even know that synthesis is needed. If a unity happens to be present that you are not seeing, the Brilliancy will arise and an instantaneous synthesis will appear as an insight. So I don't see the process as going through thesis, antithesis, and culminating in synthesis. Anyway, dialectics is a kind of logic that describes historical processes. It is a way of describing and understanding processes that happen in time. The action of Brilliancy is definitely not like that. It is a spontaneous and instantaneous happening, more of an organic process.

Spontaneity is another characteristic of the functioning of intelligence. Understanding happens spontaneously in a flash; insight is instantaneous. You can't look for it to happen; you can only be truly interested in the investigation and exploration of a situation. If you really want to understand, really want to know, and your heart and mind are engaged in the inquiry, then if Brilliancy arises, it creates synthesis spontaneously.

In my experience, it's been mysterious in its occurrence. You can't create it, but some things seem to trigger it. It comes and goes when it wants to.

Each essential aspect is part of the potential of being a human being. If you are open to that part of your potential and you don't have barriers to it, then it will arise whenever it is needed in the situation.

What makes an essential aspect arise is the objective need of the situation, not that you want it to be there. It arises only as an organic and appropriate response to the totality of the situation. Essence can intuitively read the totality of the situation and respond as some kind of innate, organic intelligence to that totality through the arising of the particular aspect needed by the situation. You might not know the quality that is needed, but in a mysterious way, Essence knows and functions by manifesting what is needed. If that happens frequently and consistently, you start experiencing brilliance in your understanding and consciousness; for this functioning of Essence is a reflection of its intelligence—which means that Brilliancy is present.

Can it happen in the dream state?

I don't see why not.

You say, "in a mysterious way." It must be mysterious to us but not to it.

The intelligence of the universe is not a thinking intelligence.

When we talk about the universe being intelligent, or God being intelligent, it doesn't mean that the universe or God is thinking about what to do next. [*Laughter*] It is not wondering about what the intelligent thing to do is. That way of seeing things is due to conceiving of intelligence as only mental. It is to avoid this misconception that I discussed intelligence as being organic.

The mystery becomes more obvious when we can perceive the intelligence of the universe, when we perceive cosmic functioning. This is seen as the Divine Intelligence, which manifests as God's thinking. However, by "God's thinking" we do not mean it is the same kind of thing that happens inside your head. For the universe, or God, the thought itself is the creation of the universe.

On that level of perception, there is no separation between thinking and action. This is a true illustration of the function of real intelligence. You don't think and then act. Intelligence is not a matter of thinking intelligently and then acting. Intelligence does not ruminate. The spontaneous action is itself the action of intelligence. So God doesn't have to think about what he's going to do before he does it. The thinking of doing it and the action itself are the same thing. So there is no set plan, no premeditation.

Brilliancy is much more intelligent than someone who needs a plan. Brilliancy doesn't need a plan because it takes in the totality of the situation and acts in the moment, instantaneously. It responds to the need of the moment with the most intelligent possibility. This is the action of a realized being.

You've been talking a lot about God and Brilliancy. I don't know if this is a true statement, but it just keeps coming into my mind that God and Brilliancy are somehow related.

You are anticipating what we will look at later on. Frequently at the beginning, when individuals first experience Brilliancy, there is an association with God—that that experience is God. This happens at a certain stage of the essential unfoldment. It is because the experiential qualities of Brilliancy—completeness, blissfulness, brightness, majesty, purity, and power—are so amazing and awe-inspiring for the individual that frequently, but not always, the person feels this must be God.

Now I would like to finish with our work on synthesis. The capacity of synthesis is something that each of us can explore for ourselves. Do we have the capacity to synthesize or not? Do we have the capacity to see the common element in an array of things? Can we discover intuitively, in a direct way, the underlying unity in our experience?

We notice that sometimes it's difficult for us to see the various elements in our experience and how they are organically and naturally connected. Because we don't see, we don't arrive at the synthetic insight. At other times, when we are feeling better and we are more present, or somebody else is helping us, right away the elements are apparent, and suddenly the flash of seeing the whole thing together occurs. It is that understanding—that flash—that creates transformation. This means that our synthetic capacity changes according to circumstance, according to our inner state, and whether there is external support. This means that we can work to free and expand this capacity by exploring what diminishes or blocks it, and what activates or enhances it.

3

Presence and Time

☙

The most significant element in the experience of realization is the direct perception that the truth of reality is Being. This recognition sets the realization experience apart from the usual experience of ego. In fact, to experience reality, or oneself, as presence is the most miraculous and amazing kind of perception. And investigating this presence—being curious, interested, and involved in finding out for oneself exactly what presence is—is the shortest path to the direct understanding of enlightenment, or realization.

Presence is what characterizes true nature and sets it apart from all the other categories of experience that fall within the realm of the ego, which is to say, the ordinary consciousness. The experience of presence negates all the fears and conflicts that the ego habitually engages in.

The primary turning point on the path to enlightenment is the realization of oneself as presence. This experience begins the whole process of realization, development, and liberation, which continues until one comes to see that presence is everything, and that everything is presence. When you experience everything as presence, then you are experiencing Universal Being, or Divine Being, or Being-as-such. But whichever way you experience it—personally or universally—the important thing about the experience is the fact of it being presence, an actual beingness. So, I want to discuss briefly what presence means.

Just hearing the word "presence", many of us think we know what it means. But nothing is really known yet because the word "presence" can mean different things. You could say that any physical object has presence because it is present: "This chair has presence because it is here now," for example, or "My body has presence." However, that is not what we mean when we say that Essence *is* presence.

It is true that Essence is present in the way a chair is present, but there are fundamental differences. Both Essence and a chair exist in a real way independent of our minds. They are not fabrications of our thoughts. In that sense, presence refers to the beingness of both Essence and the chair. So "presence" is a good way to say what Being is, where Being means the ontological condition of self-existence. The word "Being" by itself does not necessarily explain Essence in ordinary language unless you are a philosopher and you understand what Being is. So we use "presence" to delineate Being and Essence more precisely. But without further discussion, I don't think the word itself is sufficient for understanding.

We say that the chair is present, which is true. But the chair is not aware of its own presence. Essence is. We say the body is present, and we can directly be aware of and sense the presence of the body. But that is not yet an understanding of what presence is. It is true that we can be aware of the body—we can sense its presence—but that is not the same thing as the body itself being aware of its presence. When there is a consciousness that is conscious of the body, there is a subject/object dichotomy. That is not what we mean by the presence of Essence.

The presence of Essence implies that the consciousness itself is conscious of its presence. This means that the consciousness itself is directly conscious and aware of the fact of its existence not through inference but by experiencing the existence directly, by *being* its existence. So to be present as Essence—to experience oneself as presence—is to experience oneself as a self-existing consciousness, as a consciousness whose presence is identical with its consciousness of its presence. Thus, the consciousness of the presence is the same thing as the presence; the awareness of the presence is not separate from being the presence.

This is a mysterious perception to the normal mind of ego, which does not experience things that way. The normal mind is always an "I" aware of something, whereas the experience of presence has no subject/object dichotomy. But because it is possible for an "I" to be aware of the experience of presence, it is also possible to mistake that experience for the direct experience of presence. An "I," for example, could be aware of the presence of essential Joy or Strength, but that would still not be a complete knowing of the experience of the presence of Essence. The latter occurs when the Joy or the Strength is aware of itself as presence.

This, then, reflects the reality that the consciousness of presence is indistinguishable from the fact of presence itself. Beingness and consciousness are inseparable, are coemergent. This means that at the moment presence is present, who you are is simultaneously indistinguishable from the fact that you know you are presence by feeling, sensing, touching, tasting yourself as presence. The touching of yourself as presence is not different from the presence itself. The touch, the taste, the texture—in other words, the perception of the presence—*is* the presence.

Are you saying that it can sense itself?

Yes. The presence itself has a sense of itself. The presence itself is consciousness. In fact, to understand presence is to know consciousness in its purity before you separate from consciousness.

Usually consciousness is conscious of some kind of an object of perception—either outer or inner—but not of its own presence in its purity. The experience of Essence as presence is the experience of consciousness that is conscious of its own presence. Consciousness is aware of itself in a self-reflective way—but even to say "self-reflective" is not exact. It is not that consciousness turns around to know itself. It knows itself by being itself; it knows itself by complete identity with itself. It is different from the usual kind of knowing. So you see, to know presence is the same thing as to be presence, and that is the same thing as to realize presence. They are all the same thing because there is no separation.

Another thing about presence distinguishes it from the experience of ego. Whether you are experiencing an emotion, a thought, an inner state, or an action, ego cannot be separated from the imprints of the past. Ego is determined by the past. Whatever you feel, whatever you think, is largely a continuation of the past. For instance, when you say that you are aware of your body, what you are usually aware of is your body as a continuity from the past—your body was there yesterday, it was born many years ago, it has developed and changed, it is now here, and you are sensing it as you grow older, or whatever. This means that your experience of your body is inseparable from the continuity of the past.

This is true for all ego experience. Your inner sense of yourself, your beliefs about yourself, your emotions and inner states, your actions and ideas—all these are a continuation of the past. They are simply modifications of what you already know. In a real sense, your experience is not new, it is not fresh.

To know presence means to recognize yourself as completely undefined by the past. To realize presence means that your experience of yourself is not determined by memory. If memory is determining your experience when there is presence, then your experience of presence is not complete. It still has veils over it, barriers against it; it is not pure, complete. To be presence is to recognize yourself as *the* presence in the present moment. So when I say that presence is self-existing, I mean it exists right now, right at this very second, and its nature has nothing to do with whatever has happened in the past.

The way the body is has a lot to do with what happened to you in the past—the same with your mind, your personality, your emotions, your actions, and so on. They are so much determined by the past that after a while there is no presence, there is only memory instead. The more you act and experience according to memory, the more your experience lacks presence. After a while, your experience is mostly a set of reactions based on what happened in the past. And the more it becomes reactivity from the past, the more you forget presence. After a while, you don't even know what presence is. It then becomes very difficult to disengage from the past because it not only determines how you feel, it determines what you think, your sense of who you are, your very sense of existence. The understanding of presence makes clear the great gulf that exists between the experience of Essence and the experience of the ego.

Presence also has something to do with time. In one sense, presence is compacted time. It is as if you took all of time and compressed it into the present moment. Normally, your experience of yourself is spread over time—that is, into the past and the future as well as the present—in accordance with your ideas, beliefs, hopes, and fears. If you withdraw your awareness from the past and future and concentrate it solely in the present, your experience of yourself focuses into a single moment: now. To trust the now completely can lead to the experience of yourself as a self-originating presence.

Many of the ways of describing Essence refer to this awareness—Self-Originating or the Unoriginated, the Self-Arising, the Self-Existing, Pure Existence, the I AM, the pure fact of Isness—and all of them indicate that your existence is pure presence and that nothing in your experience of this existence is determined by your memories. The experience of presence is spontaneously itself, 100 percent.

You speak of an object as not having presence. The chair, you said, doesn't have presence. I was reminded of an experience I had one night of a tomato sitting on a plate on the table, and I was aware that this tomato had more than three dimensions. It seemed incredibly present, just emanating presence.

Very good. That is definitely a real experience of presence. However, I did not say that the table or the chair doesn't have presence. I said that the usual experience of the chair is not the experience of presence; it is the experience of an object that is defined by a concept we have learned in the past.

I see.

Also, the chair itself is not experiencing presence. You can perceive its presence, for presence is the nature of everything; that is possible. But to perceive the real presence of the object, you have to be present yourself.

As I said, if you become aware of your presence, after a while you will realize that everything is presence, there is nothing but presence. But we usually don't see things as presence. We perceive objects that exist in space and time as discrete and self-existing in their thinghood. We do not experience objects as full of consciousness, a consciousness that is aware of its presence. We experience them as inanimate, dead, and empty of any consciousness or awareness. We think this chair came from yesterday—somebody brought it from my office. To experience this chair as presence is to recognize that it did not come from my office; it comes from this very moment. This chair is not the chair of yesterday, it is the chair that is now—and that is a fact. But our mind has been so warped that we think it is a fact that the chair came from yesterday, from somebody's office. But that is a delusion. It can even be logically proven to be a delusion, because how can something from yesterday produce something that is now when you know that yesterday is not here anymore? The only thing that can produce something now is something that exists right now.

There's a theory of the creation of the universe that's like that. It says that the universe is not old at all; it's constantly being created moment to moment. It's kind of a wild theory because it opposes what the scientists are saying—that it's old and it's progressing through time. To say it doesn't have an age seems to reflect the viewpoint that you are talking about here.

If you look at the universe in terms of time, then everything is progressing through time. However, if you are experiencing presence, you recognize that time slows down steadily more and more. The more there is contact with presence and the more there is identity with presence, the more time slows down. And that is the point I'm trying to make: Presence has to do with freedom from time.

Time is and isn't, in the sense that if the chair is present, you can say that it is not involved in history and has no passage through time. And yet, taking a larger viewpoint, doesn't presence also include the sense in which the chair does exist in time?

In fact, it's more like the presence of the chair *is* time. Time becomes real. Real time is nothing but the ongoingness of Being, the flow of presence. That is the only real time.

I am focusing on the presence itself, the experience of presence, which is the experience of Essence, of true nature, of liberated nature, of enlightenment. It is the experience of the enlightened consciousness that is the self-existing consciousness. The consciousness is enlightened and has always been enlightened. It doesn't *become* enlightened, because it *is* itself enlightenment, liberation, freedom, reality, and truth. And what makes it be free, liberated, and true is that it is not produced by anything else. It is here right now as itself. It is self-generating. And you can't even say that it is self-generating—it just *is;* in some kind of absolute, fundamental way, it is now, this very instant, and this very instant is nothing but that.

The more we are present, the more we are in the present. The more present we are, the freer we are from the determinations of the mind, from the influence of thoughts. The mind slows down, quiets down, and becomes less important, less substantial. And since the past affects us primarily through memory, and hence through the mind, time loses its grip on our experience. This is experienced subjectively as the slowing of time. Presence slows down the conceptualizing activity, which makes us aware of what is fundamentally here, which is presence. Time slows down as if it were compacted into real time, which is the now, which is presence.

As presence takes precedence over mind, we become aware of the continuity of presence, and then we see that real time is the flow of presence. This is experienced subjectively as compacted time. It is as if the real time of presence that has been spread thin through the activity of the mind were now condensed through the greater experience of presence. All the categories of your perception, cognition, and experience start merging into each other. You no longer think of your thoughts, your feelings, your sensations, your body, and your mind as different and separate things; you begin to see how each is reflected in the others. All of them start to merge and become one thing: the flow of presence, which is real lived time.

The presence of Essence brings us to the now until we recognize that the presence of Essence *is* the now. The flow of presence—which is the same thing as the continuity of presence—is time. So, presence in the present becomes awareness of the now, not as a point in linear time but as presence. The now, which is the only real time, is recognized to be the fullness of presence. This presence of now is also seen to include all perception and experience, to include and be everything. There is nothing that exists apart from this presence. It is everything, and there is nothing separate from it; even your thoughts and ideas and beliefs are part of it. Those thoughts in fact don't really come from the past. Even the past doesn't come from the past—your memory of the past is happening right now as part of this presence. The presence becomes all-inclusive.

To arrive at that all-inclusive experience of presence, where everything is one unified presence, we first have to understand what presence is in our own personal experience, and that means understanding the experience of presence as Essence in its various aspects. The aspect of Brilliancy brings in a very precise, specific experience of presence as completely in the now. Brilliancy is a presence that slows time to a standstill. As time slows down, we experience it as the flow of presence. When time stops, we experience timelessness, and the presence is pure and complete. There is purity now because experience is completely untouched by thinking. In place of thought there is radiance and brilliance. The luminosity and magnificence of Brilliancy is the exquisite perfection of presence without time. That is why the full experience of Brilliancy is the experience of timelessness.

Before differentiation and conceptualization, before there is memory of the past or thoughts of the future, there is just the pure fact, the pure actuality, of presence with its complete radiance. Here the consciousness is aware of itself completely outside of time—consciousness and presence as the same thing. Timelessness, which is the full and complete experience of Brilliancy, becomes the entry into the now, which is universal presence.

We can think of consciousness being aware of its own actuality as a loop of self-reflection. But a loop implies time, right? Now suppose that the loop gets smaller and smaller—infinitely smaller until the loop disappears. This would mean that there is no time between actuality and the awareness of actuality. There is no longer self-reflexivity or the passage of time. It is a singularity of presence that is a singularity in time. It is completely self-aware right now; its self-existence is its self-consciousness. It is completely timeless.

It is here that we recognize Essence in its purity as a timelessness that is really you—what you are experiencing yourself to be right now. If you experience yourself purely right now—without your ideas, without your beliefs, without remembering what happened to you in the past, without referring to what you are and what you are not, without thinking where you are going, where you come from, what affected you, who your parents are, whether you are married or not, whether you are a woman or a man, whether you're young or old, sick or healthy, happy or unhappy—if all of these thoughts, beliefs, ideas, remembrances, and identifications are completely gone from your mind, completely obliterated by the radiance, and you are just here and you are just your consciousness itself, then you are in the timelessness of presence. Then you are that timelessness; then you are that presence. As this timeless moment unfolds, you recognize that this presence extends and expands until everything is included in it. This is the eternal now. Real time takes us to timelessness, and timelessness ushers us into the now.

More experience of presence will give you the feeling of having more time. You will actually start to feel that you have a great deal of time—free time—to do whatever needs to be done. This expansion of the sense of time is related to the slowing down of the mind. You no longer spend time uselessly thinking. Though it may seem magical to those caught in time (out of presence), anybody who knows presence in a deep and full way actually experiences this shift in time.

Can yearning for Brilliancy sometimes be a yearning to merge with timelessness?

It could be, yes. It might manifest that way. That is why one method, one technique, is to learn to be in the present.

Over the past few decades in the human growth movement, the practice of being in the present has been used as a developmental technique, but it has been understood and used in a somewhat incomplete way. To be in the now is understood to mean to think about just what is in the here and now, to have emotions only about what is present in this moment. Basically it has been used to situate your awareness in the present moment. In Gestalt therapy, for example, to be in the present is not taken further than that; it is not taken as far as letting go of your mind. Gestalt therapy does not understand that being in the here and now means that you will eventually recognize yourself as a presence independent of the mind. In Gestalt you still think in the kinds of categories that you learned in the past, so you are bringing the past with you into the present. However, Gestalt moves you toward the present because it asks you to look at what is right now.

So as I said, one way to get to the experience of the pure state of presence, the already liberated state, is to focus on whatever helps bring you more and more into the here and the now—to disengage from the past and the future and be in the moment. This focus is an important element in our work here, and the techniques of Gestalt therapy can provide an effective entry into the experience of presence.

Our work in the Diamond Approach is to understand with appreciation, insight, and deep feeling exactly where we are in the moment as it unfolds. In fact, we need to be completely aware and understanding of where we are at this moment for the unfoldment to occur. You cannot go about this in a theoretical way. To allow your consciousness to unfold—and, by unfolding, to shed all the layers of unclarity—you have to understand where your consciousness is at this very moment.

Are you saying that the way we are eliminating time is by studying it?

Well, that is one way of saying it. I would prefer to say that the way we are eliminating time is by clearly understanding our experience at the moment, moment to moment.

This discriminating awareness of our experience can become continuous, instead of being limited to peak experiences. To understand your experience in this way means to find the thread of where you are. When this understanding, this discriminating awareness, is complete, the thread will be a brilliant thread of presence. That is because you cannot have genuine understanding if you are not understanding what is happening in this moment; you can have only intellectual and vacuous understanding. True understanding is the understanding of what is happening now. Be aware that as we progress to deeper levels of understanding, more than just the content of experience changes; the nature of experience itself changes.

Is this like a stream of consciousness, in contrast to a sense of what your mind may be telling you?

Well, it would include that. A stream of consciousness is part of what is happening now. But the idea is more one of self-centering.

The way we work is to find out what is happening right now: What are you experiencing right now? What are you feeling right now? And then to follow that. If you don't focus on *right now*, you won't really have understanding. This is true even if you want to understand your childhood. You can't understand it by just thinking about it. The only way thinking about it would help is if that brought the childhood experience into the now so you could experience it. For example, if you were hurt by your father in childhood, you can't just think of the hurt and have it remain a memory in your mind—that doesn't do it. If you think, "I was hurt by my father in childhood," and then you feel the hurt now, in this very moment, then understanding can happen. Otherwise there is no understanding, no transformation. What matters is the experience in the moment, the lived experience, what you are actually in touch with. If it happens that you are not in touch with anything, then that lack of in-touchness is what you need to be in touch with. We have to start where we are.

If our consciousness is hovering in a place that is not deep, then by knowing where it is—I mean, knowing exactly what our consciousness is experiencing—it will drop down. When it drops down, it will expand time and become more focused in the present. And when you know precisely where your consciousness is in this next moment, it will drop down even further. The further down it drops, the more present you are, until you recognize exactly where you are in your process at this moment.

This is the way to find the thread of your unfolding, where you and presence come together. If the work we're doing, the teaching you are receiving, is falling on some kind of a mental construct of who you are—a mental part of you that is not where you truly are at this moment—then it will not take root. You will not know the real response in your soul to what we are studying. You need to recognize where you are in your process in this moment in order to really understand yourself and to use the work we are doing here. Pure presence is the gift of Brilliancy to the soul. It opens the door to timelessness—but even more important, it is the doorway to the depths of our own true nature.

4

Completeness

☙

When I refer to the essential aspects—especially when we are in intentional work situations, such as this retreat—I usually refer to them by color. I do this as a kind of shorthand because each essential aspect can be recognized in different ways through its several affects and experiential senses. For instance, the Black aspect could be experienced as peace, as stillness, or as power. So instead of calling it peace, stillness, or power, I simply say "Black."

It is the same with Brilliancy. I call it Brilliancy instead of intelligence because, while it is true that intelligence is an important way that Brilliancy is experienced, there are many other ways in which Brilliancy is experienced and recognized. These include the sense of protection, synthesis, an intelligent kind of will, real responsibility, timelessness, purity, and perfection.

In our work, we have seen that the experience of each sense, or quality, tends to raise issues that are associated with it and psychological constellations specific to it. You could have a psychological constellation around intelligence, another one around responsibility, and so on. Each sense touches a separate psychological constellation.

This morning, we want to work with another quality or characteristic of Brilliancy. It is the sense or affect of contentment, of satisfaction, of being relaxed, settled, without agitation. Usually the psyche, or soul, is agitated, seeking, excited, reactive, or not resting, not just being here in a settled, contented kind of way. There are many reasons, of course, why the psyche is like that, and most have to do with some underlying sense of deficiency. But one central cause relates to all the deficiencies. And that cause is our focus today.

The psyche is always agitated whenever there is a deficiency, a hole. Since the psyche usually can't tolerate the feeling of deficiency, it tries to do something to compensate for that feeling or to eliminate it one way or the other. If you feel there is a gap someplace in you, you start feeling uncomfortable—something is missing—and you usually feel it shouldn't be that way, right? So you work on those deficiencies, those holes, and each time you work through one of them, a specific aspect arises. You may believe that in time, with work, all of the aspects will arise and you will feel that there are no more holes, and then you will feel complete. However, the experience of completeness does not arise that way.

Brilliancy, as we have seen, is an intrinsic synthesis of all the aspects. It is experienced and recognized as a self-existing, undifferentiated gestalt of all of them. And Brilliancy addresses the specific longing or deficiency that is at the root of all the other longings to be free from holes and to close the gaps. So when Brilliancy is experienced in a full way—in the sense that you are intimately in touch with it, are being in it, being present *as* it—there is a specific affect that can be recognized. This important affect or quality is in all the aspects and is present every time you feel an aspect fully, but it only becomes specifically clear and delineated when the aspect is Brilliancy.

It is the same way with intelligence or any of the other qualities of Brilliancy. All aspects have intelligence, but only when you experience Brilliancy do you understand intelligence in a very specific way. This signifies that intelligence is implicit in all the aspects of Essence but is explicit only in the manifestation of Brilliancy. So this new quality is an experience of the already-existing unity that precedes differentiation and is a corollary to the fact that Brilliancy is a self-existing and unoriginated synthesis. The experience of this self-existing and unoriginated unity of all the aspects of Essence, which happens in the full experience of Brilliancy, is the experience of completeness. You experience yourself as being a presence that is explicitly feeling complete, with a clear and distinct recognition that nothing is missing, that there are no holes, no deficiencies.

The soul has gaps in it when it experiences itself as the personality of ego. Gaps are the holes and deficiencies that are the absences of realization of the fullness of Essence in the soul. So, one of the specific ways that completeness is recognized is in the feeling that there is no gap, which I usually call the state of no gap. When Brilliancy is fully integrated with the soul, all of the perfections of Being are present in an immanent and clear way. And then there are no gaps, no holes in the soul, because Brilliancy is a self-existing synthesis of all aspects.

The experience is that I am complete in such a way that nothing else is required. And the completeness is experienced in such an intrinsic and full way that just being here—the presence on its own—is 100 percent self-sufficient and complete; nothing needs to be taken away, to be added, to happen, or to stop happening. The sense of completeness is absolute, while being recognized and delineated in a clear and explicit manner.

When you feel an essential aspect fully, you usually do not feel that something is missing. For instance, if you are feeling love fully—the Pink aspect—you are not usually missing anything else. The aspect is complete in itself. But there is no sense or specific affect of completeness. There is no feeling of incompleteness, but there is no feeling of completeness either. By contrast, with Brilliancy there is a very specific and delineated experience of being complete. Therefore, from this insight or wisdom, we recognize that completeness does not happen by putting things together; it is not a matter of collecting all the perfections of your Being and combining them. Completeness arises by integrating the aspect of completeness into your soul.

The experience is: Your presence is completely filled, continuous—with no interruption all the way through—with the presence of completeness. Completeness means that you have not moved away from the totality of yourself in any way; there is no duality whatsoever. You are completely abiding as your nature. You don't even have any interest in looking at the completeness because there is no separation between you and the completeness of your true nature. There is no consciousness that is interested in finding out if it is complete, or in saying, "Let me experience my completeness so I can enjoy it." There isn't the interest to investigate it. There isn't even the interest to know it. Interest is eliminated, not because you are hopeless or depressed but because you are complete. Nothing else is needed or required.

But it is not as if you were complete and your mind says, "Well, now I don't need anything, so I can forget it." The completeness is so complete that the sense of "I need" or "I don't need" doesn't even occur to you. You are naturally, almost unconsciously, complete. When the completeness is fully integrated, you are not even aware that you are complete—the realization of completeness can go that far. You are just there completely, without concern or question. The consciousness is so full that there is no reason to rise out of yourself to get something or to do something or to accomplish something.

In the usual state of the psyche, some agitation or movement or excitement makes our energy go forward, away from a state of being completely settled. But completeness means that all of our outward movement has been stilled because there is contentment, for nothing is missing. If you are really the Brilliancy presence, you don't even need to know that you are Brilliancy; you don't need to know you are there; you don't need to know anything—in fact, you don't need anything.

If you are really the Brilliancy, you are in some sense not even the body; so there is no movement based on the usual instinctual promptings. Usually you want this or you want that, you like this or you like that, but all of that is a movement outside you. That is the psyche and the body doing their thing.

As the completeness, you are totally contented, unmoving. The contentment of completeness has a blissful quality that feels like a deliciousness. The deliciousness is so complete, the delicate kind of pleasure is so contented, that the mind doesn't even think about whether it is contented or not. The mind—the psyche—even forgets the memory of discontentment.

We are looking at the quality of Brilliancy when it is felt at the heart level. Brilliancy in the heart is felt as this kind of contentment, completeness, exquisite deliciousness. It is like taking vanilla ice cream and making it totally satisfying—something like that [*Laughter*] but not exactly. It is a deliciousness, a blissfulness that is very specific in its affect, in its feeling. Completeness is not the usual affect of pleasure, not the usual kind of fulfillment or satisfaction. It is not that you feel the absence of incompleteness; it is not only that incompleteness is not there. Rather, there is the definite presence of completeness with an ecstatic affect. This is Brilliancy felt in the heart; the heart is completely filled with it.

The heart of the soul is contented, full, totally nourished with milky Brilliancy. The aspect of Brilliancy has attained the nourishing milky quality of completeness. This makes the heart joyous and overflowing with all kinds of sweet love. Out of this milky kind of brilliant completeness flows colored rivers of love—pink, red, yellow, amber, gold, orange—the various colors of the heart aspects of Essence. When the Being is settled, it is not moving, it is just there; the heart is satisfied. Then the heart outflows in a natural way—not because you want it to outflow but because it is natural and it happens on its own.

Every time we feel a deficiency, a hole, a gap, there is a longing for that particular missing quality that resulted in the hole. But with that longing there is an additional subtle, underlying longing for the completeness, because each hole, each deficiency, makes you feel incomplete. So it is true that if there is a deficiency of love, for instance, you feel incomplete in your lack of love and you will long for the Love aspect. But you will also long for the completeness because the loss of Love destroyed the completeness. Likewise, the loss of Will destroys the completeness, the loss of Peace destroys the completeness, and so on.

I think it is a beautiful thing to recognize that the human soul has the potential to feel and be utterly complete. You see, the Brilliancy is our nature, the brilliance of who and what we are. That completeness, that contentment, that sort of complete deliciousness, happens by completely abiding in our nature, our Being, by not going out of ourselves. We find it by realizing presence itself. It is not found by trying to get pleasure or presence, or by trying to enjoy the presence. It is just *being* the presence.

Completeness is a contented kind of ecstasy. It is not an excited kind of ecstasy. Sometimes you are ecstatic and blissful, all excited, and you want to tell everybody about it—your hair is standing on end and your eyes are bulging [*Laughter*]—but that is more like you're on something. [*More laughter*] I wouldn't call that contentment. When you are contented, you are not even interested in saying anything about it. If you still want to say something about it, then the contentment is not complete; it is not the experience of completeness.

When you are complete, you are complete. You become a still, delicate, exquisite pool of milky Brilliancy that is luminous; and this luminosity is exquisiteness, and this exquisiteness is deliciousness, and this deliciousness is complete fulfillment. When you feel the completeness, you recognize your pure nature before you left it, before your consciousness separated from it. You are recognizing yourself in your utter purity before any disturbance happened, before any stirring occurred.

We see here that intelligence is the functioning of completeness. Brilliancy appears as an intrinsic intelligence. Because Brilliancy has everything in it, it imbues the psyche with intelligence by providing it with all the qualities it needs for its functioning. And it provides them in a synthesized way, creating a complete synthetic capacity. The psyche can now function in a complete way, which is bound to be an intelligent functioning.

Just as the longing for Brilliancy can manifest as the longing for intelligence, so it can also manifest as the longing for completeness; and the absence of Brilliancy can be experienced as incompleteness. So when you feel incomplete, you usually try to get rid of that feeling by completing yourself, right? If I feel incomplete because I feel or think I am not smart, I go to school. If I feel incomplete because I am weak, I take up weight lifting, right? If I am incomplete because I'm not compassionate enough, I go about learning to help people.

But all these activities indicate that you believe the completeness will happen by adding something to yourself. You believe that by putting things together and collecting all the necessary elements, you will then be complete. In reality that doesn't work, because completeness is an affect, a feeling, of our true nature when we experience it completely and fully—and you can't assemble your true nature from its different parts.

The completeness can happen only by confronting the incompleteness head on, by recognizing it as incompleteness, and not by acting according to the delusion that we can complete ourselves by getting this or that. Completeness happens by being honest and truthful with ourselves, acknowledging the incompleteness, allowing it to happen, exploring it, going to its source: "How do I feel incomplete? Why do I feel incomplete?" So instead of saying no to the incompleteness and wondering how you can complete yourself, you can explore the feeling: "Well, I feel incompleteness; I wonder why." You can be curious out of loving the truth, because you are interested in finding out what the truth is. You become interested in the exploration.

To confront the incompleteness, to explore it, means to acknowledge it, to let it be there, to feel it fully until you find out and understand what it's all about, why there is a sense of incompleteness. In this process, you might find out all kinds of things about incompleteness and about this or that aspect that you are out of touch with; but usually the incompleteness will continue as long as you don't realize the completeness itself. And if that incompleteness remains, it is fine to just feel that; it is better for you that you don't forget by finding a substitute.

As long as you are feeling incomplete, you are still not completely settled in yourself. You don't want to pretend to yourself that you've got it when you still aren't feeling complete. It pays to be honest—in other words, you lose by being dishonest. If you forget, or find a substitute for completeness, you might feel a little better for a while, but for the next ten billion years, you lose. [*Laughter*]

Brilliancy is a complete presence, and thus it is a presence of completeness. The greatest lesson that the soul needs to learn is how to settle into itself, because all that it wants is there in itself. The soul is always seeking, always looking, always agitating, rejecting this, accepting that. All the traditional spiritual disciplines and practices are basically for the soul to learn the inadequacy and hopelessness of ego activity and to come to the point of saying, "Okay, I won't do any of that. I give up, I'll just sit here." If you really do that, you're done—the completeness is there. The treasure is there in the simplicity of Being, but we are not aware of it because we are ahead of it. It's here, but we're going over there, so we never get it. We just need to settle back and relax; only then do we wonder, "What is all this fuss about anyway?"

But first we have to deal with the barriers to feeling incompleteness. Incompleteness is one of those things that the ego feels ashamed about, believing that it is a deficiency, a bad thing. You usually explain it with all kinds of things: I'm incomplete because I'm too little; I'm incomplete because I'm a woman; I'm incomplete because I didn't go to school; I'm incomplete because I haven't got a job—whatever you happen to feel deficient about at the time. And usually you attack yourself thoroughly for it.

So the first thing we notice about incompleteness is that superego attacks are common. The judgments need to be recognized and you need to deal with them. At some point, however, you need to understand the fundamental fact that incompleteness is not due to something missing, something wrong with you, or your not having done something. It has nothing to do with that. Completeness is really a way of experiencing your Being, so incompleteness simply means being out of touch with that experience.

The superego does not usually attack you because Brilliancy is missing. Your superego doesn't know about Brilliancy, so it attacks you about whatever sense of deficiency it finds in your experience. Under normal circumstances, there is a misinterpretation of the hole, or lack of Brilliancy; it is not seen as the absence of a certain manifestation of your Being. Instead, your superego attacks you, saying you're too short, your nose is crooked, you're dumb, you say things wrong, you never know which foot to put first—that kind of thing. That is the way your superego picks on you: It finds those little incompletenesses and attacks you for them.

But when you understand that incompleteness has nothing to do with these things, you will have a deeper handle on your superego. Completeness happens by confronting and completely tolerating the incompleteness. So your superego, by attacking you for feeling incomplete, is really preventing you from getting closer to and relaxing into your own true nature, which is complete.

Your intrinsic nature is complete, though you might not believe it now. If and when you recognize yourself—when you are really being yourself—you will find out that you are completeness. So, if you are *feeling* incomplete, that does not mean you *are* incomplete. All it means is that you are not resting in your nature.

Everybody is complete. Completeness is the deeper nature of the human soul. The more you recognize that you are really complete, the easier it becomes to accept and to experience incompleteness; for you then know that incompleteness is just some kind of ignorance. It is a symptom, it is not a true thing; it is not a true description of what and who you are. Completeness is the true description of who you are. It is not enough, however, to believe what I say. You need to have that direct experience for yourself.

Incompleteness is your path toward completeness. It is a treasure—or, more accurately, a window—that you have in your psyche. It is important to recognize the various ways you personally use to avoid the feeling of incompleteness. This may include denying your incompleteness or trying to become complete. Your spiritual search, for example, might be an attempt to cover up your incompleteness. In fact, people say that they are searching because they are incomplete. Searching for what? Completeness is not something to be sought after. Completeness is something to be relaxed into. It's like when your muscles are tense: They just need to relax, let go, and settle.

Part Two

☙

In the group of talks that make up chapter 5—the second section of this book—Brilliancy is explored from a different perspective than the material in Part One, which was from a retreat that introduced the students to Brilliancy in its various flavors. The following talks were presented several years later, as part of an ongoing teaching about the practice of inquiry and the way in which different aspects of true nature support this practice. The reader will find some of the same ground presented here as in the talks in Part One; however, the focus has shifted, and new dimensions of the Brilliancy aspect are addressed.

This chapter appeared previously in *Spacecruiser Inquiry: True Guidance for the Inner Journey*, which is based on the later teaching on inquiry. A slightly revised version is included here to present a more comprehensive picture of the essence of intelligence—the aspect of Brilliancy—all in one place, rather than asking the reader to refer to another book for this material.

Both *Spacecruiser Inquiry* and *Brilliancy* are books in the Diamond Body series, which is oriented toward the practice of the Diamond Approach. The former focuses on exploring inquiry as the spiritual practice central to this path, while *Brilliancy* offers a window through which the reader can begin to experience and understand the unfoldment of the teaching process within a group, as well as the way the teacher guides the students' individual inquiries. Part Two provides an orientation to this latter process by describing how essential intelligence functions in personal inquiry, which is then demonstrated by the transcripts of student inquiries that follow in Part Three.

5

Brilliant Inquiry

❃

Understanding and Liberation

Realization and liberation require many things: dedication and commitment, love and devotion, awareness and sensitivity. But more than anything else, they require understanding. Understanding is the central faculty needed for liberation, especially when we go very deep in our experience and arrive at subtle places. That is because when we reach the subtlety of our true nature—the real depth—what is left is our understanding. Everything else, in some sense, has dropped away by then. All that is left is our subtle capacity for discriminating what is manifesting, what is true, and what is false.

It has been acknowledged and understood by all spiritual traditions that what finally liberates the soul is to see the false as false and the true as true. This is for one simple reason: Our soul is fundamentally faithful to the truth.

Truth is the fundamental ground of our soul, so the soul is fundamentally faithful to the truth. She always lives and acts out what she believes to be true. Yes, we frequently act out of lies and falsehoods, but this is because the soul believes that they are true. When we act out being a little deficient kid, for instance, it is because the soul believes that she is a little deficient kid. When we act from anger, we really believe that the truth is that we should act out the anger. The difficulty is not that the soul loves or likes falsehood, but that she takes a falsehood as truth and lives it out faithfully. For example, the soul will not let go of identification with the ego because the soul is totally convinced that this is who she is. The soul is convinced that she is the body, that she is this person, and so this is what she is going to live, act out, and defend until death. The soul is, in a word, ignorant.

That is why at some point, the most important thing for the soul is to see what the truth really is: to see who she is and what she is, and to know the truth about the soul and about reality as a whole. Only when the soul recognizes the truth and is certain about it will she change. Before that, she will continue to behave according to what she takes to be the truth.

Of course, this situation can become quite subtle and complex because we might have an experience of true nature, recognize "Oh, that's me," and then wonder, "Well, why don't I live according to that?" The reason is that we are more convinced of other things, some of which might be held in the unconscious. We might still believe that we are more this little kid, for example, or that we are our historical identity.

Many deep convictions about what we believe is true have been crystallized in the soul and have never been challenged. Hence, our occasional insights or experiences about what true reality is do not liberate us. We still have to understand ourselves in relation to that reality in order to be liberated from the falsehoods that we take to be true. And of course, we need to see what truth itself is. This is why the role of understanding has always been recognized as the central and final factor in liberation.

For instance, if a person is identified with a particular self-image, he will not let it go before he recognizes it is just an image. It doesn't matter what anybody tells him about that image; as long as he believes the image is really him, it will not dissolve. He won't let go just because somebody loves him, or because he feels good about himself, or even because he has an experience of his true nature. He lets go only when he understands: "I am identifying with this. But it is not me, it is just an image in my mind."

Many methods do not use understanding or inquiry directly, such as those based on action or devotion, but all methods produce understanding at some point. If they don't, they won't liberate us. If at some point, through devotion and passionate love, we don't recognize and understand that we are part and parcel of the Beloved, how will we be liberated? It doesn't matter how much we love the Beloved; we will be separated as long as we do not clearly discern our inherent unity with what we love.

Understanding is our natural, inherent faculty. We see that this is all we've got when finally left to ourselves. When we forget all methods and techniques, when we just rest and be, only our own recognition of what is true is left. From this place, when we recognize our true nature, we understand who and what we are. And when we are convinced—with certainty and without question—that this truth is really our nature, then we change. So liberation is actually a change of mind. At some point, we change our mind about what reality is in a very fundamental way.

The faculty in our soul that makes it possible for our inquiry to arrive at understanding is what I call the Diamond Guidance. This faculty combines all of the essential aspects into one functioning structure of Being. Each essential aspect provides the Guidance with a specific capacity needed for the operation of inquiry and understanding. Together, all the elements of the Diamond Guidance make it possible for our inquiry to become precise enough to arrive at objective understanding. In this chapter we will explore how intelligence—the aspect of Brilliancy—is necessary for our inquiry and understanding.

We begin this exploration with the Absolute, which is the essence of our Being. The absolute essence of Being is complete in all ways, perfect in all possibilities; it is completeness and perfection in a total way. It implicitly has in it all the essential aspects, all the perfections. These perfections are the perfections of the Absolute, the explications of all the perfections inherent in our deepest nature, which is our absolute identity. All these perfections—all the essential aspects—are implicit in the Absolute. They are not only implicit and unmanifest, but they are also undifferentiated. So the Absolute is completeness, perfect in all ways in an unmanifest, implicit, and undifferentiated way.

In this context, "undifferentiated" means that the qualities of Being are not separate from each other. At this level of experience, we cannot separate or differentiate them, even though they are all there. Not only are they not differentiated, they are not manifest. In other words, we can't experience them in a positive sense; we can only know that they are there because there is no deficiency, no need, in the experience of the Absolute. The Absolute is complete when we experience it as qualityless. It is qualityless because although it implicitly has all the perfect qualities, they are all unmanifest. That is why we call it the Mystery. We know its perfections explicitly only when the Absolute is manifest.

The Brilliance of Being

At one of the stages of its manifestation, the Absolute presents itself as explicit perfection. Here, perfection and completeness are explicit, with all the various perfections present—but in this stage, the qualities are still undifferentiated. We cannot separate one from another. We can know and recognize Love in this manifestation, for example, but we cannot differentiate it from Will. And we can't differentiate Will from Clarity, Clarity from Strength, Strength from Fulfillment, or Fulfillment from Joy. All the qualities are explicit and manifest but not differentiated.

We refer to this manifestation as Brilliancy. When we experience Brilliancy, we experience perfection and completeness explicitly because our true nature is manifesting to us in a form characterized by perfection and completeness. By inquiring into Brilliancy, we recognize it as intelligence. It is the presence of pure radiance, pure brilliance. The brilliance, the radiance, is like white light that contains all the colors of the spectrum. Clear light does not manifest the prismatic colors, nor does black light. More precisely, the clarity and the blackness have all the colors in an implicit way, not explicitly. In Brilliancy, they are explicit but not differentiated, not discriminated yet. That's why when we experience manifestation directly out of the Absolute, we always see it as a radiance, as a brilliance, as illumination.

Brilliancy is a perfection in the sense that it is completely undefiled true nature, just like the Absolute. We experience and recognize this perfection directly, in a positive sense, not in an indirect or negative sense. Because it is qualityless, the Absolute is perfect, but without the feeling or concept of perfection being present. In Brilliancy, perfection is a discriminated specific quality of the Absolute. That is why we consider Brilliancy to be one of the aspects of Essence. The presence of Brilliancy is so fine, so delicate, so subtle, that it is like a substance of utmost refinement, utmost delicacy, utmost smoothness and fluidity. It is like a substance made out of brilliance itself.

As we have seen, no color can be called brilliance; brilliance is always a quality of a color. The closest experience there is to brilliant light in nature is when we look at the stars at night or look directly into the sun. The light from these bodies is actually composed of many colors, but it is so intense that our eyes can't discriminate the colors. With brilliant light, however, though the colors are all explicitly present, we cannot discriminate them because they are not differentiated. Thus, the aspect of Brilliancy doesn't exist in the physical world. Neither does clear light. We never see clear light. We never see black light. Black light, clear light, and brilliant light don't exist in nature. But they are all specific dimensions of our true nature that can manifest on their own without characterizing something else.

When we can recognize Brilliancy as the essence of intelligence, we can begin to understand the fundamental elements of intelligence. We begin to see, for instance, that when we say an action is intelligent, we mean that it is complete and perfect—it is the best way to go about something. We interpret its completeness and perfection as intelligence. An intelligent action is an effective action, whether it be mental, emotional, or physical. Why do we want action to be intelligent? Because then it will be most efficient, most economical, most expedient. It will be the most optimizing. And when Brilliancy is present, what we see is that our faculties begin to function more perfectly and completely—that is, more intelligently.

So intelligence reflects completeness, and Brilliancy is the most complete because it has all the perfections and aspects in it, undifferentiated. When we experience Brilliancy, we feel it as Love, Will, Clarity, Peace, Joy, and Truth all at the same time. Our sense of it is completeness. Whenever there is a hole in our soul, that means an aspect is missing. In Brilliancy, nothing is missing because all the aspects are present; there are no holes. We can actually feel the particular affect of completeness.

And because Brilliancy is complete, it brings about the most perfect action possible. It is the most perfect in the sense that it is the most optimizing, which means that it is the most effective in drawing us nearer to our true nature. The optimal direction for the experience of the soul is the one that leads her as close to her home as possible.

Intelligence is a very difficult concept to analyze because it includes many elements, many facets. We first need to realize that the intelligence of Brilliancy is not just mental intelligence; it is intelligence in any dimension, any action. We can have intelligence in the response to a situation, in the way we live our life, the way we think, the way we inquire, the way we interact, the way we communicate. This intelligence is organic and it underlies the actual experience of our consciousness. Brilliancy is the inherent intelligence of our Being. The more in touch we are with it, the more it penetrates and pervades our life, our perception, our experience, and our actions.

Brilliancy and the Diamond Guidance

The Diamond Guidance is a particular patterned structure of all of the various perfections, or essential aspects of Being. However, in contrast with the undifferentiated perfections of Brilliancy, the perfections of the Diamond Guidance all operate in a manifest, explicit, and differentiated way. They are explicitly differentiated, but they function together as one unit that activates understanding.

This means that the Diamond Guidance itself is an expression of Brilliancy, of intelligence. It is the brilliant light that has been differentiated and then integrated in a specific function—that of understanding. This is one way of recognizing the functioning of intelligence in the Guidance, which has prompted us to sometimes refer to the Diamond Guidance as the discriminating intelligence of Being. However, we can see that the Guidance functions intelligently in three major ways. We have been discussing the first—namely, that the whole vehicle is a manifestation of intelligent action in the sphere of understanding or discerning the truth.

A second way the Guidance acts with intelligence is by modulating its brilliance depending on the situation. Its various colors—black, red, green, yellow, and so on—can become clearer, more transparent, more intense, more brilliant. More intelligence is operating when they do so, and the Guidance is then using more intelligence and brilliance in its operation. Any color—in this case, we are referring to any essential aspect—can become more or less brilliant. If it grows brilliant enough, it becomes the pure presence of Brilliancy. The differentiated light goes back to its origin, which is undifferentiated brilliance.

In fact, as the Guidance itself becomes more brilliant, the intense luminosity will begin to feel more prominent than any of the particular colors. In other words, as the Guidance luminates more brilliantly, the aspect of intelligence becomes dominant over other qualities. When it gets very bright, we might not even see a color, just brilliance. Then the whole Diamond Guidance is brilliant, is Brilliancy.

Also, there are degrees of brilliance and color differentiation. The more that the total functioning of Brilliancy—the perfection and completeness—is necessary in inquiry, the more brilliant the Guidance becomes. By becoming more brilliant, our inquiry attains greater intelligence, to the point of becoming Brilliancy itself. Thus, through the operation of Brilliancy in the Guidance, our inquiry can become more brilliant, luminous, illuminating, penetrating, complete, comprehensive, and perfect in its functioning.

Intelligence in Inquiry

We want to emphasize in this chapter the third way that intelligence functions in the Diamond Guidance: as one of the self-existing components of the Guidance. The Diamond Guidance is a combination of every aspect in its objective or diamond form, and one of those aspects is what we call the Brilliancy diamond. In other words, intelligence functions in the Diamond Guidance as the presence of the Brilliancy diamond.

By exploring the Brilliancy diamond, we will know objectively and precisely what intelligence is and how it functions in understanding. As we have discussed, Brilliancy as an aspect is a very clear, very explicit sense of presence. Its substance is so pure, so compacted with true nature, that its presence is palpable. It is exquisitely smooth. We can feel it as a flowing luminous presence, with a density similar to mercury but infinitely smoother and finer. If we see the reflection of sunlight in a mirror, and then imagine liquefying it, we get the effect of brilliance. Brilliancy is so intense that it looks almost like a continuous explosion of light.

When we see this beautiful brilliance, we understand why and how Being is intelligent. It is intelligent not only when it manifests in thought but also as intrinsic and organic brilliance, which is the underlying intelligence in any sphere of action. It provides our faculties of inquiry and understanding with an innate intelligence, so that discriminations are subtle, connections are insightful, analysis is luminously delineated, and articulation is lucid and perfect. Brilliancy is so perfectly immediate, so complete, smooth, fluid, and free that its functioning brings ease, perfection, lucidity, and clarity to any action, whether the action is communication or thinking, interaction or analysis.

The intelligence of Being does not function in a mechanical way like a computer does—by stringing together perceptions and memories. It is not like artificial intelligence, which is why artificial intelligence will never become real intelligence. There is an innate creativity in the functioning of Brilliancy. Intelligent inquiry possesses an organic, intuitive magic in how it arrives at insights. As a result, there is always a newness in the experience, and always an efficiency in our way of understanding. The inquiry embodies a lucidity, a fluidity, and a radiance that illuminate experience and make it possible for us to see more directly. Consciousness becomes so luminous that it cannot help but see more intrinsically, more to the core of the matter, always in a very smooth, easy, and lucid way, without effort or method.

The more that Brilliancy is present, the more we see directly without having to travel the route of making a series of connections. We are able to bridge big gaps in our understanding of experience without having to go through exhaustive, methodical analysis and correlation. We can jump between places due to the intensity, the fluidity, and the smoothness that is going through our consciousness. It is as though the Brilliancy itself were flowing through our neocortex and leaping across our synapses.

In addition, our consciousness is not only clear and transparent from the clarity of Essence, but a radiance from within illuminates and highlights the various associations and connections. Connections are more readily obvious because of the intense light shining through them.

Analytic Intelligence

In its functioning, Diamond Guidance uses two primary faculties, two operations, in an organically combined way: analysis and synthesis. It combines the functioning of the right and left hemispheres of the brain in a unified action of understanding.

In order to understand something, we frequently need first to analyze it. In other words, we need to look at the various parts and components, differentiate the significant elements, and discriminate them in more subtle and minute ways. Thus, the faculty of analysis is related to separation and discrimination, which ultimately is the capacity provided by the Red essence.

The way this faculty generally manifests in the Diamond Guidance is in its diamondness—its clear, objective nature. The diamondness of the Guidance—the fact that it possesses sharp facets—is what gives it a precise capacity for discrimination and analysis. Regardless of what quality is operating, there is always a diamondness to it—always a diamondness to the Green, to the Red, to the Brilliancy, to the Black. This gives the overall diamond structure the capacity to discriminate precisely and sharply, which then becomes the capacity of analysis.

Synthetic Intelligence

Synthesis has to do with putting things together: seeing the whole picture and comprehending it as a unified truth. We take the analyzed experience—experience broken down into components—and then see the elements in a new combination. So we begin inquiry with disparate elements of experience: memories and impressions, observations and reactions. Understanding emerges only when an integration occurs—seeing all of the elements together in such a way that the whole forms a particular meaning. This meaning of the whole is what we call a synthesis.

Of course, there must be a prototype, an underlying basis for this ability to synthesize. What is that prototype? Because Brilliancy is the original synthesis of all qualities, it is the prototype and archetype of synthesis on the essential level. And because it is an inherent synthesis, an intrinsic unity, its presence makes it possible for us to see the underlying synthesis in the various elements that we have analyzed. Brilliancy functions as the capacity for synthesis in any dimension, just as the Red essence functions as the capacity for discrimination in any dimension. The dimension we are discussing here is understanding.

So analysis is related to the Red or Strength essence, and synthesis to Brilliancy. Analysis is based on separating elements in a situation or an experience—that is, discriminating parts and specifics, which brings clarity, precision, and knowledge. However, the presence of Brilliancy as the prototype of synthesis gives the soul the additional capacity to see underlying unities. This capacity appears as synthetic insights that engender understanding of larger and larger segments of reality.

The functioning of the Guidance in inquiry is primarily an interplay of analysis and synthesis. Sometimes analysis dominates, sometimes synthesis dominates. But they can also work together. We break down an object of inquiry into components and recombine certain parts; then we analyze other parts and make other combinations, until at some point an overall final synthesis emerges. We call that an insight or realization, which is the understanding of the entire matter we are inquiring into.

Intelligent Guidance

Now, what is the difference between the synthesis of Brilliancy and the synthesis of Guidance? Brilliancy can lead us to an intelligent insight because when it is present in its fluid form, flowing through our veins and nervous system, we experience an intelligence and quickness in seeing overall gestalts. Since we can operate with Brilliancy by itself and see underlying unities without the presence of the Diamond Guidance, how does synthesis change when the Guidance is present? The difference is slight but significant, and there is an overlap between the two as well.

Brilliancy makes it possible for us to perceive the already-existing, underlying inherent synthesis, the unity that is the basis of insight. This is not a matter of combining things to arrive at an understanding. The synthesis is already present; we just don't see it. When Brilliancy arises, we begin to see the synthesis that is already there. It appears as the discovery of a unity that already underlies our experience. We discover this unity with the help of the unity of the soul, which is the Brilliancy.

The insight of the Diamond Guidance derives also from a synthesis. However, unlike in Brilliancy, the aspects in the Diamond Guidance are differentiated. Therefore, the synthesis of Guidance happens by correlating the various elements in a situation. The way it works is that the elements are first analyzed, seen separately. For example, in a given situation, there may be anger, sadness, a contraction here, a memory there, this action and that defense. These are all discriminated patternings. The Guidance sees all of these and then correlates them to find the connections between them and between the various groupings. It recognizes their relationships and interactions in a precise and detailed manner. It sees how they connect to each other, how they affect each other, how one leads to another: how sadness leads to the anger, how anger leads to fear, and how the fear is related to the contraction, how the whole thing is related to what one's mother did, how what one's mother did led to marrying this or that person, how marrying that person led to having that specific kind of job, which then explains one's present financial difficulty. That is the process that happens when inquiring with the Guidance.

This is usually an organized, orderly, and clear process, a precise seeing of interrelationships and interactions. This process ultimately reveals the unity that underlies all of them. This is how the Guidance uses synthesis in its overall functioning. Why? Because the Diamond Guidance is composed of the various differentiated aspects, and those aspects are differentiated and ordered in a certain combination. So Guidance functions by seeing the various elements of experience in combination until at some point they make a coherent gestalt. Then insight shines through.

By contrast, Brilliancy arrives at insight in one shot, at a glance, as if intuitively. It doesn't need to go through the various correlations. It is fast and breathtaking. However, it does not see the details of interactions and relationships between the various elements of the situation. We arrive at insight, but most of the time we don't know how we got there. There isn't as much perception, understanding, or knowledge in the process of arriving at the insight, which often makes it difficult to communicate it to others.

However, since the Diamond Guidance has Brilliancy as an aspect, it can use the capacity for direct illumination by simply seeing the gestalt without also seeing how the illumination came about. This direct penetration to the insight is possible and sometimes necessary. But frequently what is needed is the understanding of interactions and relationships that led to the insight. This is specifically the case when one attempts to relate many insights about the same subject matter. In order to reach an overarching insight that synthesizes the knowledge in various insights, we frequently need an understanding of how we arrived at them. A more complete knowledge of the different processes and relationships is crucial for such super-insights, such as those required to develop a body of knowledge.

Intelligence operates in the Guidance both in its overall functioning as the synthetic capacity that interrelates the elements, and in the brilliant unifying visions and overarching insights that appear like lightning. Then the discriminating capacity needs to come in again to analyze and synthesize, to relate all the elements in a way that makes the insight not only communicable but usable.

The Diamond Guidance uses both kinds of synthetic capacities (that of correlation/process orientation and that of intuitive bursts) in its overall operation, and specifically in its Brilliancy diamond. Sometimes what is needed is precise discrimination and precise analysis, in order to see the specifics and how they interrelate. That is when the Guidance becomes more transparent, clear, and delicate. The diamonds become quite sharp. At other times, more luminosity, more brilliance is needed. Then all the diamonds become more intense, more brilliant. The process is organic, with one often dominating the other.

But sometimes the two intensify together. Then there is an intense sharpness with a brilliance to the diamondness. The sharpness is so sharp that it shines brilliantly. The cutting edge is not only discriminating, it is also intelligently discriminating. This is the specific arising of the Diamond Guidance in the form of the Brilliancy diamond.

Recognition of the interrelationships between analysis and synthesis, and of the different levels of synthesis, can help us understand why major scientific discoveries are normally arrived at by scientists who have a great deal of knowledge and who have already explored the field extensively. Major scientific discoveries are rarely made by ordinary people, although it may happen once in a while. We need to develop a great deal of discrimination and understanding before we can approach the underlying unity. And it is only when we approach the underlying unity of the situation being explored that the essential unity, which is the Brilliancy, will arise. Then brilliant light penetrates the various elements of the whole situation, all of them are clarified in great relief, and they are all seen united to one center. That is the unifying insight.

This is actually a description of how inquiry arrives at insight. It always functions like that, not just at times of cataclysmic insight. The process of understanding continues through analysis and synthesis, steadily reaching greater and greater unity. Based on this understanding, we can see that spiritual development is a matter of greater and greater unification, greater and greater synthesis, until finally we arrive at the primordial synthesis, the true unity, the source of Brilliancy itself—our true nature.

The Brilliancy Diamond

The Brilliancy diamond, as an aspect in the Diamond Guidance, is a wonderful smooth presence, with luminosity and preciousness inseparable from clarity, sharpness, exactness, and precision. When this diamond is present in our soul, it infuses all of our capacities with the same luminosity and precision. Our inquiry and our understanding attain these qualities of brilliance and precision, as one capacity. What does that mean?

One meaning has to do with synthesis and analysis, the unified perception and the discriminating capacity. Synthesis and discrimination happen simultaneously when the Brilliancy diamond is present. They are both present in the same act. We see the specifics of the situation and their interrelationships at the same time that we see their underlying unity. It is the synthesis of Brilliancy that is directly seeing the underlying unity. Simultaneously with this awareness, we also see precisely how the unity manifests in the various elements, the various percepts and experiences.

Consider the following example: You are beginning to experience the essential aspect of Will, the White presence. You are able to discriminate it as Will. You can stop at that—"Oh, this is Will"—or you can begin to discriminate various characteristics of it, such as the feeling of determination, the sense of confidence, the inner solidity of support, the steadfastness Will gives to the soul, and so on. This is analysis, discrimination. "Oh, I see. When I'm feeling determined in this way, I recognize in it a sense of confidence." Then, as you feel the self-confidence: "I see, this confidence is the same as what makes me steadfast. And I recognize that when I'm steadfast, it is because this Will is a sense of inner support." You begin to discriminate the qualities that are implicit in Will.

So if you have a discriminating capacity, you can analyze, you can see more details, recognize more specifics in the same experience. If your discriminating capacity is not developed, if the sharpness of the diamond isn't there, it would be difficult for you to see the various qualities that make up the aspect.

In this process, you are not only experiencing analysis, you are experiencing synthesis at the same time—understanding how all the qualities are manifestations of the same aspect. There is confidence, there's support, there's steadfastness, there's determination, there's an effortlessness and a sense of purity, there's a sense of pristineness and a sense of definiteness. At the very instant of seeing the discrimination among these, you recognize that they are all the same thing. They are just slight differentiations of the same presence.

If we have only the discriminating capacity without the synthetic one, we might sometimes experience will, sometimes confidence, sometimes determination, but it would be difficult for us to know that they all belong to the same quality, to the same aspect. In the absence of the synthetic capacity, we might even conceptualize them as different aspects that do not share an underlying unity. But if the synthetic capacity is present, we will see the underlying unity; we will see that all these properties characterize the same aspect—which is the same presence, the same Will.

In order to help you see this faculty in a larger context, I can use the example of my beginning experience of essential presence. When I first became aware of presence, I felt a sense of fullness, aliveness, and groundedness. At that time, it was simply presence for me. That was the most I could differentiate: Essence is presence. That's what I was aware of, and nobody had told me anything else before that; I had never read anywhere that presence could appear in different ways. So Essence, I found out, was presence—a fullness, an aliveness, a thereness, an I-am-ness. After a while, I would feel the experience of the presence changing. It's true that it was presence, but once in a while it felt somehow different. One day the presence would feel strong and firm, while the next day it would perhaps feel soft, sweet, and melty. That was the beginning of discrimination.

And the recognition of what that difference meant brought the jolt of insight: "Oh, Essence appears in aspects." That was the brilliant breakthrough. It was a big surprise for me, quite an eye-opener. This became a basic tenet of the Diamond Approach: Essence is not just presence but presence that presents itself in various qualities, various flavors. I could have stayed with just that, with the insight that presence appears in aspects. The exploration continued, however. At some point, I realized not only that presence has qualities and aspects, but that these arise at certain times and seem to challenge particular ego manifestations and deal with specific issues.

The Red essence, for instance, seemed related to strength and weakness, and the issue of separation anxiety. So in a context where the psychological field and the essential dimensions are seen as one—synthesized—there is more discrimination. Thus, synthesis and analysis go hand in hand. The result is the body of knowledge we now call the Diamond Approach.

The analysis kept going, and every once in a while there was a major unifying insight. But a major unifying insight by itself is useless unless the exploration continues. When synthesis and analysis work hand in hand, what arises is a great deal of knowledge, for the specifics and the connections become what we call knowledge.

But the presence of the Brilliancy diamond does more than allow us to discriminate and synthesize simultaneously; it also gives precision to our brilliance and brilliance to our precision. This means that there is sharpness and precision to synthesis. There is an exactness to it. The diamondness gives clarity, precision, and objectivity. What is synthesized are objective facts, objective manifestations.

If it were not for the precision and objectivity, our synthesis might consist of a little bit of prejudice, some reaction, an element of truth, and a touch of an essential experience, all of which would be combined into some kind of strange theory. This kind of synthesis that lacks objectivity happens frequently, especially in the spiritual sphere.

The objectivity implicit in an essential aspect when it takes on the diamond form allows us to separate our subjective, personal bias from what is actually present in the experience. Then synthesis is informed by this discrimination. That is one way the diamondness adds to the brilliance. However, when the Brilliancy diamond is functioning, the discriminating capacity itself becomes brilliant as it embodies greater luminosity and clarity, and more lucidity and speed in making the discriminations and seeing the connections between them.

When we develop this capacity to discriminate and synthesize in a single act, it can deepen our realization of presence, even the realization of nondual presence. In nondual realization, all manifestations are manifestations of the same presence. However, there are many stages of realizing nondual presence. At one stage, nondual presence can itself be diamondized, and all manifestations have sharpness, clarity, and precision. Then what we see everywhere is a unified presence that is discriminated and precisely clear.

Many of us experience the state of oneness, at least fleetingly. This experience, though profound, is two-dimensional most of the time, in that seeing another person is rather like seeing one cell of an organism where all cells sort of look the same. All is one. The dominant experience is of a unified field of nonseparateness. However, when the oneness has the precision of the diamond, what manifests is an added dimension. Everything presents itself in much greater relief; every element of the oneness becomes more uniquely itself. It is true that there is a oneness—a nonduality—but the uniqueness appears very precisely, very clearly. In this state, the other person is a particular person with his own quality, and at the same time he is part and parcel of the oneness of everything. With the precision of diamondness, uniqueness is clear; with the brilliance in the diamond, the oneness is undeniable. Both discrimination and synthesis are operative in this diamond oneness. It is all one unified field, but everything is precisely itself, clearly delineated without being separate. This is the perspective of the Brilliancy diamond as it applies to a deeper experience of realization, that of nonduality.

Discriminating the Underlying Unity

We have been discussing synthesis as the most fundamental quality of intelligence in Brilliancy. Insights seem to pop out effortlessly, connections do not require much cogitation, and the processes flow as easily as mercury. When these qualities are all present in one's functioning, we say that one is brilliant. However, there is another quality of intelligence that is significant and necessary for exploration, understanding, and synthesis. This has more to do with the completeness of intelligence than with its brilliance.

To be able to discriminate and correlate, to check things back and forth, and to synthesize, we need to hold together in our consciousness the various elements to be explored. In other words, we have all this data—percepts, sensations, feelings, memories, actions, presence, and so on—and we want to explore them by analyzing, questioning, synthesizing, seeing connections. In order to do that, we need the capacity to hold all these elements together. If we just look at one or two of the elements in isolation and forget about the others, we can never arrive at understanding. We need a way to be with all these elements in our consciousness simultaneously. To consider only some of them may not bring us to the threshold necessary for synthetic insight.

Not only do we need to hold the various elements we are exploring together, we also need to hold the right elements, not just any elements of experience. Our experience is full of things—millions of bits of data—but we need to hold in our consciousness only the particular elements, the specific data relevant for our inquiry. So we select certain elements—certain feelings, sensations, experiences, memories, actions, and situations—and hold only those; the rest remain in the background. We hold them so that we can explore them, discover significant correlations and interrelationships, and find the unity that underlies them.

But how do we know which elements need to be synthesized, and therefore which elements to hold? Since we have not yet synthesized them, we cannot see their underlying unity. So how do we know that these particular ones are the ones that are going to be synthesized? How do we discern what they are among the multitude of percepts and facts available to our experience? We normally do that selection implicitly, but did you ever ask yourself how that happens?

Let's look at a specific example: You are sitting across the table from your friend, having tea, and you are listening to her talking. You notice that you are seething with anger. You want to chop her head off. You are angry and a little bit sad. You wonder, "What am I angry about? She is talking as usual. She is always full of herself—nothing new—so why am I angry at her right now?"

As you contemplate your experience—listening to what she is saying, seeing the situation, and noticing what you are feeling—you start remembering that two nights ago when you were making love with your husband, you got a little bit irritated, a little bit hurt, in the middle of it. It was no big deal, but it affected you such that you couldn't climax after that. You didn't give it much thought at the time because that happens every once in a while. But you now realize something new about it. Somehow, listening to your friend and being mad at her reminds you of your husband. And as you contemplate all these elements together, you remember that a couple of days before that evening with your husband, when you were painting, your child threw a ball for you to catch. You realize that at that moment you almost slapped her. You knew that this was an unusual reaction to your child since you play ball with her every once in a while. So what was the big deal?

You begin to feel that all these elements are somehow connected. As you continue listening to your friend, your mind is now holding the sex scene with your husband and the painting scene with your daughter. As you do that, you start to feel empty inside, and with that emptiness comes a memory of when you were a child at home. It is a memory of your mommy busy cooking with the kids and your father reading a newspaper, and you were feeling some hurt, some anger, and also mildly empty. You never thought much about it, but it seems to be related in some way to what happened with your husband in the sex scene.

Then, in the midst of all of that, you remember your last session with your teacher and how it ended with feeling gratitude for him. You didn't think much about it at the time, but now you wonder why you were feeling so grateful to him. All these elements seem to be connected, but you don't know why you are remembering them together.

As you keep listening to your friend, you realize that something about her being full of herself is getting to you. Why does that make you mad at her? Then you remember that on the night when you made love, your husband was worried about his job. He was somewhat self-absorbed. And as you see that, you recognize that in your opinion, you are self-absorbed. However, in your childhood when you were feeling empty, you were not self-absorbed, but your parents were—your father reading his newspaper all the time and your mother always cooking and changing diapers.

"How is that related to my feeling grateful to my teacher? Something about my teacher felt positive, and with all these other people something felt painful. What is the connection? What happened in that session with my teacher?" You are drifting between all of these pieces while still listening to your friend. The memories seem to simmer, all held in your consciousness at the same time. Then you remember that in the session, as you were experiencing a clear sense of "I am" in your heart, your teacher said, "That is you." And you hadn't even said anything about your experience.

Right away, the insights explode in your consciousness. "My teacher saw me for exactly what I was in that moment!

"My friend is not seeing me, she is full of herself, fully absorbed in herself. My daughter did not see how absorbed I was while doing my painting when she threw the ball to me. When I was a kid, nobody in my family knew where I was; all of them were full of themselves, totally absorbed in themselves and their activities. They didn't see what I was feeling, or respond and relate to me according to what I needed. That is what happened to me with my husband. He started touching me right on my genitals; he wasn't attuned to where I was. I wanted him to start with the right nipple." Your hurt of not having received the right attunement opens up. All of these situations are unified by this deep wound.

So what was it that was giving you the capacity to select and hold these specific elements? You didn't recall the other times when you were angry at your husband, or angry at your child, or other hurts. You remembered only those particular situations. You were experiencing an innate capacity that can illuminate specifically those elements that have an underlying unity without you consciously or explicitly knowing the existence of that unity in advance.

If we look deeply into our consciousness, we recognize that the soul holds all the significant elements. But we can also see that there is a light, a brilliance, that underlies our consciousness; it shines through those specific elements that need to be synthesized and understood, and illuminates them in our consciousness. That brilliance is the underlying unity, and it reveals the unity in our experience even before we recognize it in our understanding.

It is Brilliancy that gives the Diamond Guidance the capacity to discriminate the right elements, the specific elements that have an underlying unity. Specifically, it is the Brilliancy diamond, because it has both the Brilliancy—which is the unity—and the diamondness, which is the discrimination. So we need both unity and discrimination; together they result in a unified act of knowing.

The content in the above example was about attunement and being seen. At other times it could be other things—the content always changes. We have considered an emotional issue, but the same capacity is needed for the exploration of any topic. Brilliancy shines through whatever elements are relevant to the particular inquiry and illuminates them in our consciousness. That way it singles them out for our recognition. Then the Diamond Guidance can use our previously acquired knowledge, our memories, and its capacities for correlating, reflecting, and analysis. In this way, exploration can reveal the underlying unity that is already beginning to shine through those particular elements in our consciousness.

This synthetic capacity makes it possible for the Diamond Guidance to explore a situation by looking at the interrelationships of the elements—analyzing some, synthesizing others—in a process that reveals their interconnections. The resulting combination leads to insight, the experience of realization that reveals the underlying unity of the situation being explored.

The process of insight is a continuing one. So in the above example, it begins when you realize, "Oh, I've got something going on about attunement. Somebody is not attuned to me." This leads to more questions: "Why am I so sensitive these days about somebody not being attuned to me? What is new about that? Those people have not been attuned to me all along."

You then realize that in the past few sessions with your private teacher, you have been working on narcissism and your sense of who you are, your sense of identity, and your feeling of being seen and supported. No wonder you feel so grateful to your teacher, because your teacher is the one who has been attuned to you, helping you, supporting you to be yourself.

And as you recognize that, you not only experience the Essential Identity, or what we refer to as simply the Point—the timeless self-recognition of "that is who I am"—as you did in your last session, but you also start to feel the inner support, the solidity that is within you. This again is an understanding: "I can have my own support, and that is what I need. So when there is no attunement, it is no big deal. I recognize that other people don't see who the hell I am since they are so busy with themselves because, obviously, they don't know who the hell *they* are. So what's new?"

Now you are not only able to disengage from all of that, but you can also be attuned to the other person and actually see what is going on for them. You can ask your friend, "There must be something bothering you. What are you really trying to say?" And it might become obvious now why your friend is talking and talking without even paying attention to you. As you see, understanding continues and can become the source of effective action. And the other person can be impacted by your understanding.

Because the realization of Brilliancy in our inquiry is usually not complete, the capacity to hold relevant experiences together does not always function perfectly. The more we have realized and integrated the Brilliancy aspect—the aspect of completeness—in the Diamond Guidance, the more we are able to hold and recognize the relevant experiences on various levels, past and present. If you do not have the capacity to tell which experiences are relevant, inquiry takes a longer time. That is one of the reasons why having a teacher helps your inquiry. A teacher can see which experiences are related because of his knowledge and sensitivity to you. Over time, you will need to learn to be able to hold your experiences for yourself and to see the thread that connects them.

This capacity to hold all the relevant material is at the opposite pole from that of another aspect—the Point's capacity to focus on one particular element. The Point gives us the ability to zero in on one thing and look at it closely, experience it with concentration, and analyze it. But we also need to have the capacity to pull back and consider all the related elements. We need both capacities—the focus and the general holding of all the relevant experiences. Frequently, inquiry needs to go back and forth between focus and the larger field.

I am aware that my personality is desperately defended against inquiry and wants to obscure that process as much as possible. There is a definite hierarchy there in the personality. Number one: The worst thing is to inquire. The second worst thing is to recognize a relevant element, and next on the priority list is holding a lot of things simultaneously. [The room bursts into laughter.]

So your personality doesn't like inquiry.

It doesn't like inquiry at all.

Personalities generally don't want to be exposed. But you want to explore for yourself whether something in your history has made you feel that it is not okay to find out, to know. There might be something specific there.

It seems to me that when you do your inquiry and you have the feeling that you have all the facts, then you have to be really brave if the synthesis doesn't happen right away. It's hard not to attack yourself. You really have to defend while you are sitting there feeling all this stuff and nothing is happening.

That's true. So when you see all the elements and the brilliant insight doesn't come shooting through, you need to be brave and you need to be able to defend yourself against the superego, as you mentioned. Both of those indicate the need for the Strength essence in inquiry. In holding our experience, we need to be able to hold pain, anger, fear, conflicts, and other elements. Maybe each one of those elements requires a particular quality. That's why Brilliancy can hold all of them. It has all the qualities. If we need to hold just one thing, such as fear or hurt, for example, then strength or compassion by itself is enough. But Brilliancy gives us the capacity to hold all the various elements at the same time.

I notice in my process that when the inquiry starts to get close to the place in my soul where I have the greatest contraction and hurt, I just go away. I push it away: "Don't do it. Let's not look here. Let's do anything except look in here."

You mean that when it gets close to yourself, you want to avoid the inquiry?

Yes, when it gets close to the place where there's the greatest hurt and contraction. So what I am also aware of is that there is a certain way that those places in my soul kind of pull my attention. So there is this tension between the pull to look at what hurts so much and absolutely not wanting to look at it, which pushes me away.

Yes, I can see that those areas will push away the inquiry because they are filled with tension or hurt. But your situation still has to do with Brilliancy because Brilliancy provides another faculty you are needing—the faculty of balance. Brilliancy has all qualities equally, so when it is present in our consciousness, it has a balancing effect. As a result, we don't prefer one thing over another. There's an equality in the way we look at the various elements of our experience. There might be hurt here, anger there; fear here, love there. Balance means that we look at all of those in an evenhanded way instead of just wanting to look at one or the other.

When we experience Brilliancy, we experience ourselves as complete and balanced. There is a sense of inner equilibrium that manifests in external life as balance. We balance the emotions with the intellect, the intellect with the body, the outer with the inner, rest with activity.

Are you using the word "balance" to mean "integration"?

I mean it in the sense of equality: One thing doesn't have more weight than another. Everything has the same importance. And balance is different from equanimity. Equanimity means an inner state of being nonreactive to anyone or anything, being peaceful—not subject to disturbance. Equanimity doesn't speak to a relationship between elements. Balance, on the other hand, means that there are various elements, and that there is an equilibrium or appropriate relationship between them. That balance then allows our development to move in an optimizing way. That's why, when I notice that people don't have balance in their life, it indicates that they're having difficulty with the aspect of Brilliancy. In fact, one indication of the absence of balance is when somebody is strange or weird.

Isn't that kind of a subjective viewpoint?

Strangeness or weirdness can be subjective, but in my perception, when people say somebody is strange and weird, frequently I notice that what they are referring to is an absence of balance, the exaggeration of certain things while other things are not paid attention to.

I've known for a long time that I've been afraid of you. I've been afraid of the Work, and I've been afraid of inquiry and analysis. Today I am understanding that the reason I am afraid of you, and the reason that I have resistance to the Work, is the same reason that I have a difficult time holding all of the elements together and synthesizing them. It is the feeling that if I do everything inquiry requires, it will mean that I have to give up my mother. If I did that, then I wouldn't know where I am. So it's just easier for me to say, "I don't understand what you're saying most of the time." It's easier for me to say, "The Work is not for me."

I get to the same point over and over again, where I have this resistance to synthesizing facts about my life in order to come to some understanding and go forward. I'm aware of this, and at this point I don't know what to do with it except to say that I have an awareness that I'm having a difficult time.

Sounds good. That's an interesting insight: If you really see the truth, you'll lose your mother, and when you lose your mother, you'll lose your sense of self, your identity; you won't know where you are. That's actually true. If you see the truth, you *will* lose your mother, and finally you will lose your identity. So your fear is justified. You just need to look at that and see if it is something desirable in the overall perspective of what you want in your life. But as far as whether truth will do that to you—definitely, that is what truth does.

It is interesting what that means. It means that having one's mother and having one's identity must be false. It must be some kind of falsehood; otherwise, why would the truth make it disappear? You say that if you see the truth, it will make you lose your mother. But truth can only destroy falsehood. So something about your relationship with your mother is false, not true. The most obvious falseness about having your mother is that in fact you don't have her.

It's false to believe that you have your mother. In your mind you're attached to an image of her, so you feel that you have her. The reason why the truth will dissolve that image is because it is not true. It is just some kind of belief, a mental position. But this kind of belief is a powerful thing. What we believe has to do with who and what we think we are, or what makes our life run, so it is very scary to have it challenged.

I am glad you are bringing this up. I'm sure many people experience this kind of fear, directly or indirectly. It's clear that behind some of the questions today there is fear, and sometimes anger. I think what I am presenting is quite challenging to deep parts of us. I think it's great that you're seeing your resistance, and that you recognize that that's *your* difficulty instead of saying, "Maybe this Work is not for me" or "This guy doesn't make sense. He's not clear today. Let *me* say it; I'll say it right." These are effective ways to protect ourselves when we sense an inner danger. I'm glad you're more objective about it today.

Penetrating Intelligence

The last question penetrated closer to the truth, which brings us to the next subject matter. I have described how Brilliancy has an intense luminosity, and also an exquisite smoothness and fluidity. Its presence has a fine, smooth texture. These two—the intense brilliance or luminosity and the exquisite smoothness—give understanding its penetrating capacity. Then we can penetrate deeply, as a surgeon does using a fine laser beam.

When we are inquiring, we are holding the content—the various facets of experience—and then interrelating those elements, seeing relationships, and analyzing and synthesizing. But our consciousness not only holds the whole interrelated field, it also sees through things; it sees through the veils, defenses, and resistances to underlying meanings, to underlying parts of our experience. We notice that our perception not only has a wider vision, but also that it can have a penetrating capacity. The penetrating capacity goes directly to the essence of the matter through brilliant illumination that pierces as it illuminates. Our consciousness is so smooth that it can move through little cracks, into tiny, subtle places. Brilliancy can seep into and penetrate those little subtle cracks and allow our consciousness to see things we wouldn't normally see.

This penetrating capacity is different from focus. The capacity of focus brings our attention to a single point. It allows us to look at just one element, and everything else becomes background. We stay concentrated, one-pointed; we can see more of the detail. That's focus. Penetration is a matter of going in: entering deep like an acupuncture needle, seeping in like fine oil, or cutting through like a surgeon's scalpel. We are not stopped at the surface, at what is presently showing itself; we see past what's conscious into what's hidden or buried. Obviously, this capacity is important for understanding our experience, especially when we are trying to see underlying meaning or underlying unity, because to do that, we have to go through many veils. Usually we do that through seeing relationships, by using analysis and synthesis. At those times, Brilliancy gives us the capacity to see underlying unity in a flash.

Sometimes, however, Brilliancy takes us to an underlying unity through penetrating insight, penetrating perception, or penetrating investigation. Even an expression can be penetrating—you can say something to somebody, you can give somebody feedback that is penetrating, and it cuts through a lot of stuff and gets to the point. Because of its utmost refinement and smoothness, Brilliancy can enter without creating resistance, static, or interference as it penetrates our consciousness. Because it is so brilliant, it can operate like the sharpest possible scalpel, the finest laser beam. Remember, you make a laser beam with very intense and coherent light of a certain wavelength, which gives the beam a penetrating quality. And the more intense the light, the finer the beam. When we use the expressions "a penetrating mind" or "a penetrating look," we are referring to this characteristic that comes specifically from Brilliancy.

Now, add the sharpness and precision of the diamond to this penetrating capacity, and we have a capacity for inquiry that approaches completeness and perfection. Not only do we have the smoothness that makes penetration effective, but that smoothness now has the sharpness and exactness of a diamond edge, which brings precision to the penetration. Not only can you drill deeply, but you can do it precisely, at the right spot, and with just the right amount of force. This is another expression of the perfection and completeness of this essential aspect.

Brilliancy is the most intense an essential aspect can be in terms of awareness—the most concentrated, immediate, and comprehensive. So the intensity gives it the penetrating capacity, but the fact of its completeness can give it the larger holding for the various contents that are needed for synthesis. In this way, Brilliancy gives us the complementary capacities of holding the relevant elements to be explored and penetrating the veils to reveal what's hidden. Both are necessary for going deeper.

We use our intelligence all the time but don't normally experience it as naturally arising from the completeness and perfection of who we are, from the Brilliancy of Being. Today we have been discriminating the various familiar qualities of intelligence such as the flash of revelation, the penetration of insight, the vision of the whole, and the radiance of illumination. Recognizing the fact that Brilliancy is the source of these capacities gives us a deeper understanding of their nature and functioning. All together, these qualities give us some sense of the functioning of the Brilliancy diamond of the Diamond Guidance. Perhaps we can now see that Brilliancy is essential for our process of inquiry and the effective unfoldment of our inner realization.

Part Three

☙

The unfolding of the subject matter on Brilliancy shifts now from the talks presented by the teacher to the individual processes of the students. The material in Part Three comes from weekend teachings presented in Colorado, where the teacher met with about thirty students for eight consecutive meetings to explore the Brilliancy material. These meetings occurred more than a year earlier than the California retreat where the talks in Part One were presented. However, the material that arose in the California students' experiences would have been similar.

In this section, we focus on the way the material impacts the process of the students. As most of the students lack the experience of Brilliancy in their lives, the dominant reality that they are all in touch with is its absence. This naturally leads to beliefs and feelings about themselves that cut them off from this aspect. Being with the truth of their experience puts the students in touch with a whole range of feelings and eventually brings them closer to the state of Brilliancy itself.

In this process, we see that the arising of particular issues related to a given aspect are not simply determined by what is presented by the teacher; they are in fact universal factors that will arise in everyone who begins to explore that territory. In this case, the students begin to explore the barriers to Brilliancy, and that exploration takes them back into their personal histories—specifically to their relationship with father.

This arising reveals another element of the Diamond Approach teaching: The material the teacher presents and the timing of the presentation are affected by the unfolding of the group process. In Part One, the talks are presented without the exercises and the group questions and exploration after the exercises, so they appear out of the context of what was unfolding in the group. The chapters were designed that way to concentrate the teaching material for the reader. In Part Three, the talks presented appear in the more complete context of the students' response to the exercises and their ensuing work with the teacher. After the initial talk, which introduced a particular perspective on the aspect of Brilliancy, the later talks were in response to what was coming up in the students' experience and what was needed for a fuller understanding of the subject matter.

The Small-Group Format

In Part Three, we are introduced to the second group-teaching structure of the Diamond Approach: groups of ten to twenty students who meet together regularly with one teacher over many years. This format supports personal inquiry based on a student's ongoing experience or his response to material brought up in the talks and exercises within the large-group format. Conceptual teaching is minimal and generally used only to elucidate or expand on what has arisen in an individual's work.

What is presented in Part Three is a combination of large- and small-group teaching formats. As in the large-group format, the teacher lectures and introduces exercises for self-exploration, but here he also engages in extensive explorations with individuals—the focus of small-group work—to take their inquiry to a deeper level. When exercises are assigned, the large group breaks up into dyads or triads. Each student has uninterrupted time to inquire into the material with the support of his partners as silent witnesses. Students are thus given the opportunity to have a personal experience of the material being discussed in the lecture. In some cases, the exercises include feedback afterward from the witnesses to deepen the understanding of what was explored.

The context of these eight meetings was two small groups that came together to explore the aspect of Brilliancy. The students had been working together in small- and large-group formats for at least five years, some much longer. Part Three includes extended transcripts of the teacher's work with individual students, giving the reader a good example of how small-group work unfolds.

The teacher guides one student at a time, supporting her inquiry into her experience, in the presence of other students. He does this by maintaining an open, curious orientation to what is arising, and at times helps the group understand the unfolding that is taking place. As the group members witness the inquiry, they learn to continue their practice of presence and to allow their own silent inquiry, which may be provoked, inspired, or affirmed by the active student's work. So the group members learn from the one who is inquiring, and at the same time provide through their presence a significant support for that individual's work. Over time, the group develops a field of committed, respectful, and appreciative holding for personal work that is increasingly deep and challenging of long-held personal beliefs. This makes room for the soul's entry into new realms of Being.

Open-Ended Inquiry

What is important in the interactions that follow is not the outcome of the dialogues or the insights arrived at, but the way each step unfolds by the inquiry turning toward the unknown. The teacher is repeatedly bringing the students back to their present experience and encouraging a sense of curiosity about what they are sensing and feeling. Often what arises from this orientation is different from what the student expected, and thus his desire for a particular outcome is confounded.

But interestingly, the students are rarely disappointed by where they eventually end up. This is not because the teacher is intent on bringing the students to some satisfying resolution of their questions. Quite the contrary. The teacher has no investment in any particular outcome of the inquiries and often encourages the exploration of some state or feeling that moves into more dissatisfaction or hurt or simply stays with discomfort. And, in fact, the students' questions and issues are not always resolved. However, the outcome is satisfying because each student feels more in touch with the reality of his experience as a result of the inquiry. One of the fundamental truths of human nature seems to be that the soul relaxes and quietly rejoices whenever it moves closer to the truth of its nature, regardless of the content of that truth.

The teacher's lack of interest in reaching an outcome also reflects his basic trust in the natural unfolding of the soul when one aligns with its truth. This law of movement in the human soul and the teacher's trust in it are both fundamental to the practice of inquiry in the Diamond Approach. Inquiry is not an activity aimed at bringing one to a particular state or capacity. Nor is it a means of discovering what stops one from arriving at a certain outcome. Inquiry is a means of inviting our true nature—which has much greater intelligence and awareness than our conscious mind will ever have—to reveal itself and guide us to a deeper understanding of reality and our own truth. True inquiry does not assume that one outcome, one experience, or one feeling state is better than any other at any given time. Inquiry invites whatever is here to show itself and reveal its truth. And each revelation, if allowed and held with respect and interest, will lead to understanding and revelation—and the further unfoldment of the soul.

6

Meeting One

☙

In previous meetings, this group has already explored the question of right action, right doing. This weekend, we want to talk about another quality that makes our action more correct, more to the point, more effective.

We begin with any everyday situation that needs to be dealt with. Many things will be required for you to deal with this situation. One is that you have to be present with the situation and aware of the factors involved. You also have to have the necessary knowledge, information, and skills to deal with that particular situation. You have to have the motivation, the desire, the willingness, and of course, you need to have the capacity or ability to deal with it.

So there is the particular situation, your presence or state in it, the knowledge, information, and skills that you have to help you deal with it, plus your ability to apply that skill and knowledge, which depends on your state at that moment. It sounds like a big deal, but this process occurs all the time. Every time you drive your car, for example, you have to deal with these different elements.

What I want to talk about has to do with all these factors: what you know; the ability to use what you know; the ability to use your skills in the correct way; the relating of your skills and what you know to what is happening in the situation; your particular state at the time; being creative in the solutions that you find; and being economical with time, material, and energy. I am interested in one identifying factor that will make all the different areas of the situation—each one and all of them together—more effective, efficient, and economical.

In the past, we have discussed a number of essential aspects in relation to right action, including Will, Strength, and presence itself. Today I will discuss intelligence in relation to right action because your capacity to deal well with a situation depends a lot on how smart you are. In other words, intelligence makes a person able to deal with a situation more or less effectively. So what is intelligence? How does it manifest? Can it be developed? Or are we just born dumb or smart, and that's it?

Everybody knows that intelligence has a lot to do with learning any subject matter. The more intelligent you are, the easier it is for you to learn. Furthermore, when learning is easier for you, you can learn more and your learning is more efficient. However, the learning of material is just one area where intelligence manifests. Another area is in the application of what you learn to the situation at hand.

Intelligence is not just for your intellect, for your mind, so that you can read or hear something and understand it more easily. There is something called intelligent action. You can be intelligent in the way you act, behave, run your life, and deal with situations. So although having qualities of will, strength, and presence, as well as certain skills, is basic and necessary in dealing with a given situation, intelligence will add more effectiveness and more efficiency.

Certainly, intelligence is useful for learning, reasoning, absorbing, deduction, induction, understanding things, correlating facts, and connecting one thing to another. But intelligence is also an important factor in actually dealing with any practical situation. Sometimes intelligence can mean the difference between finding and not finding a solution: If you do not apply your intelligence, you may not be able to deal with the situation. And the more intelligent you are and the more you can apply your intelligence, the more effective the solution will be. This means that the way you do something will be more efficient, your functioning will be more economical, and your action will be more elegant.

Some people are intelligent intellectually. When they are in school, they can read all the books, do well on the exams, get As and A-pluses. But when it comes to their life in the world, they become stupid; they cannot apply their intelligence. Yet intelligence is integral to the application of knowledge, such as in seeing alternatives. The more intelligent you are and the brighter you are, the more alternatives and shortcuts you will see. The more shortcuts you can see, the more you can conserve energy and time, and the more you will think of solutions that are creative, even unexpected.

Intelligence is related to the functioning of all our capacities, not just the intellectual ones. It is relevant to any functioning regardless of the area and plane of reality. Remember, intelligence is an innate element of every living consciousness—machines cannot be truly intelligent.

When faced with a situation that has the usual alternatives that are commonly known, if you apply a greater intelligence to that situation, you will find solutions that are not obvious, that nobody ever thought of, that are not directly observable in the facts, and that are not in your memory. Intelligence allows creative and original solutions that are not direct applications of or deductions from what you already know.

So true intelligence gives us the capacity to function in ways that cannot be deduced from preexisting facts. It gives us the capacity to make completely original leaps, to be truly creative. The functioning of this capacity points to a quality in us that is not in a given situation to start with. It is something that we can bring to it through our presence. This functioning of intelligence is not a direct application of knowledge or skill. You can learn a skill and then merely apply it correctly; or you can apply it with intelligence, and the intelligence will add something that you never learned in developing the skill.

Intelligence is not something you are taught in school. School learning may exercise your capacity for intelligence, but nothing in schooling itself really teaches you how to be intelligent. Intelligence is one of our capacities, one of our potentials, just as love is one of our potentials. Nobody can really teach you how to love. Love is something you have to find in yourself. People may allow you to exercise the capacity for love, but nobody can ever really define love such that if you practice that definition, you will become loving. It isn't like that. Love is something you have to open to in yourself and then bring to the situation. The same is true with intelligence.

Intelligence transcends the mechanical part of our consciousness, the physiological apparatus of the nervous system. Many of you think that intelligence has to do with how many cells are operating in your brain. That factor may have something to do with its level of functioning, just as the thymus gland becomes more operative the more love manifests. But that doesn't mean that you can do something mechanical with your thymus gland and become more loving. Neither can you do something with your brain—inject it with some kind of chemical to activate more of the cells—and become more intelligent, at least not at the present level of scientific knowledge. Intelligence is something innate, organic—part of your very consciousness, part of your very beingness—that when present can affect your brain and allow more cells to be active. It's as though more of a certain part of you has to be present in your brain for your brain to respond and function intelligently.

Intelligence needs the physical apparatus of the brain in order to express itself. So if you have brain damage, your capacity for intelligence will probably be limited. This is because even though you have innate intelligence, the vehicle through which it expresses itself isn't functioning optimally. It is as if you had a great capacity to sing but something was wrong with your vocal cords—you would be unable to sing, regardless of how wonderful your innate singing capacity was. Likewise, you could be very intelligent, but if you have brain damage, you won't be able to express that intelligence. The point is that intelligence is not an innate property of the brain cells; it is a property of your consciousness, your soul.

Because intelligence is an aspect of your true nature, it is something you can bring to any situation. It is part of you that you can actualize and bring to bear in whatever capacities you have. Intelligence is a certain quality that is different from other capacities in the sense that it can affect all other capacities. Each capacity can be more or less infused with intelligence.

For instance, take the capacities for discrimination and analysis. Everybody has these, and they can be more or less effective, more or less developed. Intelligence will affect the effectiveness, expansiveness, and development of the ability to discriminate and analyze. So you could apply your intelligence to those capacities and you might become a real genius. Your capacity for analyzing and discriminating could become refined, thorough, precise, clear, and sharp, and thus lead to brilliant understanding and knowledge. Enhancement of these capacities has no limit in terms of refinement or sharpness; it can reach heights of amazing brilliance. Or you could be sloppy; your capacity of analysis could be dull. You analyze, but things remain jumbled up and indistinct in your thinking. The discrimination doesn't become fine or sharp, and hence is not so useful.

I think that anybody who has applied themselves to this capacity of discrimination and analysis can see that it is not a matter of either/or, of having the capacities or not. Regardless of how good you are at it already, you could always become more discriminating, and your analysis could always become sharper and more to the point. And the more that happens, the more there is a sense of precision—not only a sense of precision but elegance as well.

Many people like mathematics and math problems and get hooked on them in school, because of the elegance involved. You could take a mathematical problem and solve it in three or four pages. But if you could apply your intelligence, you might solve it in one page. If somebody comes along who is even more brilliant, he or she could solve it in maybe one or two lines.

That was the genius of Einstein, for instance. He believed that the solutions to scientific problems should be elegant. And he believed that the more elegant, the more aesthetically appealing, and the simpler the solution is, the more real and true it is. So, for Einstein, the elegance, simplicity, succinctness, and aesthetics of a solution had a lot to do with its truth. You are actually closer to the truth the more elegant your perception is, the more beautiful your formulation is, the more aesthetically appealing your understanding is, the simpler and shorter your solution is.

This sense of beauty and elegance became one of the guiding principles of Einstein's work. People would bring him the solution to a problem, and if it was cumbersome, complicated, and many pages long, he would say that it couldn't be the solution. "But it *is* the solution," they would say. Einstein responded, "It can't be the *best* solution." They asked him why, and he replied, "It's not elegant enough. It's not beautiful. It looks ugly." And they said, "So what?" His answer was, "Well, God doesn't make things like that. When God makes things, He makes them very beautiful. The equation has to look elegant and concise; it has to be just right." The presence of elegance is the clearest indication that you are being more intelligent. Elegance is a beauty that has to do with economy, succinctness, precision, gracefulness, and aesthetics.

If you look at Einstein's discoveries, at his general theory of relativity, for instance, you will see that he reduced things to only one equation. What people take years and years to understand, he could express in one equation. And from that one equation, he could expand and deduce the whole huge theory that explains the universe for us. This tells you something about intelligence. Another example is his equation that defines the relationship of energy and matter. It is the simplest you can find in science: $E = mc^2$. E represents the quantity of energy, m the mass of matter, and c the speed of light.

Intelligence goes beyond helping us to solve problems better and deal with situations more effectively; it actually helps us get to the truth. The more intelligent a solution is, the closer you are to the truth. The brighter and more intelligent we are at perceiving or understanding a situation, the more we feel satisfied in our solution, and the more likely that our solution is true. Conversely, the more cumbersome it is, the more complicated it seems, the more we are dissatisfied, the more likely our solution has missed the mark of truth. So intelligence is useful for dealing with a situation and, as a quality of our Being characterized by elegance, simplicity, and economy, it makes our interaction with the situation more effective and easier.

But now we are seeing that the quality of intelligence also has a lot to do with the truth. It's as if intelligence were the part of us—the quality of our Being, of our essence—that can discern the truth most directly. The more intelligent I am, the more directly I can perceive the truth of the situation. So it is not just a matter of awareness; it is a matter of adding another quality to awareness that makes us brighter and more intelligent. It's as if you had a dimmer switch; you turn the light on with it and it's a little dim at the beginning. More intelligence means turning the dimmer switch up, which makes the light brighter. The more intelligent you are, the brighter the light is; and the brighter the light is, the more you will see, the more you will discriminate, the closer things will appear to you, and the more clearly their nature will be revealed.

Intelligence is something we bring from within ourselves that makes us apprehend and perceive situations in a more direct and intimate way. So what does it mean if intelligence is like a light that can become brighter, more intense, more brilliant, thus revealing the situation more clearly to us? It means that we can bring this quality into any situation and it has the property or capacity to dissolve the veils, the barriers, between us and what we are experiencing, perceiving, and contemplating. The more intelligence there is, the less there is a dullness, a thickness, and a barrier, and there are fewer layers of debris between us and what we are studying. Intelligence is something that can penetrate obscurations by lighting everything up. The fewer barriers there are, the more we are directly, intimately in contact with the situation.

Suppose you see a path in dealing with a situation. As you get closer to it, you start to see that the one path is really three or more paths that you could take. Some of them seem to be easier, shorter. The more you bring in the quality of intelligence, the more paths are revealed—there are twenty paths now, everywhere. You can see some paths that are much shorter, more elegant, easier, and more economical than the ones you saw before. This is the quality of revelation in intelligence, and it doesn't have an end.

Intelligence can infuse any part of our life, and we can bring it to bear in any situation. If your intelligence can infuse the situation with brightness, so that you act more effectively, you will see how much time can be saved. That's what I mean by economy: You are saving time, you are saving energy.

Intelligence can penetrate, support, and open up any capacity and any endeavor in any situation. There is no limitation on the amount of intelligence that can be present, on how much light can be shed, on how many alternatives can be revealed.

Another sign of the presence of intelligence has to do with a sense of brilliance. If your mind is operating in an intelligent way, after a while you notice that there is pleasure in your brain, as though the cells themselves were having orgasms. They are illuminating from within, bursting with living intelligence and brightness. And using the intelligence of your mind will feel smooth and pleasurable. Things start to happen easily, and your thoughts, ideas, and perceptions begin to have the smoothness and the freedom of movement through a fluid medium. The operation of intelligence becomes like the flow of mercury.

Such smoothness is the basis of the penetrating power of intelligence. This penetrating power has to do with the fluidity and delicacy of the movement and physiognomic properties of intelligence. The capacity to pierce to the heart of the matter is seldom as evident in other aspects as it is in Brilliancy. The presence of intelligence has a delicacy and smoothness that is so refined, so exquisite, and of such gentleness that there is nothing it cannot pierce and penetrate.

When your mind or any of your capacities function that way—imbued with intelligence—you feel that you are using yourself correctly, which means the way you are supposed to be using yourself. The power of your cells and the capacity of your mind—to think and decide, to see and act, to discriminate and organize—are working perfectly. There is a sense of perfection, of elegance, of precision, of ease; things feel like they are flowing naturally, in the best way for them to flow. It is similar to the way a brook flows downhill: The water will flow right around any rocks or barriers in the easiest and most efficient way as it continues in its descent.

In this state, your consciousness is impeccable in its functioning, such that nothing attaches to it, nothing holds it back. It has no stickiness that will let it get caught here and there. It is so easy and smooth, so refined, that nothing can cling to it. You see how mercurial it is? Even if you were to catch some drops, you wouldn't be able to hold on to them—the mercury would slip right out of your fingers. Now imagine intelligence going through your brain just like that—nothing holding on to it. It just slips through things, penetrating and piercing them.

Intelligence, this presence of consciousness, is not only delicate, smooth, and impeccable; it is also bright. It is a brilliance that illuminates the way. As it is flowing through, it is illuminating its way; and by illuminating it, it is flowing through it. The illumination and the flow are the same thing. This illumination can get brighter and brighter so that the minutest possible cracks can be seen. And it is so refined that it can penetrate those minute cracks. Regardless of how small, delicate, or subtle the situation is, your intelligence is so piercing that it can penetrate and go through it. There is no limitation on this capacity of penetrating illumination.

Are you getting a feeling for how intelligence works? It is a sense of brilliance, of brightness, that can open things up. It is a smoothness, delicacy, and slipperiness, a sense of exquisiteness and refinement that keeps our functioning from getting stuck.

Remember that intelligence is a quality of our true nature, one of the aspects of Essence. Essence can manifest in such a deep way that it becomes pure radiance—the aspect of Brilliancy—which we find to be intelligence. Essence can manifest as this intelligence, which becomes ever more brilliant, ever more radiant, ever more luminous. It can become luminous in a way that is beyond sharp—beyond excitement and intensity—in a way that is smooth, gentle, delicate, settled. And I mean settled in a very refined way, like the essence of refinement, the essence of delicacy, the essence of elegance. I don't know how to say it exactly. The elegance has to do with the refinement, and the refinement has to do with the smoothness, and the smoothness has to do with an exquisiteness of texture. The texture is so extremely smooth that it luminates brilliantly.

The aspect of Brilliancy is the deepest differentiated nature of our consciousness. If you really let your consciousness emerge, and be purely itself, you realize that it manifests more and more of that brilliance, smoothness, delicacy, elegance, impeccability, and intelligence. And because that is the true inner nature of our consciousness, it can infuse any of the other aspects and capacities. It can make our actions more intelligent, our thinking more intelligent, our responses more intelligent, our decisions more intelligent, our timing more intelligent, our organization more intelligent, our analysis more intelligent—everything actualizes more of its capacity. Intelligence is not just something that functions on its own. It is more like a fuel additive, a quality you can add to any of the capacities to make them function more efficiently, more elegantly, more smoothly, and more easily.

We are seeing here that the question of intelligence is not merely, "Am I smart or am I not smart? If I am smart, I can do this and that and that; if I am not, I'll just do other things." Intelligence is much more basic. It is something you are always using, one way or another. We tend to apply it in some areas and not others. Some of us don't recognize that we have it. But I don't believe there is anybody who doesn't have it. Actually, it is not possible not to be intelligent. Intelligence is such a basic quality of our consciousness, of our Being, of our essence, that we cannot function without it. Life, in its very nature, is intelligent. Without intelligence, you can't survive.

We are applying our intelligence all the time. We are always making subtle decisions about things: "Should I put on these clothes or those clothes today?" Intelligence will have to be working to help you deal with that question. The more intelligent you are, the more factors you will consider in your decision, such as the weather, where you are going and what kind of activities you are going to be doing, what impression you want to make, and so forth. And with intelligence, you might make the decision in two seconds.

Now that we have more of a feel for intelligence, let's get a little more practical and look at how it functions in our lives. How is intelligence part of us? Are we experiencing it or not? How do we feel about it? Do we allow ourselves to bring that part of us, that inner heart of our consciousness, into our life, into our experience? We want to find out what holds us back from the full realization of intelligence.

We also want to discover how can we apply our intelligence. How can we make our actions in the world be an expression of right living, and not just right living but intelligent living, elegant living? How can all our actions have an intelligence and elegance? We want to learn about an elegance that not only looks and seems beautiful but is also efficient. We want to learn about an elegance that actually conserves energy, time, space, money, and material.

Through our work in the rest of this retreat, you will find out that you have inhibitions in various areas of your life that block intelligence from functioning there. We will be dealing with these inhibitions in our continuing work in the School; but at this retreat, we want to deal specifically with the inhibitions about intelligence itself. Why don't we allow ourselves to be intelligent? Why not allow the Brilliancy to come out? Why not allow that brightness, that brilliance, to pervade us, our capacities, our life?

An exercise is given to help the students become aware of their unconscious beliefs about intelligence. They do this by exploring their associations with being smart. After the exercise, the students reassemble.

A. H. Almaas: Any comments or questions?
Student: Two things came to my mind. Sometimes I'm doing landscaping, and I am trying to figure out where to set things so they have a harmony and a flow to them. It doesn't seem like an intellectual exercise; it seems more like an instinct. Afterward, I can intellectually recognize why it works or feels good, but at the time it didn't feel smart or intellectual. Another experience is when I work on peoples' bodies chiropractically. Some of the best work I do does not have a plan or an intelligent—in a way I would call intelligent—approach to it. It's like I'll feel led to do something, and I'll recognize the intelligence in it after the session. So I have a tendency to believe that intelligence is intellectual, but I experience it in life as a handmaid to instinct or intuition.

AH: Well, as I have said, intelligence is a quality of Being, an essential aspect. It can pervade or influence any capacity. That capacity can be intellectual, physical, intuitive—it doesn't matter. So intelligence is not just intellectual. It actually has to do with action. It makes available the possibility of intelligent action.

So, as intelligence flows in action, the action becomes more intelligent. The intelligence can also manifest as a sense of guidance. The guidance and the intelligence are inseparable within our actions—in terms of what we do and how we do it—without our thinking about it. And when intelligence is pervasive, the intellectual is no longer just intellectual, in the sense that even mental capacities also reflect true nature as they manifest guidance and intelligence. As I have said, intelligence can affect any capacity—physical, emotional, intellectual, or spiritual. Some of us experience it in certain capacities but not in others, but it can manifest in any of our capacities. Yet it is not a part of any of those capacities. Intelligence is a quality on its own, and it is something that can infuse and expand those capacities.

So, yes, intelligence can infuse your instinctual and intuitive functioning. When your physical capacities and sensitivities are operating intelligently, you may think of them as functioning intuitively or instinctually. I believe this is a common tendency. And in fact, what we frequently call instinctual or intuitive is nothing but the absence of mechanical or linear functioning. And, as we are seeing, it is a property of functioning based in organic intelligence. Instinctual functioning also indicates that intelligence is not just a mental activity but is a quality of the functioning of our consciousness, of our soul.

S: How do you do this type of exercise without getting hung up in the mind? I find that a lot of my experience is filtered through the mind. And I find that sometimes I tend to dwell in the mind.

AH: Which experience are you talking about?

S: The whole aspect of intelligence.

AH: In this culture, we tend to see intelligence as existing primarily in relation to mental functioning. We tend to believe that it is only the mind that can be intelligent. It doesn't have to be that way. For instance, I said to let yourself be spontaneous in doing the exercise, to let whatever happens to be there come up on its own. The exercise was basically emotional, for we are exploring emotional issues about intelligence. You see, you might think of intelligence as only mental, but it is not necessarily so. Some people use their mental faculties more than anything else and tend to use their intelligence mostly that way, but all of our functioning can be imbued with intelligence, as we are starting to see. That leads us to the next exercise.

In this exercise, the students explore their relationship to Brilliancy, which is the essence of intelligence. They take turns investigating for themselves what they feel about Brilliancy, to what degree they know it, and how and when they experience it. The exercise involves uncovering the student's attitudes and beliefs about Brilliancy as well as areas where it is restricted. Afterward, the students reassemble.

AH: Time for questions and comments.
S: What I found in doing the exercise and listening to everyone else in my group is that I had to come up with a new definition of Brilliancy. At the beginning of the exercise, Brilliancy to me meant a condition that is always external, and the people I was relating to had a preconceived idea of what it meant to be brilliant. By the end, I felt a new sense of Brilliancy that was very different from any other conceptions I have had about it.
AH: So when you say that you saw it as external, did you mean an external manifestation? Actions? How other people see it?
S: The latter. I was looking for approval externally. I was getting feedback for being bright, for whether I did something that was brilliant.
AH: I see. So intelligence is used to get something from the outside. That was your way of being seen and approved of.
S: It was never a feeling or a sense of being. It was always striving, difficult.
AH: Something you have to work for. Be brilliant so people will think you're brilliant—a nonbrilliant thing to do! So how did it feel, seeing that?
S: It felt like I was just opening up and seeing that for the first time. I felt sort of like a little baby somehow.
AH: How did that feel?
S: It felt really warm and kind of integrated and whole. It made me feel a lot more present. I didn't find myself fading at all. When I have to sit

and listen during exercises, every once in a while I'll catch myself fading away from listening. This time, I felt really whole when I experienced the new sense of Brilliancy.

AH: It's important to have a direct taste. It seems that you were able to have a taste of Brilliancy by seeing how your mind usually looks at it.

Anybody else want to share their experience in the exercise?

Another student begins to work.

S: Along the same lines as the previous student, my experience is that I don't own any of my own intelligence, or don't see that I have any brilliance. I found out that I don't own it for myself, and that I really dissociate myself from it by projecting it out toward other people. And the only way that I can own it, experience it, or have it for myself is by having it fed back from others. So I see this huge split inside myself: I almost feel torn, because I don't know how to have the intelligence and the Being and the things you've talked about, without them having to be mirrored back by other people. It became really obvious to me in the exercise that that's the case.

AH: You mean that you're aware of the Brilliancy, but you are also aware that you don't own it?

S: Right. See, it doesn't mean anything to me unless someone says, "Hey, that's really great."

AH: So the feedback is what is important, not the Brilliancy itself.

S: Right.

AH: If you shine, other people will see. That's the idea we are getting here, right? If you radiate, if you shine, other people will see it and will think that you are brilliant and wonderful.

S: I don't have the experience of the bursting sun inside myself, and enjoying that. It's like it got cold or something.

AH: Might be. And maybe the first step to reowning that part of us is to see how we want it to be seen from the outside. We might first need to see our external orientation, how we don't really care for our Brilliancy itself. What we want is some kind of validation or admiration from the outside. We need to recognize this before we can integrate that part of us. This is an important issue that many of us face about

Essence in general or about some of its aspects. Essence is seen as less important than getting some feedback for the ego, and is even used to get this feedback. Many of us have to confront such an inverted value system in order to be able to integrate our essential nature, and that is not easy.

AH comments: *It might seem to the reader that the reports of the students are quite deep for such a short and simple exercise, but this is not unusual. This depth is partly due to the fact that these students have been doing this work for several years, partly due to their deep commitment to finding the truth of their experience, and partly due to the greater intimacy and openness they have with each other after being in the same group for such a long time.*

Another factor is that their exploration is of an aspect of Essence. Most of the individuals in the group have had some experience of one aspect or another, which gives them the capacity to be open to Essence in general when it manifests in the environment. This capacity develops as one becomes more empty of one's own issues and ego structures. This is also experienced as a greater realization of the empathic capacity, which becomes the main capacity that allows for learning from a teacher, especially in the spiritual domain.

The teacher is not merely lecturing about Brilliancy; he is also embodying the aspect while talking. He is presenting the aspect both in words and in its actuality. This is in fact the central way a teacher of Essence transmits his or her knowledge of that realization. The teacher is not exactly giving the student an experience of Essence; rather the presence of the teacher activates the student's own presence in whatever essential aspect or dimension is being studied. This process, which is sometimes called direct transmission, makes it possible for the receptive individual to get a glimpse of the quality. This can either be through a direct experience of the aspect or through an experience of the various psychological constellations that are brought to consciousness by the impact of the presence of Essence on the student's soul.

AH: Anybody else wish to work?

Another student begins.

S: For me it is different. I don't want anybody to see my Brilliancy. It brings up sheer terror and a lot of hurt, and it's like my mind just starts fading away. And I feel it, I mean I really feel it. But it's very difficult for me to have other people see it.

AH: Is it okay for you to express it in action?

S: Yeah. I think that's been happening.

AH: So it's okay to express it as long as nobody recognizes it.

S: I don't want anyone to see it. I don't want anybody to say anything about it. That's what's scary.

AH: It's scary if someone sees it.

S: It is.

AH: Maybe they are seeing you, then, in a deep way.

S: I think so.

AH: Do you mean that if they see you, they might realize that you are twinkling from inside? [*Laughter*]

S: Well, I mean it's okay if I'm twinkling, but I don't want anyone else to know. It's not funny either.

AH: So you cannot be this way with others. Then we want to explore the things that prevent us from being that way with others, since it is part of who we are.

A different student speaks up.

S: It almost seems to be identification. What I mean is, the anatomy of it seems to be that when you are really little, you are not as smart as someone who's been around and attached to the Earth a little bit longer. Comparatively, you look like you are not too smart, so you pick up this identification of being not very brilliant; not being so brilliant becomes part of your identity. Later on, it's almost scary to think of being really brilliant because then it's going to upset your identifications, which is really disturbing.

AH: So that means there has already been an identity built up based on being not brilliant. To be brilliant, then, means that you have to let go of that identification.

S: It can be embarrassing, threatening—all sorts of things.

Another student begins.

S: I don't want to let go of a parent.

AH: Of a parent? Who do you mean?

S: I didn't realize how attached to my father's impression of me I've become. And to the emotion of that, the feeling that I am not really very smart . . . you know—I am kind of smart, but not real smart. And maybe it's a way of hanging on to Daddy.

AH: Maybe. So, you see, there is a lot more to this than is obvious at first.

S: But I am amazed at the—it sounds so trite—the emotional block to it.

AH: Yes, and that's a very good thing to see. That's what I was trying to say earlier. The resistances and the blockages against being brilliant are mostly emotional. It's not that we don't have Brilliancy or that we don't have intelligence; it is rather that there are emotional issues and conflicts about this capacity. This has to do with various relationships you had in childhood that prevent you from being the Brilliancy that you can be.

Children in general are very smart; they have an intrinsic and innate intelligence. If you look at how little kids are, you see that they are intelligent in a real way, the way Brilliancy is, in the sense that the intelligence is very flexible, organic. They are always coming up with different kinds of ideas and solutions than you would expect. It is frequently quite amazing how kids deal with their situation.

Two nights ago, we were having dinner, and Tanya, my five-year-old daughter, didn't like what was being served. So her mom said, "That's our dinner tonight—there is nothing we can do about it." And she answered, "Yes we can; we can do something about it." And I asked "What?" And she said, "Throw it in the garbage."

S: There is an innocence.

AH: There is an innocence. Very good insight. Innocence is one of the qualities of Brilliancy. You have to be innocent to allow it. It's like the innocence allows brilliancy to be organic and free flowing. You don't expect the ideas that come and the Brilliancy in those ideas and the actions you then take. And that's how children are in the beginning. They lose this living intelligence little by little; but in their early years, there is spontaneity and innocence as part of that intelligence. The kinds of things that kids come up with can amaze you, even shock you.

Brilliancy, as you see, does need that flexibility and innocence. The rigidity that starts to set in as the ego develops tends to eliminate these qualities, tends to block them. And you can't use your intelligence if you have to be rigid. The very nature of intelligence is that it opens up new possibilities and alternatives. You start to see various situations in creative and unexpectedly different ways.

Intelligence has a great deal to do with expansion and flexibility. And in doing this retreat, many of us might remember those times in our past when we were brilliant, intelligent, and right on—in our perceptions and comments, in what we did, in what we chose. We might also find that some parts of the relationships with your parents contributed to the dampening of the Brilliancy, as some of you have shared so far.

S: In our group, we noticed that each of us felt that someplace way back we made a decision about Brilliancy. In my case it was, "I'm not that." We all felt that we did make some decision, "Well, that's not me." So there's no more innocence when I am making a decision. The action is not flexible—and that became reality for me. And this inflexible intelligence is with me every day.

AH: You might want to see what made you do that. What made you think every day that you are not brilliant? Why should true Brilliancy only be for a few special people? These are some of our ideas, some of our assumptions, that need to be questioned and challenged.

S: It is something that I did. I did it.

AH: That might be true. What I am saying is that there must be some reason why you did that. There must be some psychodynamic basis for you feeling you had to do it that way. I mean, it's true that as a kid, for instance, you saw—or more accurately, you believed—that your parents were more intelligent than you were. But that was not always true. Parents are not necessarily more intelligent. Rather, they are most often more knowledgeable. You have to differentiate between being knowledgeable and being intelligent. They are not the same thing. A child can see that her parents know more about what to do. They have had more experience. But the child might notice that her parents are not smart. "Why are they doing that?" the child will think.

Frequently kids have feelings like, "I don't know why Daddy is always working. He's just working every day. He leaves in the morning and comes in at night, and is always tired and complaining of being tired and not having any fun. He is either working or tired and sleeping. Why? It seems like a dumb thing to do." These are some very intelligent perceptions because it is frequently obvious that our parents don't seem to be happy in what they are doing. It's true that the child might not know that you need to make a living, but that is not an absence of intelligence; it's an absence of knowledge. The reality is that the child's feelings indicate a very brilliant perception. Why would anyone spend most of their time doing something that they are always complaining about? I think most adults need to ask themselves this question.

It is very disquieting to parents if their children actually voice these perceptions. One reason is because when we develop an identity—if we really become that person we think we are and need to hold on to that identity—intelligence is perceived to be very threatening, as some of us are starting to see. It's not just that we don't believe in such an intelligence, and not just that we can't have it; it is actually very threatening. Intelligence can and will reveal parts of us that we don't want to reveal.

S: It seemed like when I was allowing the Brilliancy to be there, to open up, I would be hit with this doubt: "Oh, this isn't real." It was like I was scared of something—and that makes me really doubt the Brilliancy a lot. I am scared of letting it be there. The fear stops me.

AH: So for you there is doubt.

S: Self-doubt.

AH: You doubt yourself. This doubt could be investigated more. It's good that you see there is doubt. The next step is to see what that doubt is about. What makes you doubt yourself? Where does this doubt come from?

S: What comes to mind is just being challenged by my parents a lot. I'd say something, and they would challenge it, whether I was right or wrong.

AH: I see. That made you doubt yourself. How do you feel now when you realize that your parents squashed your intelligence that way?

S: Well, there is a part of me that's angry about it. And I feel like I just really want to expand.

AH: Are you angry at one of your parents or both of them?

S: Right now I see it more in terms of my father.

AH: Your father. What about your father? What are you angry at him for?

S: I am pissed at the part of him that just was so overbearing.

AH: I see. He was overbearing and questioned you, which made you doubt yourself.

S: He questioned many things I did, what I said, my ideas. He questioned things like what I was feeling.

AH: So instead of supporting your insights and intelligence, he questioned and doubted you. Why do you think he did that?

S: He himself wanted to be the intelligent one.

AH: I understand. It's understandable to be very angry about that. There might be other feelings about it. You might want to explore this issue more in your own time. We are seeing the beginning of the issue of Brilliancy for you.

Another student starts to work.

S: The feeling in the exercise, and what came up afterward, is that I talk *about* it; I talk all the way around the subject matter. I never got to the very center of it. And I was just thinking about that in relationship to my father. There would be this dialogue between us, and as long as I could work all the way around the dialogue, it was okay. But when it came to the center, or the emotional-feeling part of it, he wouldn't touch it or allow me to touch it.

AH: He wouldn't let you touch the emotional part of the dialogue?

S: Yeah. It was okay to verbalize around everything, but not the emotional part, not the feeling part.

AH: What does it make you feel when you see that?

S: Well, I think that what it made me feel and makes me feel is separate from others. Like I can experience it for myself but not in connection with others.

AH: The emotions?

S: No, the Brilliancy.

AH: Oh, the Brilliancy. What are you experiencing right at this moment?

S: I mean it's difficult to even talk. I felt real emotional about it.

AH: You feel the difficulty. What's the difficulty like? What is the difficulty?

S: Afraid. It is similar to what the last person was talking about—my father was the smart one and I was the dumb one. So it's safer to keep quiet.

AH: What's the fear about?

S: I don't know.

AH: What does the fear tell you when you feel it now, when you let it happen, when you realize that you are afraid to talk about it?

S: It's more in connection with the world. I am afraid to let people know about this part of me.

AH: So, to talk about that part of yourself is exposing yourself in some way. Why is it dangerous to expose yourself? There must be a certain kind of risk.

S: It is all those judgments.

AH: What is the world going to judge you as? What is the judgment?

S: My father comes to mind—he must have had some judgment.

AH: So your father is the world in this instance.

S: Sure.

AH: How do you feel now?

S: How do I feel? Nervous. And I feel sad and I feel angry about that, too. I am also aware of the Brilliancy.

AH: That's a precious part of you. When you feel that part of you, the Brilliancy, what is it like for you?

S: It's like my mind is not there. It's just happening, and there's some kind of light about it. The light is bright and luminous, very brilliant.

AH: So you feel light inside you?

S: It happens a lot when I am doing my artwork.

AH: So you have areas in your life where you could express it—in your artwork, for example—but you keep the world outside of it.

S: That's right. I saw in the exercise that when I was a child, I found that Brilliancy mostly by myself, not when I was with my parents.

Another student starts to relate his experience.

S: Brilliancy felt like something real simple, very innocent. It felt almost ethereal to me, in the sense that it doesn't seem like it's possible to direct. It is almost self-directing. Is there a relationship between Brilliancy and mother, like in the symbiotic phase where things just kind of flow along simply?

AH: What makes you think of that? What is it in your experience that makes you think that it might be related to the symbiotic phase and mother?

S: It feels tremendously comfortable.

AH: Oh, it feels comfortable.

S: Also when I feel those feelings, other feelings come, like gratitude.

AH: All essential aspects feel comfortable if you don't have reactions to them.

S: As I think about it, as the feelings come up, many times gratitude will come up.

AH: The more you experience Brilliancy, the more likely it is that you will experience the other aspects. It's like the source. What you say is true: that it cannot be directed, that it directs itself. How can you direct intelligence? Intelligence should be what directs. And if you appreciate the experience, it makes sense that gratitude would arise.

S: How does it come into action?

AH: That's the next step. The first step is to be able to experience it. The next step is for it to come into action in your life. That's the integration part of it. How it comes into action is a whole process on its own. And as you see, it has to do with innocence. If you act in an innocent way, it will tend to be there, to function. The more you stay with it, the more you have insight and an understanding of how it works. You get into the groove of it, the feel of it. The more you deal with the issues around it, and the more it's allowed, the more it will be able to penetrate your actions and your life.

Another student starts at this point.

S: I get real pissed. And that's just a cover for the hurt. I am sitting here feeling hurt, and I realize that I bought into the belief that my father is smarter than I am. You can't feel hurt unless you buy into that bullshit. Then it occurred to me that he projected his stupidity on me, and I've been carrying that around.

AH: I see.

S: I mean it's really kind of comical.

AH: It's hurtful. It hurts to see him projecting his stupidity on you and making you believe you're not smart, that he's the smart one. It's bound to hurt you, and I understand that you'd be angry. I think it is good that you are feeling that there is a hurt about it, a deep hurt. It is deep because this part, the intelligence, is a very deep and very precious part of who you are.

AH comments: *The depth of the hurt is not obvious in the words of the student, but is quite obvious to the teacher because of the expression he sees on the student's face. The teacher is also aware of the depth of the feeling due to the empathic capacity that allows an open and sympathetic person to feel the quality and depth of another human being's feelings.*

Another student starts sharing her experience.

S: During the exercise, I was aware of all the attitudes that my father made me feel. Basically, Brilliancy to me is something that other people have and that I'll never have. It was interesting what happened after the exercise. I was giving feedback to Rod, and Jane came down and sat at our table; she wanted to know what happened this morning. I told her in about a minute, and then Rod said to me, "That was brilliant." And I felt real embarrassed. Kind of like no one ever told me that.

AH: So that part was not recognized in you.

I am getting quite curious about people's experiences. How come everybody is talking about their fathers? Did somebody tell you to talk about your fathers? No? Did anybody know that we were going to work on father this weekend? I was planning to leave father until tomorrow, but daddy is already coming in very strongly.

7

Meeting Two

☙

Questions and comments followed the meditation period at the beginning of the session.

AH: Any questions?
S: Could you say something about intellect?
AH: In some sense, it has to do with intelligence. Intellect, however, is not an essential aspect; it is a certain capacity that we have, that the soul has—the capacity for reasoning and arriving at understanding. Intellect questions, ponders, investigates, contemplates, discerns, discriminates, and so on, as a process of arriving at insight. This capacity can use or embody intelligence or not. The intellect can function more or less intelligently, with more or less intelligence. However, there is a higher intellect, which is a traditional name for the quality that I call Diamond Guidance.

Another student begins to work.

S: In discussing Brilliancy, I noticed a lot of emptiness inside. I felt much emptiness inside.
AH: Do you still feel that?
S: Ah, it's . . . there. I also feel sad.

AH: Do you know what the sadness is about?

S: I was curious about that. I wasn't very good at deciding what it was. It has something to do with being on my own, having my own strength and my own Brilliancy. In the last week or so, I've seen something about how I have given up a lot of things for my father. For example, I have given up my relationships with women because of what my father's relationship to my mother was like, and things like that.

AH: What is it you feel now?

S: Sort of that emptiness in my head.

AH: In your head. You feel the emptiness in the head. How does that affect you? How does it make you feel?

S: There is some fear involved. And it seems that if I stay with the fear, I am able to see things more clearly. And it seems to bring more space.

AH: What's the fear about?

S: That emptiness makes me feel like I'm . . . like there is no sense of self.

AH: That's what it feels like, that emptiness, that there is no sense of self?

S: Yes, and physically, sort of deficient, weak.

AH: Do you feel actually weak, or you think that emptiness means being weak?

S: In this moment, I don't actually feel weak.

AH: I wonder what will happen if you just feel the emptiness and don't have any ideas about it. Then see what it feels like.

S: It's kind of still.

AH: So there is a stillness to it. It doesn't feel bad then, when you don't have ideas about it.

S: It's like I got stuck by trying to avoid it. It actually isn't that unpleasant.

AH: When you stay with this peaceful and still emptiness in your head, what happens?

S: It expands. When I just stay with it and don't do anything to it—when I just relax—it seems to get bigger and bigger.

AH: How big does it get?

S: Hmm . . . no size. I just feel empty and spacious all over.

AH comments: *The absence of any aspect of Essence, when such absence is not avoided or defended against, will be experienced as an emptiness. The emptiness will have a deficient feeling, an affect of* *something missing. This fact is the basis of the theory of holes in the Diamond Approach. Whenever an aspect is missing in one's conscious experience, one experiences this absence as a hole in the psyche. In the above instance, the absence of Brilliancy in the consciousness of the student appeared as a deficient emptiness in the head. The location of the emptiness most likely means that the student was considering Brilliancy to be located in his mental capacities. Also, when the emptiness is not rejected or defended against—which necessitates recognizing and suspending one's judgments and various ideas about it—it transforms into a spacious emptiness, which is the experience of the presence of space. That happened in this case when the teacher suggested that the student experience the emptiness without preconceived ideas.**

AH: I wonder what happens if you just remain this way without reacting to the experience of this spaciousness?

S: I start feeling something in my head.

AH: What kind of something?

S: It feels bright. I feel bright in my head.

AH: Bright in your head. Do you mean you see brightness in your head?

S: Well, let me see. I guess that is what I mean. But not exactly. I feel brightness in my head, and I also sort of see something shining in there.

AH: What is the feeling of this brightness in the head?

S: The emptiness in the head is getting pervaded by this beautiful light. It is quite luminous. It is like my brain is exploding with Brilliancy.

AH: Brilliancy. How do you feel psychologically? If you remember, the deficient emptiness appeared when you were doing the exercise about Brilliancy. How do you feel now? Does this experience mean anything to that deficient emptiness?

S: I feel somehow something new that I have never felt before. I feel full of brightness. I feel bright, as if my brain is exploding with light. I also do not feel deficient. In fact, I am starting to see how I am intelligent. It is not new, but I did not see these expressions of mine as intelligent. I do feel brighter than usual though. I mean . . . well, I mean I feel smart. This makes me nervous, but I like it. I feel that it is my intelligence.

---

* See *The Void: Inner Spaciousness and Ego Structure* (1986; reissued by Shambhala Publications, 2000).

AH: So the brightness is both visual and psychological.

S: The brightness actually is more substantial than light. It is light, but it is like liquid light that is bright. It is also not just in the head; it seems to be spreading.

AH: Okay. Just stay with this experience and find out for yourself what it means to you.

AH comments: *The theory of holes states that the transformation of the deficient emptiness into the inner experience of space is the step that precedes the arising of a missing aspect of Essence. Space becomes the clearing where Essence manifests. (See* The Void.*) It is also significant that the student started to see that the aspect of Brilliancy is not just a bright light but actually a presence, something more substantial than light—more like liquid light.*

Another student now starts working.

S: My relationship to Brilliancy seems to be directly connected to my relationship with my mother, and in a larger sense, to the world. That's what came out of doing the exercise.

AH: So you are seeing something about your mother that is related to Brilliancy?

S: As a child, it was threatening to her. She pushed me away.

AH: So if you were brilliant, she'd push you away?

S: Well, that's how it happened. In my actual experience, the Brilliancy that I have brings a direct feeling of rejection and, probably deeper, a direct experience of humiliation. I just wanted to say these things.

AH: That is fine. What is it you feel now?

S: Right now, I don't really feel it that much.

AH: So you are just telling us about your experience.

S: It is hard for me to actually emotionally feel in the exercises, to really feel it.

AH: But you're saying your mommy didn't like you to have that quality.

S: It seems like . . . I don't know. During lunch, I was trying to stay with what had happened for me at the end of the last exercise, and it seemed like there was some sadness about feeling the Brilliancy or anything else

I recognized in myself. It feels like I put things that were part of me away because I didn't want to hurt my parents. I feel in touch with that. It feels like it was a compassionate thing. And yet it feels like the hurt is my own hurt for having done that. I have a sense of the melancholy and the tragedy in all of this. It seems like it's all directly connected with the Brilliancy.

AH: You're saying that you sacrificed something in yourself so that you wouldn't hurt your parents.

S: And all I got—what I am left with—is this tragic sense of myself, which is nothing. And it feels as though being myself, in a sense, feels deficient because I am not being anything that they wanted me to be. And there is a real sense of deficiency, which is tragic.

AH: So if you are yourself, then it's not what they want, and that makes you feel deficient.

S: In a sense, yeah. That's exactly what it feels like.

AH: Deficient in what sense?

S: It's like being . . . I don't know, I just feel like I'm gone. I feel empty, and there is this sadness.

AH: Is the sadness about hurting yourself or what? What is it about?

S: The biggest sadness is about what I did to myself. But there is also this sadness about not living up to their expectations. It seems that both are there.

AH: So you partly feel sad that you couldn't satisfy their expectations.

S: I couldn't really be what they wanted me to be.

AH: And that hurts them. If you don't become what they want you to be, you'll be hurting them.

S: And by being myself . . .

AH: . . . you'll be hurting them.

S: Yeah, either way.

AH: You feel you can't be yourself because that will hurt them, so you try to be something else.

S: But that hurts them, too.

AH: Because it didn't work, you mean.

S: Right. Now, though, it seems like it's such a . . . I mean, if I feel the hurt, it feels like there is such a sense of longing just to be myself, just to *be*, no matter what they feel. No matter what anyone else feels.

AH: So, being yourself would confront them with their situation and make them see the truth, you mean. I see. So you believe that the truth will hurt them.

S: I believe the truth will hurt everybody.

AH: I see. That's where you got it. What we are seeing here is that you think the truth will hurt other people, so better to get away from the truth. How do you feel now when you see that?

S: I don't know, it brings a sense of . . . well, somehow I feel more mature, I feel stronger, I feel different. It's been funny today: While we've been doing this, the truth has been there. I have been tasting it. When I did the second exercise, I had a sense about how the Brilliancy would hurt someone or would hurt me. That is where the pain began.

AH: You thought, "It's better that they don't hurt, even if that means no truth."

S: Even if it was a lie.

AH: So, avoiding hurt is the priority there; hurt is the worst thing.

S: Especially, it seems, for other people.

AH: But what we are seeing here is that you are hurting yourself by cutting off the truth. What do you think will happen to people if they don't see the truth, if they are cut off from the truth?

S: Well, I think they won't feel hurt.

AH: I see, that's what you think. But do you think they will be different from you? I am asking this because when you are cut off from the truth, you seem to feel hurt.

S: I don't know. It's like some kind of childish belief that if they don't see the truth, they won't feel the hurt that I still feel.

AH: That's the belief you had as a child. But what is the actual perception?

S: The actual perception is that they are still going to feel it even if they are cut off from it.

AH: But how about the cutting off from the truth? That doesn't hurt?

S: No, it does hurt.

AH: Well, which one is the deeper hurt?

S: The cutting off.

AH: So when you figure out a way so that people don't see the truth, what is that doing to them, in reality?

S: Hurting them.

AH: As children, we think we are protecting our parents by covering up the truth; but in doing that, we could be hurting them even more. The truth might hurt, but the truth always brings in more integration, really. This is something we learn the more we look objectively at those situations.

S: I am feeling hurt.

AH: So that's what you are feeling now? Hurt?

S: Yes.

AH: What about?

S: Feeling separate from the truth.

AH: That's the deeper hurt: feeling separate from the truth.

S: And it feels like it relates somehow to not wanting to be recognized, because there is so much that is not true. Having one thing seen brings up all the things that aren't true.

AH: You don't want other people to see the untrue as well?

S: It all comes together.

AH: The basis of hurt is the sense of being cut off from oneself, from one's own truth. That has to happen first, before you can be hurt in other ways. If you are not cut off from truth, you can't be truly hurt. But if you are cut off from truth, then you will be hurt by all sorts of things. But those hurts are just provoking the deeper hurt. They're a reflection of it.

That's really a dilemma in life. What we see is that most people do get hurt by the truth, and so we think the best thing is to cover up the truth, to forget the truth. However, the fact is that the more you see, the more you recognize that it is really the other way around. Although the truth might hurt for a while, seeing the truth will actually eliminate much more hurt in the future. It is a difficult lesson to learn. Learning it brings a kind of maturity. It means that you have to believe and act according to the perception that the loss of truth is really the biggest hurt.

S: It helps a lot to experience the way it feels.

AH: What happens when you stay with this hurt?

S: I feel sad. I feel some kind of compassion for myself for being cut off from the truth. Also, compassion for others. I have to experience the hurt of being cut off from the truth to know how bad it is.

AH: That's how you know it: You see what's it like to be cut off from the truth. Imagine your life without truth in it. What is there then, what is left?

S: What we are talking about here is a taboo that runs really deep in our society. It seems to me that there is a taboo against knowing and living and shining with your truth, even more so than there is about sexual things. I mean, it's okay to get into art, and to get really intellectual and to succeed in this and that, but when it comes to actually embodying the truth, and Being, that's just for cats like Jesus—that's not for you. And so it seems that if you start to exercise any kind of Brilliancy or intelligence, there is a really deep taboo in society that says it is not okay.

This comes not only from our parents, but it's everywhere you turn. I can see that when you are two or three years old, there is so much coming at you to shut you down. And then to try to recapture that intelligence and live it, it just seems like I am not only involved with hurting people, but that I am asking for attack. Wilhelm Reich refers to this a lot in his book *The Murder of Christ*. My experience is that there is a lot of attack out there, not just putting you down or hushing you up. It is absolutely not okay to be the truth.

AH: That has a lot of truth to it. However, what that can do for us is give us greater motivation to be more intelligent about living our truth.

How do we deal with this? We need to be more intelligent in handling the situation without getting cut off from the truth. It is true that society doesn't recognize or support truth in a deep way. But that is not new; society has always been like that, and it's probably going to be like that for the next few million years. You can take that as a given.

The fact is, when we discuss society in relationship to truth or anything of deep significance, most of the time we'll find that society doesn't know, doesn't recognize, doesn't approve, doesn't support whatever it is—and that's not because we are modern-day Americans. It was the case in the Middle Ages, in Rome, in Greece. What did they do to Socrates? What did they do to Christ? It's always like that. My guess is, it's going to continue like that. In fact, I do not see many signs of improvement. And maybe that's the way it's supposed to be anyway—who knows? We can look gloomily at this situation and spend time feeling bad about it or we can simply recognize the fact that that is how society is. We can know that society is the way it is and take that into consideration.

So if we are really interested in working on ourselves, if we care about the truth enough, if we care about our true nature enough to be in touch with it, we will do what is necessary to actualize it. This is not the same as setting ourselves up to change society or impose something on it.

Instead we can ask ourselves, "What is the most intelligent way to go about this so we can be the truth of what we are? How can we use the present situation in the most intelligent way possible to support ourselves and our endeavor—and hopefully benefit society as well?"

I am saying that we first need to connect ourselves to the truth before we even think about the truth in terms of the larger society. Don't you think that would be more intelligent?

S: It's a lot more intelligent than trying to project Brilliancy onto the world and get approval from it.

AH: You need to see that your feelings about society at large, although generally accurate, are partly a reflection of your feelings about your parents, who found the truth hurtful. It might actually not be possible for you to be objective about society before you become clear about this issue with your parents. So how do you feel now?

S: I feel like I've got a lot of work to do this weekend.

AH: What do you mean? What kind? Are you sure or is that just another idea?

S: No. I struggle a lot with trying to be myself in situations, whatever that means—I find myself trying to please people, conform to them, get along with them, be relational, and still be who I am and express myself. It is a very difficult problem. I feel like I can't be myself 95 percent of the time.

AH: That is not bad.

S: It may be higher than that.

AH: I mean that being yourself 5 percent of the time is pretty good for most people. Really. I am not kidding. If you can be yourself 5 percent of the time, you at least know what it is like to be yourself. A lot of people haven't even got the vaguest idea what it is like to be themselves. In fact, the majority of people don't even know when they are not being themselves.

S: For me, it's actually in my consciousness. I am saying that I am in touch with what I think and what I feel, and I am always asking myself, "Can I say this or not? Can I express this or not? Will this person relate to this or not?"

AH: But that is a particular and specific issue, you see. One does not need to express everything to be oneself. There are many things I know that I can't express, and I don't. And I don't feel that it is a problem that I can't express them.

S: For me it is a problem when I can't express them.

AH: Yes, and that's what we need to understand. Why is it that you need to express them? What for? Obviously, you want something from the situation. That's one avenue of investigation here.

By working on intelligence—which is one of the ways of experiencing the Brilliancy aspect—we start to see a great deal about our relationship to ourselves, to other people, to the world, to our parents. However, I think the important thing here for us to explore further is the understanding that Brilliancy is not a characteristic; it's not something that describes you; it's not a qualitative aspect of you. It's not that you can be or not be brilliant.

We are realizing that Brilliancy is an actual part of who we are. It's like your stomach. You don't say a person is stomachy. A person has a stomach. It's part of being a person, of having a body, that you have a stomach. It is the same with Brilliancy. You can't say a person is brilliant or not brilliant. You say that a person is not being that part of themselves, that they are not in touch with their Brilliancy.

We are talking about being or not being in touch with the truth, being or not being cut off from the truth. The way I see it is that Brilliancy, or intelligence, is a way of being. It is actually your presence in one of its qualities. Brilliancy is not something you attain one of these days. Brilliancy is a part of you that you realize is you. That is why I said that you cannot learn intelligence in school. Nobody can teach you to be intelligent. Intelligence is something that is part of your makeup, of your very constitution. This understanding points to what we mean by Essence. Essence is not something that describes you—it's not a quality of how you are. Essence is *who* you are.

This is a very important insight to see in regard to intelligence. Yes, I can be intelligent; but deeper than that, I can be *intelligence*. If you allow yourself to embody the Brilliancy, you can experience yourself as that beautiful, delicate presence that is Brilliancy, that is intelligence. Our essence, our beingness, our soul, our very consciousness, is actually Brilliancy. At a very deep level of our essential existence, we find that we are *intelligence*—not that we are *intelligent*, but that intelligence is our self-nature, our ipseity. In fact, our capacities and our other qualities issue out of intelligence, are differentiations out of intelligence. Intelligence is not one of those little things you can have or not have. It is a core, a center, a source of who we are.

Brilliancy is who I am. Other things I experience are things that come out of me. And because I am the Being of intelligence, because I am pure Brilliancy, there is light, there is brightness, in my other qualities. Consciousness, without the Brilliancy, is a dullness. It is dull, heavy, dark. The fact that at the deepest level I am Brilliancy itself makes it possible for there to be light in my consciousness, in my experience of my consciousness.

Brilliancy, in other words, is a very basic fact of my consciousness. It is the actual physiognomy of the substance of my being. At a very deep place, and in a fundamental way, I am Brilliancy. The truth of the human soul is that its essence is ultimately Brilliancy, its self-nature is fundamentally intelligence.

Another student now begins to work.

S: I am having a flood of clarity. I am seeing some things quite clearly right now as I sit here listening to you. One of the things that just came to me in the last couple of minutes was how close an identity there has been between this issue about intelligence and the general issue of potency and castration. I find myself in the same damn dilemma around intelligence that I am frequently in about potency in general. The issue that I see is that my father was always putting me down, always minimizing me in relation to intelligence or any kind of potency. In the case of my mother, intelligence was somehow always for her; it was never something that was just mine.

Many feelings are coming up in my chest. I think I am feeling some anger. I've had times when I experienced my potency in general—and sometimes my intelligence—simply for myself. But I see that that is only an occasional gift. Elements of needing to perform come in so much of the rest of the time, as in the situation with my mother. The other part of the issue is that I have to minimize my intelligence, or my potency in general, in some way, for my father. I had only seen this in terms of castration issues before. Now I am seeing this issue in terms of intelligence. I am seeing that this is one of the basic dilemmas of my life. I find the same kind of dilemma in just about every area in my life.

AH: When you see it that way—that you have to minimize yourself, that you have to minimize your intelligence—what does that make you feel? How does it make you feel that you've had to do that all of your life?

S: I feel angry.

AH: So there is anger, okay. Whom do you feel angry at?

S: My dad.

AH: Does the anger become specific when you feel it like that, when you just let it be? What specifically are you angry at him for?

S: No, actually. When I stay with it, it turns into sadness.

AH: So there is sadness now instead of the anger. What is it like when you feel the sadness?

S: It's like a deep hurt.

AH: There is hurt.

S: I feel there is just a whole part of me that my dad didn't know.

AH: I see. Which part?

S: Well, really, it comes down to every part. Any part that . . . well, every part. I felt that there was nothing he really saw or knew.

AH: So you really couldn't be yourself with him. You had to contract when you were around him. Who you are was not accepted, wasn't okay. It appears that that's what the hurt was about. When you feel the hurt, when you look within the hurt, what happens? What do you find inside the hurt, if there is anything beside the pain itself?

AH comments: *The teacher might seem to be interpreting the student's experience too deeply. This was not the impression in the meeting. It is difficult to get a feeling from the written transcript for the actual emotional and energetic atmosphere. In the meeting itself, the interpretation had quite a natural flow with the process of the student.*

The teacher can discern much more from the total presentation of the student than the small part that is available to the reader through the words that were spoken. In addition, the teacher is familiar with the student's general character and personality. So he is responding not only to the spoken words of the student, but also to the totality of the stu-

dent's presentation, to the totality of the student's consciousness as it is manifesting in the room.

The teacher is also knowledgeable about the universal characteristics of the issue being discussed, and hence is familiar with its various ramifications. All of these factors taken together will explain the apparent jump in depth the teacher took in his response to this student. As the reader, you will need to take into consideration all of these points as you experience apparent jumps in the working process between the teacher and his students as they explore the material here in Part Three.

Of course, it is possible for the teacher to interpret too much or too fast, which did happen in some moments during the course of working with students at this retreat. However, the important point to keep in mind is that the teacher's response can only facilitate or impede the naturally unfolding inner process of the student. The teacher sees his function as primarily that of clarifying what is happening in the experience of the student so that the consciousness of the student is supported to unfold according to its own patterns, revealing increasingly deeper levels of its reality.

This process is based on the understanding—which is an intrinsic part of the Diamond Approach—that the consciousness of the soul will naturally move to deeper aspects of its own reality when the experience that is manifesting is understood completely and accurately. Understanding the truth of present experience naturally leads to the revelation of the rest of the truth about a particular soul. This deeper truth is hidden from one's conscious experience until the full truth of the present moment is completely perceived. This will then be the complete understanding of the situation that will unfold as a process, continuing until the soul's potential is fully realized.

S: I just kind of feel lost, and void.
AH: Okay, so there is a sense of lostness and voidness. Let's see what you find out if you just feel that.
S: It's kind of like an emptiness.
AH: Very well. What is the sense to that emptiness when you feel it?
S: It's kind of floating. There is darkness to it.

AH: Darkness. Sense that emptiness, that darkness. Just sense it, be there, feel it in a gentle way.

[*Pause*]

S: It starts to change.

AH: That's what happens. The moment you let it be, it changes.

S: When I stopped being afraid of it, I felt an expansion. And then as I expand, I feel some kind of resistance to the expansion. The sense of it is like leaving my father, letting my father go.

AH: I see. You need to let go of your father to allow that expansion. So then, to have him means you have to be contracted, small. That is the relationship you had with your father. To allow the expansion, in this case, means to let go of that relationship. [*Pause*] How about now—what is your experience?

S: I feel a lot of trembling in my body. I am feeling a lot of expansion and some resistance to it. I see that's where the trembling comes from.

AH: I see; there is some resistance to letting go of that relationship with your father. What do you think will happen if you let go of it?

S: It just feels like mourning, like mourning what never was.

AH: So you are mourning the father you didn't have.

S: Yeah. And when you talk about that, there is sadness.

AH: I see. Let yourself feel the hurt for not having the father that you needed, that you wanted.

[*Pause*]

S: When I stay with it, it smoothes out, and I feel more expansion.

AH: I see, you needed to allow the sadness of the loss for the expansion to go on. What is the feeling in the expansion? What is the sense?

S: It is literally like I am brightened.

AH: Brightened. The expansion brings brightness.

S: And a smooth sensation. I get a smooth sense. It's interesting: I expand again to a certain level, then I can feel . . . It's like I get to a place where I can't expand any further, and I feel the trembling start in my body again. It's like more resistance to letting go.

AH: It's okay for the resistance to be there. Just be aware of what the resistance is about. What is it that stops you from expanding?

[*Pause*]

S: Again, it's like another level of my letting go of him.

AH: Right. It would be interesting to see what it's like to let go of him. I know you want that freedom, but it is also obvious that the letting go is not so easy. It means going through many difficult emotions.

S: As you said that, I felt more expansion.

AH: All right, that's fine.

S: It's happening in increments.

AH: What's the quality in the expansion? You said smoothness, right?

S: It's funny; I had a taste of something. I feel more of a sense of strength.

AH: Expansion, strength, smoothness.

S: And the trembling gets more intense again.

AH: Feel the trembling. Let's see what it's about. Let's see what we find out when you let the trembling happen. The trembling is part of what is happening, so let's follow it by allowing it.

S: It feels like a kind of hanging on. And then it feels like a huge void. I just can't imagine what it would be if I let go completely. It feels as if it would be going into the dark. I just had a sense of the work I did yesterday—it was falling into a dark space. I saw that falling into the dark space was like falling into Mom. There seems to be a connection here.

AH: I see. So if you let go of your dad, you fall into Mom.

S: Yeah, and then I'll be absorbed.

AH: I see. Other feelings arise as you let go. Now roll your eyes.

AH comments: *This exercise is merely to relax the eyes and loosen the tense muscles in the whole ocular area. The teacher became aware of the student's tensing up in the area around the head and suggested the exercise to see what would happen when there was more relaxation in the face.*

AH: Okay. How about now—what do you experience?

S: Different. One of the things that I am aware of is some of the feedback I got earlier in the exercise about how I focus on other people's reactions to me. I didn't realize it was going to go this far. And one of the things that I've been struck with is how I'm not feeling very self-conscious. Normally, I'd be feeling more self-conscious about doing this work in front of people I don't know. It feels like a relief.

AH: Yes, it seems to me that's exactly what you are letting go of.

S: I feel kind of bright, and I feel young.

AH: Tell me more about that. What's it like?

S: It feels like a veil got lifted. Like I am seeing without a block there, without something between me and the world. I feel that I am more direct. It also feels like there is more in me, more brightness, more coming from inside of me, and also more contact with the outside.

AH: So the brightness is something you are bringing into the world. Now when you feel that sense of brightness, when you let yourself be it and experience it, what do you see in terms of the father you never had? How is it related to that?

S: Well, he either didn't see the brightness, or when he saw it he attacked it. And partly there was a thing about the fact that he was sick a lot. I felt that I didn't have a right to feel good around him if he felt bad. I felt I didn't have a right to this energy, to this life, because his was so clouded.

AH: So you couldn't have this brightness when you were around him.

S: No. Now I feel I can, for it is my brightness. It's my own.

AH: It is your own, right?

S: It has always been mine, but it got covered over. And now I can feel that it is mine again.

AH: What is it like just to be it?

S: It feels very powerful, and I am very trembly again.

AH: That's part of the trembling—the power that comes with it. When the Brilliancy comes, it is a powerful sense of presence, a sense of power and immensity. The energy that comes from it is quite powerful.

S: It feels good. It's a strange feeling. It feels really wonderful, and it just feels like all the muscles are charging and discharging.

AH: I understand. I remember when I first experienced Brilliancy. I didn't know about it then; I didn't know there was such a thing. I was standing in the middle of a room with some people, and I started shaking all over the place. I wasn't scared of it; it's just that my body was shaking. "Now, why am I shaking?" I wondered. After a while of just staying with the shaking, there appeared this immense and powerful presence. It had a sense of being big and expanded, a thereness that is big and expansive. It seems that as Brilliancy begins to arise, many people feel a kind of shaking, trembling.

S: As you were talking, I started feeling soft. There is a soft and sweet feeling in the room. I see you being soft and sweet as you talk. I feel understood, like you understood what I was feeling. And I feel comforted.

AH: Yes, that's part of what you didn't have from your father: the love and sweetness, and the understanding. You can see that I see you, see your brightness. I understand your brightness in a way that your father did not. That comforts you.

S: Yeah, he didn't understand me. He didn't see me or understand me, or want to understand me.

AH: It's an interesting thing to see that Brilliancy manifests in many ways. One of the ways it manifests is as a powerful presence. It's like Brilliancy is really presence in its purest form—pure presence—so pure that it is brilliant, so pure that it is luminous. But it is just presence, presence in a powerful way. Dense presence, very palpable presence.

S: It seems like there is such a clarity. My eyes are clear and the atmosphere seems different; the light looks brighter.

AH: That's what I meant, you see, when I said this morning that it will affect your capacities. Your seeing is now clearer, brighter. Things like that will happen. Everything will start looking brighter, more shiny. There is more shine in the world.

S: I am still sitting over here trembling.

AH: Maybe it will expand more. Let's see how big it will be if you don't decide for it—as big as this room, or as big as the city, or what? Since Brilliancy is intelligence, let intelligence guide.

S: I was getting into it, and all of a sudden I felt my whole body was charged on the outside. It's a different feeling; it's not inside. It felt like it was outside my body, up and down my arms and legs—almost as if my hair were standing on end.

AH: So you are getting energized, charged up. Let yourself be the presence of it.

S: The whole feeling of it is changing. It becomes like jelly.

AH: Where do you feel the jelly?

S: It feels like it's in my torso.

AH: In the torso.

S: As soon as I say that, I start to contract again against it. I just felt very strong, and then I start to shake again.

AH: There needs to be a readjustment in your system for that kind of energy. It is interesting. You said it has to do with letting go of your relationship with your father. You said you have to let go of your father to be this part.

S: I couldn't let go this much with my father until I saw those issues in the work I did about my mother, because the alternative was to be lost in her. Maybe I held on to that as a way to counterbalance her.

AH: We frequently use father to separate from mother. So if we lose the relation to our father, we feel that we will fall in Mommy's lap, and God knows what will happen there! I think it is important for you to remember what you said at the beginning: that your father put you down and attacked you for your intelligence. You felt that the same thing happened in relation to your power and potency. As a result, you couldn't be intelligent or powerful around your father. So you had to let go of that relation with him to regain those qualities. Not the real present relationship, but the emotional one you retain in your mind. That is what you felt in the expansion.

The expansion is the space that resulted from letting go of that relationship. You felt the grief about the loss. You had to feel that for the expansion to happen. In that expansion, a brightness manifested. That was the Brilliancy aspect of Essence. It is interesting that the brightness made you feel powerful. Brilliancy manifested in a form to fit your situation exactly. It manifested in its powerful form, for you felt that your father did not see—or he put down—not only your intelligence but also your potency. So the Essence that manifested is both bright and powerful. It is a resolution of both the issue of intelligence and the issue of potency.

It is also interesting that you were working on intelligence, and the aspect that manifested is brightness. This shows that intelligence is truly a bright presence, a Brilliancy.

AH turns back to the group.

As you see, there is a lot of connection between intelligence, Brilliancy, and one's father. The mother figures in it, but father seems to figure more prominently. So one of the ways of learning to realize this part of us is to understand the relationship with one's father and to work through that.

We will continue to explore the ways in which this issue of Brilliancy is connected to father.

Understanding your relationship with your father will help us a lot in understanding your relationship to intelligence, as some of you have already seen. I didn't mention the word "father" this morning, and yet after the first exercise, everybody was talking about their father. I just thought we'd discuss intelligence, for that was what I was talking about at the start of the meeting. It is obvious that there must be some connection between intelligence and father, a mysterious one. What is this relationship? How come you found that the question of Brilliancy and intelligence is connected to father? This might become more evident by understanding one's relationship to one's father.

So, before I say any more, I would like you to explore that. Each person needs to look more deeply into this so you can see it for yourselves. The understanding should come from you, rather than from my telling you. So we are going to do an exercise now.

The students are asked to explore as personally and deeply as possible their relationship with their father—in other words, its closeness or distance, positive or negative qualities, emotional dynamics, and so on— as it exists in them based on their childhood experience. After the exercise, the students reassemble.

AH: Any questions?

S: This gets worse and worse. I looked at my father, and there was what I assumed was Brilliancy. I realized that I assumed or believed, somehow, that he embodied intelligence. But then the more I explored and talked about it, it didn't have any presence; it didn't have any Being.

AH: What is it that didn't have presence or Being?

S: My father's Brilliancy.

AH: This means you were seeing him as representing Brilliancy, but now you are finding out that he didn't really have it.

S: Yeah, right. But I wondered. I mean, that's what I saw when he died. Now I see that Brilliancy was what I saw in him in life. It seemed to have more flesh then. And now it feels that it really wasn't there, although I thought it was there. I projected it.

AH: It appears that what you did to your aspect of Brilliancy is that you projected it onto your father: "He's a brilliant person." This means you can have the Brilliancy only by having him.

S: And then, as I explored it some more, at the end of the exercise, I felt like I have never had a father. Boy, it didn't feel that good. I never really had a father. It's sort of grim, you know. But I mean it was interesting.

AH: I keep smiling because people are saying the things I am planning to talk about before I say them.

S: I guess what I was feeling is that I would do almost anything to feel that I did have a father, including be like him, project Brilliancy on him, or whatever.

AH: It sounds like in your mind your father and Brilliancy were the same, and that Brilliancy *was* your father. And discovering that he wasn't that Brilliancy means to you now that you didn't have your father; it means the loss of the father you had. Brilliancy is the father for you, then.

S: That's the other thing I felt. I mean, I saw him as the source, and so if I didn't have a father, I didn't have a source.

AH: Does that mean that if he wasn't the source, you didn't have a father?

S: The same, either way. I knew I associated intelligence and Brilliancy with my father before, but I didn't recognize it went that deep.

AH: So you felt you lost your father today.

S: Yes.

AH: That's the same thing that was happening to Lenny this afternoon. He had to let go of his father to experience that part of himself.

Another student begins to work.

S: I have a question. I am real aware of how I perceived that my father was brilliant and that I was not. The problem is that I don't want to let go.

AH: Of your father?

S: Yeah. You talked about the support. Projecting my Brilliancy on my father is how I got support for me. I'm just feeling a lot of fear around this, thinking of how I am doing it myself.

AH: So you feel your fear now?

S: Yeah. Like a lightning bolt that hit me as I said that.

AH: How about now? What are you feeling?

S: Sort of used to it.

AH: You are not as scared now.

S: I am really seeing the damage that has been done by giving the Brilliancy to someone else.

AH: You gave a very important part of you away. You put it outside, on him. And that's the way you had it—by having your father, yes?

S: And he's dead. He's not in the world.

AH: This whole drama is only in your mind, obviously. It doesn't matter whether he is dead or not. It is the father in your mind that matters in this case. What do you think will happen if you let go of your father?

S: I might forget to get up in the morning or eat properly. I might forget how to move to get things done.

AH: You mean you wouldn't know how to take care of yourself.

S: And that is totally ridiculous.

AH: But that's what your mind says—that you wouldn't be able to take care of yourself. That's why you keep his image in your mind. The image of your brilliant father makes you feel supported, which you seem to believe you need in order to take care of yourself. How about right now—what's happening now?

S: I am feeling nervous. I am seeing that to perpetuate this inner figure is to support this little "chit-chit-chit"—it keeps this inner mental noise going.

AH: Just be aware of that; that's all you need to do—that's what is happening. You're keeping your father with this "chit-chit-chit," and in that way, you feel supported. If you are just aware of that fact, what happens? What do you feel?

[*Pause*]

S: I see that this is how I make myself get up in the morning. I do it by keeping my head talking to me, and that's absurd.

AH: That's what we do—that's what most people do. We think we can't learn how to deal with the world and take care of things unless we have Daddy telling us in our head how we are not doing it right, or how we should do it faster, better. This way we feel, "Daddy's here, Daddy's here—good. I don't have to be scared. The world doesn't have to scare me." Many people feel safe only while Daddy is whipping them in the background of their consciousness: "Go on! Why are you sitting on your ass? No—no—no, that's wrong! Dummy!" Right? You complain, you do therapy for it, but at the same time, you don't want to let it go. "Sit here, Daddy. That's good. What will I do without you?"

Of course, then, we do it with people outside, too. We can project that image on somebody outside, on a man who will do the same thing. You can either project that image of Daddy outside and relate to somebody else as Daddy, or you yourself try to become like Daddy. That way you know how to be smart, how to be worldly wise. You feel that you know how to take care of yourself—not because you have your own intelligence but because you have the image of a brilliant father in the deep recesses of your mind. That becomes a way for many of us to have Brilliancy.

After a pause, a different student begins to work.

S: Is there a tendency for a person to lean more toward the father that whips and chains us and is more judgmental? I had a very strange situation: When I was little, I was raised by two men: my biological father and a man who was a friend of the family since I was two and whom I lived with when I was nine. My biological father was very critical and judgmental, and I always had to be perfect. I was not allowed to feel in that house. The other man who raised me was loving and really supported me and taught me how to have a good time. I loved him more than I loved my real father. In between all of this, I lived in Japan for a year and a half; and when I came back, I ended up completely denying the friend-father any affection or acknowledgment that he existed. I just completely hung out with my real father. So it seemed that I just hung on to the criticism or something instead of leaning toward what I thought was more brilliant, more loving.

AH: What do you think would have happened if you had leaned more toward the loving part?

S: I probably would have become more loving.

AH: Is that why you didn't do it, because you didn't want to be more loving?

S: Well, maybe, because my real father was saying, "No, you can't be expressive."

AH: There might be some complexity here we don't see. Sometimes, people seem to go this way or that way, but it's not necessarily one way or the other. The circumstances, which can be understood, are what determined your choice. But understanding those circumstances would bring in another issue about the relationship with father that we haven't talked about yet. Since we do not have time now to pursue your process, I'll just mention the idea briefly.

What this points to is the issue of splitting the father in our mind into a good father and a bad father. It's just like with mommy: There is a good mommy and a bad mommy. The mind engages in this kind of splitting early on in life for certain purposes, some of them defensive. The splitting becomes especially easy to do when you have two different people, two different fathers. You can find something in reality, then, that will support you in this splitting. This is something we will explore more tonight.

Now it's time for dinner.

8

Meeting Three

☙

After a sitting meditation, a student raises his hand.

AH: So, what's happening?

S: Something kind of strange. It seems like for much of my life—from my teenage years until just a while back—I held on to this thought that I hated my father, and I blamed him. Through the process of the Work, I have somehow changed. He died two years ago, and ever since then I have been idealizing him. Both sides have really screwed up my relationships with men, or I have allowed them to interfere. I am not sure how to get the balance. It seems like I hold on to one side or the other as a way of keeping him.

 And what I have been doing the last couple of years is longing and wanting and missing that relationship—him—and just idealizing it, like it was just this almost perfect fantasy. And today it sort of popped out in the room, and I realized some of the bad things, too. But I don't seem to be able to integrate the good and the bad. I don't know what gets in my way, but it is either/or, one or the other.

AH: So, it starts by first seeing that it is either/or—by seeing how you split your father—and by seeing how each time you do that, it is unrealistic. Because by doing it that way, there is a defensiveness about it.

S: Yeah. It's a way of keeping me away from my emptiness, because I feel like I wouldn't exist if I just felt that. Either the hatred (and that is very possible) or the idealization (if I want to put a judgment on it) is kind of yucky. It's all that wanting and longing for the frustrating object. But it keeps me from feeling empty, as if I don't exist, and I know I have that emptiness in myself.

AH: So maybe that's what you need to feel: that emptiness. Do you feel that sometimes?

S: Yeah. Actually, it's like what someone was talking about earlier: When I feel the emptiness at all, it is peace for me. It's a relief from all that noise in my head, and frustration, once I allow myself to get into it. I sometimes feel that I don't exist, though, and I am real afraid of that when I feel empty. It feels like I'm not there, and I don't know what would happen. There is no me anymore.

AH: So what's scary about it is not just that it is empty, but that you feel you don't exist?

S: Yeah, I think that's what is scary. The emptiness itself, the pure emptiness that feels peaceful and still. It's a welcome relief from all the noise, and my mind disappears. But then it's like I don't know who or what I am, or if I have any boundaries, or if I exist. I guess that's what is so terrifying for me.

AH: Splitting is always to defend against that. Otherwise, what do you think it is for? It's a defense.

S: Yeah, I know it's a defense.

AH: Yes, and it's basically a defense against losing yourself, to stop feeling that you don't exist. And that state where you feel you don't exist is not an easy state to tolerate.

S: Although every time I do, I notice that I still function. I mean, I'm walking around doing work and making decisions without my mind. I think it's a gas! It's nice to be amused and not terrified.

AH: And it is interesting: You don't exist, but you keep going and do all sorts of things.

S: Yeah. There I am, making all these decisions.

AH: Right. How does this person who doesn't exist do all these things?

S: I don't know . . . Yeah, and when I can get out of the terror, step away from it, I sort of laugh. It's amusing to me, you know; I sound like that for days.

AH: But there is a lesson there.

S: That it's okay?

AH: What does it mean when you feel you don't exist? What is it that doesn't exist?

S: The personality.

AH: But which part? You need to see specifically what is missing at that time. There is something that is not there at that time, and somehow you believe that that is you. But when that goes away, you continue going around doing your thing. You may realize, "Oh, that's not really me," you see? Because you are still doing what you are doing, although you don't exist. If you think of it logically, saying, "I don't exist," that's one statement. The other statement is, "I am doing what I am doing." Now these statements don't go together. So the only conclusion you could draw from that is that there must be two people. When one doesn't exist, the other one starts existing. See that?

S: Yeah.

AH: One of them you believe is you. Your mind is really convinced that that is you. But when it is not there, you are still living, talking and walking, and all that. Still, you go around saying, "I don't exist, I don't exist; isn't that terrifying? Isn't that terrible? I don't exist!" Who is saying, "I don't exist"? I mean, if you just think about it logically, you will catch yourself in the act and say, "Wait a minute! What am I doing saying that I don't exist? All I can say is that there is a feeling of not existing." Because that is what is happening. There is a feeling, there is a state of nonexistence, but that doesn't mean you don't exist. Does that make sense?

S: Yeah, it does. Not when I am in it though, I guess.

AH: But that indicates that you really believe that what you call the "I" is really you.

S: Say that again.

AH: You believe that it is really you—that part that is not existing.

S: Yeah, I really do. I mean that's what I see every time I say that.

AH: That's what you need to look at: What is it that you believe is you? Really investigate it, look at it very closely, very accurately. "I think this is me, but sometimes it goes away, and still I am functioning. What does that mean? How can that be me, if it goes away and I am still functioning?"

S: That's just really puzzling to my mind. It's like I can't figure it out.

AH: What I am saying, however, is that you could investigate and know more specifically what that part is, what it feels like. Right? You could understand it so that the fear doesn't have to be there. [*Pause*] What is it you are feeling now?

S: A tight band around my solar plexus. And butterflies in my stomach ... but some kind of contraction.

AH: Does that feel like you?

S: Well, yeah. I guess I walk around that way.

AH: Yeah. You feel that's you.

S: Yeah.

AH: This contracted something that's there because you walk around with it—that's you. When that goes away, you freak out: "Oh, I'm gone. I'm dead." But all that goes away is this contraction. But for thirty years you've lived with that contraction—"It feels like me." Well, you're going to miss it when it goes away. [*Laughter*] It might be something like a beetle's back. Have you ever seen a beetle's back?

S: Yeah. Hard shell.

AH: Exactly. You need to look at that very closely, see what it is you are taking to be you. It's a serious matter. I am not kidding. This is your life. If you take this to be you, then see what the implications are. I mean, that's how I investigate things. If I feel that I am disappeared and gone, but I am still talking, you know, to me that's very unusual. [*Laughter*]

S: It's curious.

AH: It is curious. There must be a contradiction someplace here. "What do I mean, that I don't exist but I am talking? It doesn't make sense." So I try to make sense of it. And by trying to make sense out of it, I realize there is something there I am calling me that could go away, and I am still talking, which means—logically speaking, completely logically—that what went away can't be me. And if you remind yourself of that every morning, every time it comes back—"Here it is; that's not me"—maybe in time you will learn that it is really not you. It is something that got attached to you. You could change the relationship to it so that you feel you are walking around with a floppy something hanging behind you, until one of these days you'd be relieved if it just falls off. But as long as you believe it is you, you don't want it to fall off.

So as you see, this needs a deep, honest, intellectual kind of curiosity about the situation. Not how you feel about it—you need to use your mind here. Think about it: "What is this business? Every once in a while, I go around feeling that I don't exist while I do things, but then I get scared that I don't exist. That doesn't make sense at all." Be intellectually curious about it. That is a time when the mind could be useful. If you just get scared, or you get carried away with your emotions, you won't see what is happening; you won't understand it.

And you'd be surprised at what kinds of things you take to be you. All of us take ourselves to be things that are strange. You know if you really investigate what most people are taking themselves to be, if they were to see what that is, they would think they're loonies. I mean, they would think they are people who should be locked up. Some people walk around thinking that they are a thing, for instance; some people walk around thinking that they are a monster; some people walk around thinking that they are God; some people walk around thinking they are a man without a woman—things like that. These are hallucinations, a pure disregard of reality. And we need to find out what all these stories are that we tell ourselves, while we pretend at the same time that we are normal. If you are really normal, you won't have to take yourself to be anything; you won't bother about what it is that is you. Who you are, whatever you are—you won't need to think of it.

Anyway, the way to solve the splitting—any kind of splitting—is by being able to tolerate that sense of disappearing, of disintegrating. If you allow that to happen and accept it, then something else will happen.

After a pause, another student begins to work.

S: In the exercise where I went into my relationship with my father, what came up is the fact that I never really had the kind of relationship that I wanted with my father. There is emptiness and longing for him.
AH: Yes.
S: And I noticed that in the work I did, what came up for me was still really wanting to have him, hoping that there is still something I can say or do to relate to him in a new way or something, to have him. But also in a way knowing that he's probably not going to change at sixty and that I may

never have him. So it seems that to just let go of father, and to be free of him, does bring up the emptiness and the longing. And it just seems like when you're still really wanting father, to go cold turkey on him and then embrace the emptiness and the longing, it just seems difficult. The tendency is to still want father, and yet what I am picking up on is that what this is about is the ability to let go of father.

AH: No, that's not true.

S: No?

AH: I said that because I happened to be working with people where that's what the issue was. The exercise was to find out what your relationship with your father is and how you experience it. It seems that you found out for yourself that your relationship with your father is that you are longing for him, you want him. That is the truth. You stay with what is true for you.

S: Right.

AH: You stay with the truth. See? You don't try to let go.

S: There is just a lot of conflict and frustration about that, because I have tried for thirty-five years to have that with him and it's not happened. So what comes up for me is that maybe it isn't worth still pursuing that. Maybe that's just acting out a childish thing, and maybe I should be letting go of that.

AH: Well, maybe at some point you will let go, but the letting go will not happen by trying to let go. The letting go will happen by staying with the truth, understanding the longing, where the longing takes you. You don't let go of anything, or anybody, by trying to let go. The letting go is a natural process of dropping away when the situation is understood completely. Does that make sense?

S: Yes.

AH: But you never let go. I never experienced myself letting go, never in my life—that never happened. I understood certain things, and through the understanding, transformation happened, things changed, see? But I didn't feel, "I am letting go of this." It is not exactly like that. It's more like through understanding, a certain part starts dissolving or changing. So it seems that what you're feeling is the important thing.

So you are feeling the emptiness and the longing for the father you did not have. Right? So you feel you've wanted it for a long time. [*Stu-*

dent is nodding.] What is it specifically you wanted that you didn't have?

S: I just wanted him to love me, and to have contact with him and to have him love me. And to just be who I am and have him get it.

AH: So he didn't do that?

S: Well, it's kind of a double whammy because he always said he loved me, and he even did things with me that gave the appearance that he loved me. But what I discovered is that all that was sort of a disguise, for the sake of appearance, and that what was actually so was that he didn't.

AH: So it was a show, you mean.

S: Right.

AH: And how do you feel when you think of that? There was a show of love, but no real love.

S: Well, I feel two things. He encouraged me to do things, and he indicated that if I did those things, I would get love. So I performed in all these different ways, and accomplished all these things, and then he didn't love me like he said he would. So I feel really angry about that. And then the fact that I have done all that efforting, and accomplished all those things and done this and that and still haven't gotten the love, that also makes me feel really sad.

AH: So you feel the sadness now?

S: Um-hum.

AH: So you feel the sadness for not being loved by him?

S: Right.

AH: For the absence of that love.

S: Yes.

AH: When you sense that sadness, when you feel it, what happens, where does it take you?

S: It takes me toward longing for him and wanting him even more.

AH: Feel the longing and the wanting. If you feel that, and allow that to happen, where does that take you?

[*Pause*]

S: You see, at that point, what happens is that I want to do something to have him. My tendency is to not want to go deeper into the longing but to do something.

AH: So you don't want to feel the longing anymore. You want to act on it.

S: Right.

AH: So you stop feeling the longing. This is your usual pattern. How about if you just stay with the longing and don't try to do anything about it? Just recognize that that's what you feel—the longing for your daddy and his love. It's quite understandable. If you feel that without trying to change it or do something about it, what happens?

[*Pause*]

S: Right now, I am sensing that I feel fear.

AH: Interesting. Let the fear happen. Let's find out what's bringing up the fear. You feel longing, you stay with the longing, and you start feeling fear. Any idea what the fear is about?

S: I just want to be with it for a minute here. [*Pause*] Yeah, it's like really being abandoned and really being alone. It's like it's very scary; the feeling of abandonment is real scary.

AH: So that's what's scary, the aloneness and the abandonment. Because that is the source of the longing, right? You are longing because you don't have him.

S: Right.

AH: So if you let yourself feel the longing, it will take you to the feeling of not having him, which will feel like an abandonment, right?

S: Right.

AH: And aloneness. What's scary about the feeling of abandonment and aloneness?

S: It just feels real disorienting, and it feels like there is nothing to stand on. It kind of reminds me about what you were sharing before about tolerating the emptiness, because it just feels really empty. I mean, no structure at all.

AH: Right. So, if you feel the abandonment, the structure will be lost. There will be emptiness, no support, nothing to stand on—you'll feel lost. And that's what's scary about it.

S: Right.

AH: So when you are trying to get your father, and acting out the longing, it is a way of not feeling that state of abandonment.

S: Right. It's like I really tend to avoid it.

AH: Well it's understandable. You didn't know how to handle it in the past, right? It's scary. You start feeling yourself, and you start feeling that the floor is disappearing from under your feet. You are getting empty. You probably have ideas about that kind of emptiness. But if you don't have ideas, and if you see that there is this emptiness, try to find out what it is really about without judging whether it is good or bad.

So be curious, investigate it: What is this emptiness? What is it about? What does it really feel like? Can you feel it without your reactions to it so that you can know it objectively? You don't know if it is really scary or not because there is a reaction to the emptiness that is mixed with it.

We don't know it on its own. So I am saying, let's see; maybe we could find out. If you let it be on its own, if you don't have ideas about it, we might see it more accurately for what it is. Maybe you'll find out that it is scary; maybe you'll find out that it is not. We don't know. So we want to see what happens if you just feel that emptiness, that state, without taking a position about it.

[*Pause*]

S: Now I can do that. It just feels calm and still.

AH: Interesting. So the emptiness that felt disorienting becomes calmer, more still, when there is no reaction to it. Okay, now roll your eyes. [*Pause*] How about now—what are you experiencing?

S: A sense of calmness and stillness. I feel also much more awake, and I feel more present. And it seems that there is more clarity.

AH: Where do you feel the presence? Is there any specific place?

S: It's right in my belly—actually in the chest and the belly.

AH: When you feel that sense of presence, what does it feel like?

S: It feels like strength and power. And it has a sense of running adrenaline also—there's an adrenaline kind of feeling with it.

AH: It has an energetic quality to it.

S: Yes.

AH: And how do you feel about your father from this place?

S: Actually, I experience compassion for him. I get a sense of his tremendous suffering.

AH: Right. So now that you are more separate from him, you can see him as he is. So we can see now that that space that you were running away from—you felt it had a disorientation, which is really the disorientation of feeling no boundary or no support—that is a transitional space. That's the emptiness when the emptiness is not completely allowed. It is the state with the structure dissolving, becoming empty, but the emptiness hasn't happened completely. That's how it feels.

S: Right.

AH: Transition is always like that...

S: I usually always stop there, and then what comes up is, "What am I going to do?"

AH: ... in order to support that structure, to keep it going. You go back to your usual pattern. Right? But when you allow it, you realize there is something that arises, takes its place. That is the true warrior strength, the strength that has compassion, has energy. And I think it is significant for all of us to see these processes. Seeing these processes and understanding them, we understand ourselves. We understand how our mind works, how our soul works, what its relationship is to its essence, what the process of transformation is. For instance, a couple of years ago, would you have believed that this would happen?

S: No.

AH: If I talked to you then about this, would this have happened?

S: Probably not.

AH: It took some time, took some work, right? In fact you didn't even know if it would happen or not. In this way, it seems you were able to go through it step by step, right? There were the feelings there, but it didn't have to be that difficult.

S: In my individual bodywork and all the things we do, gradually I get a little more insight and understanding about different parts of this.

AH: Right. And every time you understand something scary, it's not scary anymore, see? Understanding something means you don't have to be scared of it, because fear comes from misunderstanding. And each time you have a new experience like this, you have less fear about going inside, about letting yourself dissolve, go to a deeper state, or feel fear. In time, you get used to it; you realize it's fine. But it takes time, as you see, to learn and understand and experience deeply.

It is important to see that learning and understanding take time—they don't come in one gulp. That's one part of it. The other part is seeing the actual forces of transformation. First, you experience the ego state, the structure itself. The particular sector of the personality, in this case, is the part of you that has a relationship with father, that object relation in which part of you wants father, longs for him; and it includes the anger about all of that. Then you realize after a while that that structure covers up an emptiness, or a hole. And when you get into the emptiness and the hole and accept it, there arises naturally, on its own, a certain essential presence. Now, when you feel that essential presence—here it's strength and energy—does that feel more like you or like the part that you started with?

[*Pause*]

S: The strength and power feels more like me.

AH: That is interesting. What about it makes it feel more like you?

S: It has substance and it's inside of me, and I can feel it, and it has some presence to it.

AH: Is there anything about it, the way it feels, that makes it feel it is more like you?

S: Instead of being something added on, it feels like it wells up from inside.

AH: Okay. It wells up from within.

S: A word that comes to mind is, it kind of "emanates."

AH: Emanates. Okay. So you see it as something emerging from within you.

S: Right.

AH: So it's more of a core thing.

S: Right.

AH: So it's deeper than the other part.

S: Yes, and it doesn't come from any particular place. It kind of has an unknown source, but it comes up from deep inside.

AH: Right. But notice, "deep and inner" is not a relationship to the body. Inner means an inner dimension. It doesn't mean inside your body necessarily, or deep inside your body. I mean, how deep can you go in the body—six inches, right? So it's much deeper than that. So when we say "inner" or "deep" here, we usually think in terms of physical space, three dimensions; "inside" means inside this body. But the feeling of inner, if you pay attention to it, means something different. You go to the inner of your consciousness, and the inner of one's consciousness is not a spatial inner. It's an inner in terms of depth, in terms of shifting to a different dimension. See what I am saying? All of this just shows you how many things you can learn from an experience like that—there is a lot of food in it.

You could start from any one of those places and think of it, pursue it, feel it, and you could learn different kinds of things. Like you learned about personality, how it works; you learned how understanding works. You could learn about what you mean by inner, what you mean by deep, what you mean by you. And the more I ask you questions, the more you see things and the more you understand.

And in this experience, you can also understand what presence is. Right? You can see that presence really means something; it's not an empty word.

After a silence, another student has a question.

S: What is the difference between letting go and surrendering?

AH: There is no such thing as letting go, and there is no such thing as surrendering.

S: I've been getting some bad information. [*Laughter*]

AH: There are certain experiences we call letting go and surrendering. That's when you are feeling relaxed and things are dissolving and tension is melting. We call that surrendering, but that doesn't mean that there is somebody there surrendering. It means that certain tensions, certain holdings, are just falling apart, melting, dissolving like butter. They are disappearing like ice in water.

S: But even that is through understanding, isn't it? It is not a conscious act.

AH: No, it's not a conscious act.

S: You don't say, "I'm going to dissolve now."

AH: No, you don't do that. That's what I am trying to say. You don't say, "I am going to dissolve." You don't say, "I am going to surrender." You don't say, "I am going to let go." You look at the situation, understand it, and recognize when you are resisting it; you see how you are holding on to something. That's all you can do.

So if you see it that way, the method of work becomes easier, more obvious. When you think of surrendering, it's very hard to tell somebody, "Surrender." What does that mean? How do you surrender? Nobody knows how to surrender. Nobody ever knew how to surrender. But you could definitely observe yourself, be curious, understand yourself, and the understanding will make parts of you not take certain positions; you will not stand behind certain positions.

The experience is more that you stop fighting, you stop resisting. And in fact, we don't stop resisting and fighting by deciding, "I'm going to stop resisting and fighting." It's more like you see the resistance, see the fighting, see that it is destructive and doesn't really work. That by itself seems to do something—it's like your instincts themselves change. So when that change happens, people say there is surrender, or that a person surrendered. So you could use the word "surrender" as long as you understand what it means. Surrender and letting go are not actions you take. They are more the absence of internal action.

After a long silence, another student begins to work.

S: I am really ashamed of my father. He wasn't a good father figure at all. He let my mom emasculate him. He was real impotent and wasn't a good source of information about how the world works, how to take care of money, how to value knowledge or intelligence. So, it's like he wasn't a real father.

AH: So, you didn't have a real father, the father you needed. You got a wimp for a father.

S: Yeah, he was very weak.

AH: Sounds like you are disappointed in him.

S: Very disappointed. Yes.

AH: So how does that make you feel?

S: Mostly just a lot of hurt, and wishing that he would have been different, and feeling the loss of that influence in my life.

AH: Right. So you feel that loss sometimes?

S: Yeah, a lot.

AH: How about right now, what do you feel?

[*Pause*]

S: I feel a lot of sensations in my chest. Fear and hurt.

AH: What is the fear about?

S: Working in the group—that's part of it. Feeling ashamed is hard for me to feel, too. Feeling ashamed of him is like an identity I have taken on. It's a feeling of being ashamed of myself and not knowing certain things, or seeing how that lack in my life has influenced my life and feeling ashamed of it.

AH: So it makes you ashamed of yourself.

S: And ashamed of my mother for castrating him all the time and of him for letting her do that. And witnessing it. And me doing that with other men, too, acting like my mother did. Just the whole thing.

AH: You were let down by your dad, so you couldn't respect him.

S: He didn't respect himself at all. My mother didn't respect him. His children really didn't respect him by the time he died.

AH: Sounds like you wanted a daddy that you could respect.

S: Yes. I feel that a lot.

AH: You missed having him?

S: Yeah. And during the exercise, we were talking about being ashamed of our fathers and having castrating bitches for mothers. All of us. It was really interesting.

AH: Yeah? All of you were the same? Do you still feel afraid?

S: Yeah. I do.

AH: What is scary about working?

S: I am always afraid of working in group. I'm afraid I am going to cry—my face gets red—and feeling emotions and people being here.

AH: Is it bad to cry?

S: Yeah. It's uncomfortable. It's just uncomfortable to feel my feelings in front of other people.

AH: There must be something about it that makes you uncomfortable.

S: Well, it's just feeling out of control.

AH: So it's okay to be out of control by yourself but not in front of other people?

S: Well, I don't like to do it by myself either.

AH: Oh, so you just don't like being out of control.

S: No, I don't like to be out of control.

AH: So we understand this slightly differently now. You don't like being out of control; it's uncomfortable.

S: Yes. My dad was out of control; my mom was out of control. That feels bad.

AH: So what does it mean if you are out of control?

S: Oh, you don't have self-discipline, you don't have enough strength or will to control yourself, to not lash out. I don't just think about sitting here crying. Out of control means attacking other people.

AH: So are you afraid that you will do that?

S: No, actually, I'm just afraid that I will cry. But to be out of control means attacking other people.

AH: But that is not what you are afraid of.

S: No, I am afraid of being out of control and crying.

AH: So crying is out of control?

S: It can be that way, yeah.

AH: And it means you don't have any discipline? No will, you said?

S: I am getting confused. No, it doesn't mean that. Just to cry here, and to look at all this, isn't really being out of control.

AH: So how do you feel now?

S: I still feel a little afraid.

AH: So, maybe you are afraid of something else?

S: No.

AH: What happens if you just let the fear be there, let the fear reveal its secrets? What's it about?

S: I feel afraid of being humiliated by working on my father and how I was ashamed of him.

AH: So the fear is because of the shame?

S: It's just very hard for me to stay with this shame.

AH: So you feel humiliated if you reveal the story of your father.

S: Or just being exposed to that feeling.

AH: So what do you think people will think if you talk about your father and your relationship with him?

S: I feel . . . I wonder if they'll see how I'm like him and how I'm identified with him, and you know, see me as weak.

AH: Well, how will they feel about you?

S: Probably disgust, you know. That's how I felt toward my father, so I imagine they will be disgusted with me.

AH: So they'll feel toward you the way you felt toward your father? It sounds like you are projecting yourself on people—being like your father, and projecting yourself on other people.

S: Projecting my reaction toward my father onto other people so I could be independent?

AH: Yes.

S: Um-hum.

AH: So it seems you felt disgusted with him, ashamed of him?

S: Um-hum.

AH: What's happening now?

[*Pause*]

S: I just feel sad and hurt.

AH: So there's sadness and hurt.

S: Yes. It's like I want to keep him secret.

AH: So it's painful to reveal.

S: Very painful.

AH: So it seems that there is part of your life that you are really very ashamed of, that you try to keep secret. Does it go away if you keep it secret?

S: No, I think I act it out more. Or else I just repress it. I see how I have repressed it.

AH: Let's see what happens if you stay with the hurt and the sadness.

[*There is a long pause in the room.*]

S: It feels like a burden in my chest, a caved-in feeling in my solar plexus, like it is a burning hurt.

[*Again, there is a long silence.*]

And I am very aware of my head. My head feels like it's moving, clogged up, and painful, and it goes between feeling foggy and painful.

AH: Now roll your eyes. Whatever feelings happen, let them happen. [*Pause while student does the exercise*] Okay, how about now?

S: Well, it feels a lot clearer in my head.

AH: And what is it you feel?

S: I still feel afraid. Partly I wish I had never started talking. I really want to retreat.

AH: Want to retreat? Okay, if that's what you want, that's fine.

S: I just feel a cowardice, and there is part of me that says, "Deal with it," you know.

AH: Well, if you are afraid, that is fine. Your fear is fine, whatever you are experiencing. Do you want to stop? It's up to you.

S: I don't want to be a coward.

AH: So if you stop, that means you are a coward? [*Pause*] So you feel you shouldn't have any limitations?

S: I already have a lot, yeah. I just feel hot and really afraid.

AH: What are you afraid of?

[*Pause*]

S: Well, I don't know.

AH: You feel hot and afraid?

S: And I feel some contraction in my chest.

AH: Do you feel hot all over?

S: No. My arms and legs, my neck.

AH: So what happens when you feel the heat?

S: Just more heat, more awareness all over of my body.

AH: Does the heat make you feel any particular way? Or is it just temperature, just heat?

S: I just feel alive. I was feeling really foggy before I was talking, like I had a really heavy feeling in my head and my eyes; it was hard to see. But now I can see people across the room again. I feel more alive right now.

AH: So the heat gives you more aliveness?

S: The feeling of fear is more like retracting. This is more expansive.

AH: This is more of the opposite. Your energy is expanding instead of contracting. So, you get hot when you decide not to retract, huh? Is it all right?

S: It makes more room for the pain.

AH: So it seems there's a lot of pain in your relationship with your daddy?

S: Yes.

AH: So one thing you could do is to see all the feelings you have about it, like disappointment, shame, and being hurt. And there is also the longing for the good daddy that you didn't have, right? You can let both of those be present. Do you feel that, too?

S: Yes.

After a long silence, another student raises her hand.

AH: Yes?

S: In the exercise, when I was talking about my relationship to my father, it was like I was telling a story about the things that he did to me, and all of the sudden I was just hit with this shock. It feels like a disbelief, because I was talking about the abusive things that he did. And I have known all along that he was abusive—it was just part of my life—but this was in relation to me when I was three and couldn't talk. So I came across this terrifying fear. I went from disbelief, sadness, and hurt to fear. And I've just been staying with that. I don't know if fear is what my relationship to my father is, or what I'm afraid of.

AH: So that is what you are experiencing now, the fear?

S: Yeah, just a real shakiness. A fear of life.

AH: See what happens if you just stay with the fear and don't do anything about it; just be in it.

[*Pause*]

S: It seems like it is real deep. It feels like I am going to die.

AH: That's interesting. In what sense? Or what is going to make you die?

S: I just feel struck by this awful image of him, a monster. It's like this shock.

AH: So it's like a realization of how it was.

S: Yes.

AH: So what does it make you feel that he was that way? What did that do to you?

[*Pause*]

S: What I was saying in the exercise was that I felt like I was being wired. And now I'm just shaking and I feel sick.

AH: So you are believing it more?

S: Yeah.

AH: It sounds like you didn't want to believe it completely before.

S: Yeah, because I was talking about it intellectually.

AH: Now you are feeling it. I'd like you to move your knees.

AH comments: *This exercise is to relax the pelvis and sacrum, and to loosen the tense muscles in the whole pelvic and genital area. I had be-*

come aware that the student was more directly in contact with her experience than earlier, and at the same time, that her attention was concentrated in the upper part of her body. I made the suggestion to see what would happen when there was more relaxation and energy in the lower body.

S: I'm starting to feel really disorganized.
AH: That's what will happen, it seems. That's what you are afraid of, right?
S: Yes.
AH: Right. Like if you let yourself feel the reality of the situation, you're just going to start feeling disorganized. But let's find out what that's about. Okay? What else besides disorganized?
[*Pause*]
S: I know that when he was violent I felt really, you know, like I didn't know what was going on. It's like I'm just remembering that—just this sense of not knowing what's happening.
AH: So it seems it changes your sense of yourself—right?—if you see the situation, and how hard it is.
S: Yeah, it does. I see him as the monster instead of seeing me as the monster.
AH: When he is the monster, how do you feel then? How do you see yourself?
S: Like this little warrior, trying to protect me.
AH: That's how you feel now? Or is that how you felt?
S: That was the original feeling that came up, and I am still shaking.
AH: Do you still feel disorganization?
S: No. It felt like I was going to lose it.
AH: Is that bad?
S: Yeah.
AH: To be disorganized, you mean?
S: Yeah.
AH: My impression is that if you really see the situation as it is, you might lose him.
S: Lose my father?
AH: Yeah. Like by not believing it, you still have a father you can depend

on and relate to, no? To see him as a monster means that then you can't relate to him. Does that make sense?

S: Um-hum.

AH: Maybe that's the reason you didn't want to completely acknowledge it.

[*Pause*]

S: Yes, it felt more like a complete realization for me.

AH: And maybe a complete realization means the loss of a certain kind of relationship. At least in your mind. Or a loss of some kind of security or safety, or an illusion that gave you some kind of safety, no? What's happening now?

S: I am just really shaky.

AH: Does the shaking have feelings or is it just shaking?

S: It's just shaking.

[*Pause*]

AH: What do you feel in the belly?

S: It's a rock.

AH: A rock. Now move your knees again. Let's get some relaxation there and see what happens.

[*The student does the exercise.*]

Okay.

S: Sadness. I feel like I have never had anything of my own; it's always in reaction to him.

AH: I see. Is it okay to feel that sadness?

S: Uh-huh.

AH: What happens when you stay with the sadness?

S: It's like he is just gone, my father's just gone.

AH: Yeah. Right. What does that feel like?

S: It feels like I am an undiscovered person.

AH: Right. Who you are is still undiscovered. What is that like?

S: It has—it's sort of exciting.

AH: Uh-huh. Exciting possibilities. How do you feel in the belly now?

S: I'm shaking all the way to the floor now.

AH: Um-hum. That's good. So shaking seems good. It opens things up. It might be a little scary, but it opens things up. It happens today that a lot of people are shaking. It's the retreat to be remembered for the shakes. But this is usual when working on Brilliancy.

So it seems that by seeing your relationship with your father in a certain way, you kept a certain relationship to him, which also gave you a sense of who you are. So when that is gone, not only is he gone but that sense of who you are is gone, which allows a new possibility for who you are.

S: It's like I am still talking about who I think I am.

AH: Yeah, right. But if you allow that sense that you are undiscovered yet, what does that feel like?

S: I like it. But it's like it doesn't make for a whole lot of conversation. [*Laughter*]

AH: We could talk about what it might be, what might arise. We could talk about mystery. But I mean in your body—how does it feel?

S: It feels freer. I feel embodied. Before, I was saying, "No, this isn't real," and I sort of fell asleep. I do feel more embodied.

AH: More embodied, more relaxed in your body. Do you feel more present?

S: Yeah, I do. It's really clear.

AH: So we see it is starting to happen ... the possibilities. The first thing that happens is that you start appearing to yourself as more here, more present, more embodied, right? The more you feel you are embodied, the more you know you are being here and the more there is a sense of presence. The sense of presence always makes you feel like you are really here, embodied. If you have experiences—spiritual experiences—that make you feel distant from your body, you know to perhaps be suspicious of them, regardless of how transcendent they are. But if you feel you are more here, more present in your body, you realize the experience is definitely real.

S: It feels real to me. It feels crisp.

AH: You are new? A new person, huh?

S: I am seeing things new.

AH: Yes. The same thing. When you are new, you see things in a newer way. So you see things more crisply, more clearly. Presence. More clarity, more crispness. More organization?

S: It's like that doesn't really matter.

AH: Right. Like maybe the sense of organization is more of a wholesomeness.

S: It feels wholesome.

AH: Instead of an organization of parts. So, that's you? When you are being yourself, that's how you feel: present, full, wholesome, solid, here, present. And then you could study yourself, taste yourself from the inside, right? What does it taste like? Full, solid, subtle, smooth, and so on. "Oh, I like myself. This is a nice person to hold and hug." Doesn't it feel good?

S: It feels cleansing.

AH: So it is amazing what we find, what lies beneath the relationship with daddy. All kinds of treasures—hidden, unrecognized all this time, hidden by all the fears, the problems, the longing, the anger, the deprivation, the idealization.

A student has a question.

S: Is the Brilliancy we have been working on what makes this all seem so smooth, so easy? It's like there is just . . . I don't know, it's like there is such an openness. And it just seems like these things are coming up and being presented and they are being worked on and things are happening. I mean, it's just so smooth, just so easy.

AH: That is true, the quality of the Brilliancy is like that. Smooth, easy, gets into all the cracks with ease. It's pretty smooth—smooth and smoothing.

Another student wishes to work.

AH: Yes?

S: What I said earlier about my mother . . . afterward I felt like I was completely missing the point. And somehow I still feel like I am missing the heart of me. I think that one main factor is missing: not connecting with my father. It's that my father wasn't there, he physically wasn't there. He was missing from when I was a three-month-old baby to almost three; and then two and a half years later, he died.

AH: So you didn't have a daddy, really.

S: Yeah, right, exactly. Like I don't have the real actual experience of contact; and during the times he was there, he had tuberculosis, so we weren't allowed to be close to him physically. And it was two-and-a-half years' time. So my experience of him is as a completely rejecting kid, not being able to handle the situation I saw, or the sadness. Like what I did was completely reject him.

AH: Reject him, I see.

S: So I have always felt that part of me was missing.

AH: It's understandable. So you will feel things about your mother as a result, because she was the one who was there.

S: And I saw her react, too, about her husband dying and all this.

AH: You didn't have much personal relationship with your father, right? But it sounds like you do have a relationship.

S: Yes, not having a relationship becomes the relationship.

AH: Yeah, sure. Not only that, there is a rejection. Rejecting and missing father.

S: It always feels like part of me is missing. The emotional part of it.

AH: Do you feel it sometimes, like there is something missing?

S: Yeah, I feel it like a shell, an empty shell. How I see my father is like an empty shell. That was all he had—no body. I always saw him as distant.

AH: So when you see your father that way, how do you feel?

S: The shell.

AH: Oh, I see. If you see your father like a shell, you become like a shell.

S: Right, I become the relationship.

AH: Well, no wonder you don't want to think about it.

S: Like today ... being here is not really being here.

AH: Right. Dealing with father, you become an empty shell. How about now—what do you feel now?

S: Well, just listening to other people dealing with their own issues about their fathers gives me more of an idea about what a father might be.

AH: Right. Something that you didn't even think about ...

S: No.

AH: ... what a father might be. But the more you see that, the more it makes you feel that there is something missing.

S: Yeah, right. The more I think about it, the more I miss him. At six years old, I just completely wanted to eradicate all the feeling. It was hard for me to even remember his name. It makes me nervous to even talk about him.

AH: So you wanted to forget about that part of your life. It must be a painful part.

S: It's hard for me to even think about "Yes, he was Daddy."

AH: Yeah, that's what I mean. What is difficult about it is that it makes you feel empty, like a shell, as you said. It's not necessarily painful in the sense that it causes direct pain, but it is difficult to feel that something is missing, no?

S: Yes, it is. That part, that emotional part that feels more painful—that emotional part is what's missing.

AH: So that is how you feel now, that the emotional part is missing?

S: Yes.

AH: So, it seems that to forget about your father, you have to forget about the part that feels anything about him, right?

S: Yes, um-hum.

AH: Otherwise, you won't forget about him. The two go together.

S: It's like chasing a shadow.

AH: I understand.

S: Not having an object.

AH: So what does that feel like, that you're chasing a shadow, that there is nobody there to touch?

S: Well, there is a lot of frustration. I usually don't work with it.

AH: What about right now?

S: There is a sense of deficiency, that that is a part missing.

AH: So you become aware of that sense of deficiency, that something is missing.

S: There is a big part of the puzzle that's missing.

AH: Well, just be aware of that, that something is missing. I know it is a difficult thing to be aware of; but as you see, you are already aware of it, that something is missing. A big part of the puzzle is missing, a part of you is missing. [*Pause*] What happens when you just let yourself be aware of that?

S: I see a dark shadow over . . . it doesn't have any depth.

AH: But how does that make you feel? How does that affect you?

S: Deficient.

AH: Deficient. In what sense? In what way?

S: Deficient, empty. But I know it's just emotionally deficient. I can't say to you I'm angry or sad.

AH: So, deficient means there are no emotions.

S: Yes.

AH: Okay. What does that feel like? What do you feel in the chest?

S: The chest is feeling warm and a little trembly; it's feeling warm, and hot, trembly, and there's a lot of movement. That's the part that is missing. I'm missing my father. Little feeling or sensation—it's protected, and nothing inside. Nothing to connect to.

AH: Yeah. But when you feel yourself, you feel some warmth?

S: Right now, yes, I feel warmth and a little bit of trembling.

AH: So when you feel the warmth, and those feelings, how does your perception change about your father?

S: I can put some pieces together. I looked at his picture a year ago, and my brother is quite a bit like him in looks, and the way he—his development. When my father passed away, my brother was five or something like that. And I talked for the first time . . . my brother and I talked about my—I mean our—father and how difficult it was. A sense of compassion for how he must have felt.

AH: How about now? Now, how do you feel about yourself and this situation?

S: I could put his face together, but it's still hard. Like putting puzzles of some figures together.

AH: It doesn't have body or heart, huh?

S: It's hard for me to even pick up the pieces or look further.

AH: What's difficult about it?

S: The difficult part is that as I put it together, he will start . . . perhaps he will become alive again. And I feel the moments that I remember having contact with him.

AH: Are you saying that you do not want to remember those experiences of contact with him?

S: Not actually feeling him. Talking about them is all right.

AH: But not feeling them?

S: No, I don't want to feel them.

AH: So what's difficult about feeling them?

S: The most difficult is that I did want him.

AH: I see. So that's what the difficulty is—to feel the wanting.

S: Um-hum.

AH: How about now, what is it you feel?

S: It's putting back a sense of aliveness in me. It's like allowing myself this wanting.

AH: Being absent does not really eliminate your wanting; it probably makes it even greater, because you didn't have him.

S: Yes. It just meant I didn't know my mind anymore.

AH: Um-hum.

S: Yes. To acknowledge that means you are alive more.

AH: You are acknowledging yourself, letting yourself have your feelings. They are all buried feelings about your father.

[*Pause*]

S: It feels like I've had a shadow of him with me all this time, and now it feels like I'm putting him into a real figure, and acting, saying about . . . [*Student becomes silent.*]

AH: Is it okay to feel that way?

S: Yes.

AH: So is it okay to feel that you want him?

S: Yes. I think that he also would have wanted to know that before he died. He died in agony.

AH: So you are aware of his agony now.

S: Yes. I think that as a child, I saw his pain.

AH: And maybe that was difficult.

S: It was difficult to handle his anger.

AH: So it seems like you have tried to avoid feeling all these feelings about him because it was painful. His pain, and your pain about it, and your needs. A lot of difficult feelings for a little child. So you handled it by making it less real. See?

S: By making myself less real.

AH: By making him—which means you have to make yourself—less real. The more you feel your feelings, the more you're real, as you see.

S: I feel softer and I feel more real, like I have real feelings.

AH: Um-hum. It seems you are regaining your heart.

[*Period of silence*]

S: Thank you.

AH: You're welcome.

Another student indicates she wants to work.

AH: Yes?

S: I have been recognizing how much I identify with my father, and I also transfer my father, like a lot of people. And I have apparently a very strong need to have that identification. It seems as if I am being my strength by being my father and having my father. I feel really jelly-like now.

AH: Uh-huh.

S: I feel powerless without him. This entire day, I have felt so heavy in my chest. And when we did the exercise, I found that I could get in touch with the sadness to some degree. I didn't need to shut that off. And it seems so obvious to me that I am trying to reach him, that I need him. But at the same time, I recognize the difficulty this is creating for me. That I wanted him with me.

AH: How about right now—what do you feel?

S: I feel a lot of heaviness in my chest and my shoulders.

AH: So, when you identify with your father, you become like him. Now if you become like him, that prevents you from feeling certain feelings about him. No? Do you know which one in particular?

S: Pain.

AH: Yes? There is a specific feeling that is more important, if you feel like him.

S: That prevents me from feeling?

AH: If you feel like him, that prevents you from feeling certain things toward him. Right? Well, if you are like him then wherever you go, father is around.

S: My strength?

AH: It's true, but father is more than just strength. What I am trying to say is that if you become like your father, it is giving you strength; but it is also giving you your father. Do you see that?

S: Um-hum. So I don't have the feeling that he's gone.

AH: Or the feeling that you want him. If you are being like father, father is here, father is around. You don't have to feel like you want him—you've already got him. If you are like him, you've got him, right? So I am wondering whether you're being like him so you don't have to feel how much you want him.

S: I am sure I do, because whenever I get into that, that wanting Daddy, it is very, very painful.

AH: How about now: What do you feel in the chest?

S: Sadness.

AH: Um-hum. Now roll your eyes. [*Pause*] How about now—what are you experiencing?

S: Loss.

AH: Loss? Sadness and loss. If you stay with the sadness, what do you feel? Loss of what? What kind of loss?

[*Pause*]

S: No support.

AH: And how do you know it is loss of support? Do you feel that you have no support?

S: I think it's a wanting.

AH: A wanting, okay. So the sadness has a wanting in it. Good, just stay with the feeling. It's important to see exactly what the feeling is. If there is a wanting in it, that is fine. That's what you're feeling, a wanting.

[*There is a period of silence.*]

Are you still feeling the wanting?

S: No.

AH: No? What is it you feel now?

S: Some expansion.

AH: So when you feel the wanting, the chest expanded. That is interesting. So it feels easier, lighter in the chest. So it seems the heaviness was there because you were blocking the wanting.

S: Is it possible to be aware of it intellectually and be blocking it still?

AH: Yes. You might know in your mind that's what is happening, but feeling-wise you are not letting it happen. That is a form of defense. So when you feel more expanded in the chest, what is that like for you?

S: There's this center, and it's radiating warmth.

AH: Pretty good. A center radiating warmth. So when you feel that warmth, how do you feel about your father?

S: I don't feel as if I need him as strongly.

AH: How about in terms of being present or being more present—do you feel present now? Do you feel more you in a calm light way?

[*Student nods head and is quiet.*]

So we want to explore a little more specifically our relationship with father, which we've been doing, and the many ways we relate to father; as we have seen, different people relate to father in different ways. One of the ways, obviously, is feeling that you want things from father, right? Wanting love, approval, support, recognition—seeing father as an object, as a person you want something from. Maybe you didn't get enough of the right thing. Another way of relating to father that happens is wanting to be with him—not just wanting something from him but wanting to be with him, wanting closeness, merging with father, intimacy with father. The intimacy could go to any depth—just wanting to be with him, do things with him, or wanting to be completely merged with him, not separate from him.

Another way of relating to father we have seen is actually being like him, identifying with him. Basically, the identification is a way of having father, and it fulfills many functions. One of them is having what we think we want from father—the strength, the support, whatever. But it also provides a defense against the feelings of wanting him, of feeling that you want to merge with him, want to have intimacy with him. Because you know, if he is here, he's here, and then you don't have to feel you want him. Everybody has some identification with his or her father.

So now we want to do an exercise to specifically work on seeing the identification. When you have completed the exercise, we'll come back here.

In the exercise, the students explore all the ways in which they are like their father. After the exercise, the students reassemble.

AH: Well, what is happening?

A student indicates that he wishes to work.

AH: Yes?
S: I feel like I have made great progress in seeing my identification with Father. I saw I'm spending a lot of time and energy in being exactly not like my father. It's taken me two years to see this. It's just amazing to me that I've spent many years of my life doing this and that it is actually the same thing as being like him, except that on the surface—where I was so sure that I was not like him—I was very different. Then I had a sense

recently of identifying more with him. And lately I've just felt like a clone. It's really very uncomfortable.

AH: It is?

S: Part of the time, I don't believe half of it, and in this last exercise I could just feel it. And I guess one main part that stands out from when people were talking earlier about projecting their brilliance is that my experience was not of projecting my brilliance out, but rather taking in the dullness from my father.

AH: So what does it do to you when you see how much you became like him?

S: I get angry.

AH: Angry, I see. Um-hum.

S: It's a rebellious kind of anger. I can feel myself wanting to rebel, to set it all up so that I'm not like him, so that I can prove that I'm not.

AH: What happens when you just feel the energy of the anger, without having to do anything?

S: I get very hot. It almost feels like I am burning in a fire. And I feel some expansion.

AH: So when you feel the energy of the anger, you feel more of a sense of expansion. When you feel that sense of expansion, how do you feel about your father?

S: Like he's different.

AH: Right. That's the trick. When you feel the anger and don't act on it, there is a real separation. The rebellion is just a sham separation, as you were seeing, not a real separation. But feeling the energy of the anger brings in the energy of the true separateness, which gives you a sense of expansion, warmth, strength. How is it to feel separate, if you are not like him, if you are not him? Is that okay?

S: It's better than okay.

AH: I was just being cautious; I didn't want to presume. So you see, you can feel separate without having to do anything, just by staying with what you feel.

S: Well, I have to admit it's a lot easier, more conducive in a session like this, or a private session, or whatever. I find that pretty difficult during the day—like at work—I lose my focus.

AH: Yes. Usually you rebel to not be like him. But that way doesn't work and you end up being like him. However, if you just stay with the energy itself, you become separate. Then the next question will be: What makes you want to be like him, become like him? There must be a force that makes you be like him. That will be the next question, to question that force. What is the motive behind it? Because, obviously, you could feel separate, as you see now.

S: Yeah, it seems like I am just beginning to yearn for him, to want him.

AH: So that is what comes out?

S: I'm surprised.

AH: So that is what is underneath it: a yearning for a closeness. Now there is a yearning for a closeness, but you didn't want to feel it. Why not? What is it about the yearning that made you not want to feel it?

S: My experience with my father was that he didn't respond to my need for closeness.

AH: I see ... so the yearning won't work.

S: That was my experience.

AH: You know, you might allow the yearning because the yearning might be for the real father—for the father that you wanted, not necessarily for the father that you got. So you don't let yourself feel the yearning because, if you feel it, you believe you will get what you usually got, which made you feel, "Why yearn?" But maybe if you feel the yearning—your heart wants something—your yearning might take you to what your heart really wants, not necessarily to what your father gave you.

S: I think I have really been into denying the whole experience of my father. Like I realized today, when I talk about him, I either have to joke about the way he was or I really get into the experience of what it was like to be around him. And it is really painful. And I think it was painful in the last exercise to see how much I am like him.

AH: So what is it like now, when you see how much you are like him?

S: I feel a lot of heat and a lot of anger. By just feeling the feelings I have felt today it kind of got me in touch with a different place.

AH: So you are realizing you had more of a relationship with your father than you thought.

S: Yeah, I think I just wrote him off as being an asshole, and I didn't see why anyone could like him. He was filled with a lot of hate and resentment.

AH: Seems like we are in a situation of having realizations about our fathers that we didn't expect.

After a pause, another student wishes to work.

AH: Yes?

S: I have a similar experience to the person who was just working. I always just thought my father was terrible. And I am really amazed today at seeing that in order to defend against how much I missed him and wanted him, I became like him. I never ever knew that. I just feel a rage of anger and hatred—so hot, and all this stuff . . . like how could I have bought into it? You know, all this time I thought I had retired it. It's quite a revelation to see how charged this is.

AH: Well, that tells you he was very important for you.

S: More than I admitted.

AH: Right. That is what you are starting to see. Still feel all these feelings?

S: Oh yes, very much. They have been building up all day. Oh, a horrible flush, a heat wave, turmoil.

AH: When you think of him, what do you feel?

S: Well it's a combination; that's part of the dilemma. There is a lot of love and hatred at the same time, yes.

AH: At the same time, yeah.

S: And to have those two feelings together . . .

AH: It sounds like you are having them.

S: Yeah, and it feels very disorienting. I don't understand how they can exist side by side.

AH: Well, usually you split them. That is how they didn't exist side by side.

S: They are both here now, though.

AH: Right, and if you have both, that means you are not splitting. But let that happen, let the disorientation happen. Just let yourself feel the hatred and the love together and see what happens.

S: It feels almost like an emotional overload, a supercharge. It feels almost bigger than my existence.

AH: Now roll your eyes. [*Pause*] Okay. How about now—what are you experiencing?

S: Sort of a light-headedness. Not so much the heat and electricity, but more just lightness.

AH: Feel that lightness.

S: There is a bit of anxiety about it. It still feels like if I get too light-headed, I'll pass out.

AH: And it is not okay to pass out?

S: No. But on the other hand, the lightness definitely reduces the sense of anxiety.

AH: Maybe the anxiety is because of the lightness. Feel the lightness. The more you accept the lightness, the more that means there is no need for the fear. Right? Let the light-headedness happen—don't fight it. [*Pause*] So what happens when you let it happen?

S: There is a sense that the emotion—the heat charge that I have been running around with all day—maybe it could fall away.

AH: It that bad?

S: No, that is very good! It is just kind of surprising to me. I didn't expect that to go away.

AH: But maybe there is a reason for keeping those two things apart.

S: What, the lightness and the heat?

AH: The two kinds of feelings you have.

S: I don't understand that relationship.

AH: What I am saying about the two opposing feelings of love and hate is that maybe the reason for keeping them apart is so that you don't feel the lightness.

S: Well, yes, because the openness doesn't have to feel the obsessive way that it usually does.

AH: Right.

S: So what will I do with my spare time?

AH: Just be open and have fun. There might be other things, but obviously there is something about that openness that you are saying no to, right? Otherwise, there wouldn't be the question, "What am I going to do?" There is an issue there because, as I said before, splitting is a defense. The more the split comes together, the more there is a possibility of some kind of lightness and emptiness. And you'll see that the lightness is very nice. So light-headed that one doesn't even know it's there. Wouldn't it be nice to be light like that?

S: Oh, it would be wonderful. I'll take it.

AH: It's a deal. So we will start here tomorrow.

9

Meeting Four

☙

Yesterday we saw how, in exploring or studying intelligence and our relationship to it, we invariably start to deal with our relationship with father. There seems to be a mysterious connection between intelligence—and more specifically, Brilliancy—and father. So I want to talk about this area so that we can have some idea about what this aspect of Essence is, what a father is, and some of the reasons why they become connected in our experience.

Two of the many manifestations of Being—two major essential aspects—are associated with the parents. If we look at our formative experience in childhood, we can see why. In the first few months and years of life the infant's primary relationship is a dyadic one, mostly with the mother. This insight is now generally accepted in depth psychology, especially after Margaret Mahler's research, which culminated in her theory of separation and individuation. As a natural continuation of the bond formed during pregnancy, the early relationship of the child is primarily with the mother. The mother's intimate physical relationship with the child is expressed through the whole nurturing process and represents the central element of maternal care.

The maternal functions are directly related to the essential aspect of the Merging Essence, which therefore becomes the primary aspect associated with the mother. Merging Essence is a kind of love that has a relaxing, merging, and melting quality. It is a heart manifestation in the sense that it feels like love, contentment, nourishment, softness, and warmth. Thus, the longing for mother often reflects a disconnection from the Merging Essence.

But that maternal relationship doesn't mean that the father is not needed or that he does not have a place or function. He is needed as a presence of strength and support that makes the relationship between the child and mother comfortable and optimal, or at least possible. Ideally, the father acts as a protective and supportive umbrella over and around the mother and child. He is experienced as a presence that contains both mother and child. His presence gives that primary mother-child relationship a sense of security, a sense of protection that allows the two to be involved in their early interaction without having to worry about the rest of the world. The father takes care of the worldly part. These have been the traditional roles of mother and father; and although the situation has been changing due to variations in the nuclear family situation, parts of these maternal and paternal roles remain fundamental due to the biological components dominant in the infant's early life.

Our discussion this morning will reflect the situation most of you probably encountered in childhood, at least in the very early period of life, where the mother is the primary caretaker of the infant and the father is in the environment but is not the primary parent directly relating to the infant. The mother has her energies tied up with the direct care and nurturance of the baby.

In this situation, the father becomes the child's link or connection to the world outside. The child is with its mother, but the child observes the father coming and going, maybe working, but as part of and connected with the outside world. The father also becomes the support for the nourishing relationship with the mother, the protector of the family, and the provider for the house and home. When this happens, the father becomes connected in the child's mind with the sense of there being a strong presence that is a background support, a source of knowledge and skill, and a presence that allows security and safety.

Brilliancy is the aspect that has those same qualities of a strong presence that gives support, protection, security, and safety, and thus is the one most strongly associated with father. The Merging Essence is golden, sweet, nourishing, and loving, while Brilliancy has a sense of a strength and power, and of presence that is not only impeccable but immaculate and immovable. It has a sense of will to it, and a sense of purity too. But this purity is different and beyond the intimate sense of the loving relationship characteristic of the Merging Essence. The purity of Brilliancy is connected with the purity of whiteness rather than the warm gold of the Merging Essence.

Brilliancy is a brilliance beyond whiteness, like light reflecting off a mirror in the sun; it is so brilliant that you can't look at it. So Brilliancy doesn't really have a color; it is the brilliance of all colors combined. That brilliance gives it a sense of purity and also of innocence, for it is an actual presence. And that presence has a sense of power and strength that the individual usually responds to by feeling protected, feeling taken care of—not taken care of because one is fed, cleaned, dressed, or held, but because one feels safe and protected, enveloped by a presence that makes one feel secure and safe to be in the world.

If you then experience the aspect of Brilliancy more fully, you realize that it not only has a sense of security and protection, but it also provides some sense of guidance, which arises from the intelligence that is fundamental to Brilliancy. This intelligence acts as guidance because it is intelligence about functioning, about the world, about how to act and how to deal with life. This intelligence and guidance has historically been the father's function.

Traditionally—and here we are not critiquing traditional roles—the mother's function is to nurse, bathe, and clothe the child, while providing love, nourishment, and warmth, all the things most needed by the infant. But as the child gets a little older, the father begins to come into the picture to guide and support the child in learning how to deal with things and how to be in the world.

In showing the child how to do things on its own, the father becomes a support for the child's separation and autonomy from the mother, because from the beginning, the child sees father as outside the symbiotic and merging orbit of infant and mother. The child tends to identify with the father in order to be more grown up—to learn how to take care of things, to learn independence, and to be more responsible. Responsibility is also part of the aspect of Brilliancy. The father is responsible for the family in a more enveloping sense; the mother is responsible for the family in a more inward sense.

I don't know how much biological endowment accounts for these differences and how much is culturally determined, but these are the usual roles taken on by father and mother, as becomes apparent when one studies the situation. In the Diamond Approach, we don't know whether essential aspects create such associations or if they are culturally formed; when something has been in place for thousands of years, it is hard to tell. But we do know that the aspect of intelligence, of Brilliancy, definitely gives one the sense of being protected and supported, the sense that it is safe to be out in the world doing what one wants to do, and a sense that one is being guided.

Furthermore, we observe that the different qualities of Brilliancy are needed by the child at different stages of its development. The infant needs the sense of protection, security, and safety in the form of a strong, responsible, and capable presence that envelops both mother and child. Later on the child needs the father as support for separation and individuation from the mother in order to develop and become herself. Still later she needs him to guide her in navigating the external world. In time, this evolving support from father matures into her own personal sense of responsibility.

We are not giving an opinion here or presenting a view or theory. What we are discussing now are observations, the raw data of our explorations. This is an area that is open for everybody to explore and confirm personally, as some of you have already found out in the exercises. We find that the father role is associated with certain specific functions. We also find that the presence of Brilliancy has qualities that closely resemble those functions. Lastly, we also discover that the mind associates the father with the aspect of Brilliancy. This is a discovery we have made from observation, one that so far seems to be universally true.

Most people's development results in them choosing to identify with one parent over the other—they either want mother or they want father. Generally speaking, mother means more nourishment, more coziness, more warmth, more sweetness, and more melting. Father means more independence, more responsibility, more grown up–ness, and more practical capacity. However, both are needed for human beings. Maybe these needs arise at different times, and in various combinations, but both are needed for a child to really mature and become a responsible human being.

The soul desires the presence of Brilliancy because the soul needs it in order to feel safe to come out and meet the world, to learn to have a life of her own. The soul has an innate need to see the aspect of Brilliancy, which is a part of herself, because as you know, the soul learns first by seeing things outside herself. As children, we don't know that we have Essence, with all its aspects and qualities. A young child cannot express and embody the functions of the essential aspects. She needs them to be expressed, to be shown, by the human beings who take care of her. She first sees them in her parents, who, as they embody and express these qualities and functions, become mirrors for her own innate qualities. Then, by identification with her parents, she can manifest those qualities and become more that way. Thus, there is an intrinsic need for modeling of what the child can be by both father and mother. In other words, the child's need for the presence and functioning of the father is actually the need for a part of her essential self—the aspect of Brilliancy and its qualities and capacities.

However, as a child, you don't see this as the need for yourself; you experience it as the need for your father. People often talk about their father not being there for them in childhood, or say that the father who was there wasn't the father they wanted. The more deeply you explore what kind of father you wanted, the more you start to describe the qualities of Brilliancy. And the more you know what qualities you needed in your father, the more you recognize the qualities of Brilliancy. That is the reason many of you started talking about your relationship with your father as we began to explore this essential aspect.

It seems mysterious and miraculous, but these are the facts as we have found them in twenty-five years of work with thousands of students. I take it to mean that our universe has an implicit order that we can perceive if we are interested in exploring the truth of our experience.

I think that our experience of the properties and qualities of Brilliancy is one reason this aspect becomes connected with God the father for many individuals. God in the Judeo-Christian sense is more of the father, the masculine kind of God. God the father has the sense of overseeing and enveloping, of being an overarching and full presence, a presence that is both powerful and intelligent. These qualities also characterize Brilliancy, as we have seen. So as with Brilliancy, your relationship to God becomes, at least in part, a reflection of the relationship to your father. As a result, you can't really see what your relationship to God is; you can only see your relationship to your father reflected in it. So clarifying your relationship to

God—and more specifically, your relationship to Brilliancy—becomes a matter of dealing with the relationship with your father. Thus, in order to be able to finally know the truth of your relationship to God in an objective sense—which means specifically to truly embody the aspect of Brilliancy—you have to deal with your father issues. Otherwise the relationship of your soul to that protective source, which is the Brilliancy of Being, will not be harmonious; or the relationship will not exist; or there may exist all kinds of splittings and reactivities and defenses that will prevent you from openly being in touch with that presence.

The interesting thing about Brilliancy is that it is one of those aspects that forms a whole dimension, a whole universe of Essence, because it can exist in many forms, depending on the kind of father you need in the moment. The sense then is more that of a source of Beingness with many forms than of one particular quality. It can be an immense, powerful presence if what is needed is support, protection, or strength. Or it can manifest as a very delicate, smooth, gentle, and exquisite presence when guidance and intelligence are needed. Or it can manifest as a very soft and responsive immediacy when what is needed is a father who is flexible and soft, who has gentleness, attentiveness, and love. So Brilliancy can change its form depending on the need of the soul at any given moment.

Each one of these qualities is usually projected on father; but when they have become integrated in us, we are affected in a different way as each manifests. The various forms of Brilliancy will give us capacities that are embodied in our own souls, instead of having them by identification with father. If Brilliancy manifests in us as immensity and power, density and strength, it will imbue all our capacities, all our functioning, with a sense of endurance, strength, and power—all of which can feel like a will that has intelligence. If what is needed is some kind of very delicate and refined functioning and operation, then the Brilliancy becomes more subtle and exquisite, filling our capacities with a refined discrimination and penetrating intelligence.

So Brilliancy can change in its form and therefore its influences on all of our capacities, depending on our need in the moment. In the same way a father needs to be a different kind of father at different times, depending on the needs of the child at the moment, or at different stages of development. Your father needs to fulfill different functions at different times and stages.

And when those different functions become internalized, you will become the father of yourself. Then your capacities will take on various forms and manifestations according to the needs of the moment.

This understanding of the relationship between Brilliancy and father, and how one integrates and embodies the various qualities and capacities as one reowns one's own Brilliancy, gives a more adequate understanding of the internalization of parental functions than is available through depth psychology. The view in depth psychology, as in psychoanalytic theory, is that the child develops most of his capacities and functions by internalizing them from the parents, the father in our present case. That view does not recognize the human child's innate qualities, but gives him only the capacity to learn those qualities from the parents. It is as if the child begins his life possessing no qualities of strength, support, guidance, and responsibility, but develops them only by acquiring them from the father.

In the understanding we are working with, we see that the child has all of the qualities and capacities in potential as part of his own Brilliancy. He cannot, however, utilize or express them because of the immaturity of his physical and psychic apparatuses. So he needs to have them reflected in his environment until he is able to fully embody them. This embodiment occurs partially through the process of internalization and identification. However, this is not a matter of getting from outside something he did not have to start with, but rather a process of learning to use what he already has by seeing it reflected outside himself in his parents. In other words, he discovers and develops what he already has by seeing his parents utilizing and expressing the same qualities and capacities he innately possesses.

This shows not only how, but also why, the integration of what the father represents is important. Because of the connection between the aspect of Brilliancy and the father, we found that everybody tends to project this aspect on father—the father that is there, or the father you never had. There is always an image of father. Usually it is the "good father" that we project those qualities on, but not exclusively. Sometimes we project some of the qualities—like those of power, density, and immensity—on a father that seems aggressive and angry, and we end up associating power and immensity with some kind of negativity. Then we tend to resist Brilliancy because of such associations.

So far in this exploration of the relationship with father we have seen how we identify with him, how much we become like him. But you need to remember that identification is partially a way to defend against the desire and longing for father; it is a way to feel we have father. If we feel that we have father, we don't need to feel that we want him and thereby avoid acknowledging our longing for him. But having father means having all the qualities of Brilliancy: a sense of being safe, a sense of intelligence and guidance, a sense of capacity, responsibility, and brilliance. We believe we are getting all of these by becoming like father, which is why we often become like father without even knowing it. There is a deep, inner need for those qualities; and because in one way or another we associate them with father, we believe that the only way to have them is to become like our father. But to be able to truly embody these qualities, you need to see what you really want when you identify with your father in that way. Then, by seeing what you really want with this identification, it is possible for you to regain, or reown, that part of yourself.

Now we will continue with our exploration of the relationship of father with Brilliancy. Yesterday, we explored the overall personal relationship with your father; we also studied your identification with your father. Now we go to the next step and do an exercise.

In this exercise, the students explore why they resist experiencing their desire for father. After the exercise, the students reassemble.

AH: Very good. So, what have you found out?
S: I realized that I had really seen everything from my father's eyes, and it was like having that position leave when I was doing the exercise. I mean it's like everything looks so different at this moment.

I was noticing this morning before we started that it seemed like a lot of stuff came up between last night and today, and a lot of it was anxiety. What I seemed to find out about the anxiety in the exercise was that I was anxious because there wasn't that overall protective sense, so I felt exposed. This started last night when I saw my identifications with my father. The identifications that made me see things through his eyes seem to have fallen away by merely seeing them. After that, here I felt my own sense of being safe, protected, powerful, empowered. I felt them without having to be like my father. And it felt really nice because I had seen the split in my father and seen him together, like the two pieces together. And it felt like I was able to look at him and appreciate what he had done, and my identification with him was just gone. And it wasn't me pushing him away, or being angry.

AH: We find this frequently. When you become realistic about the relationship, when you see it as it is—both the good and the bad—that object relation generally just falls away. It is usually the splitting and the defenses that keep it there. So you said you were seeing things through his eyes?

S: It was that sense.

AH: How does it feel now?

S: It feels wonderful.

AH: Yes, so you got your eyes back.

S: Yeah. That is exactly what it feels like. And it is so nice in my head because everything connects. It's like before I had to work for connections, and now it's like everything is connected to everything else and it feels really happy, really right.

AH: That is what usually happens when you own your eyes. The Brilliancy is then able to go through your eyes and empower that capacity. You can then see the connections that are already present. The Brilliancy is like the sap that goes through everything.

S: That is the connection.

AH: That is the connection, the inner core of all that is. So if you could see from Brilliancy itself, you could see it everywhere. You could find out that it can function as the consciousness that really connects everything.

S: So then I was wondering what the connection is between Brilliancy and the Point. I am sure you have talked about this, but I do not have it right now.

AH: Brilliancy is the father of the Point. The Point is you; it is your essential self and identity.

The Point is different from Brilliancy. The Point, when you experience it, has a living quality to it—it's living, alive, and responsive—while Brilliancy is just a presence, a brilliant presence. We've talked about many ways that Brilliancy manifests. Now, you can attain a quality of Brilliancy where it becomes like the Point. That is more like what people call God, where you see the whole universe as a living, breathing, pulsing presence—just like the Point, but infinite. That's what we call the Father of the Point, which is a sense of a very immense presence. You experience it by perceiving that at the core of everything there is a living, brilliant intelligence. It is manifesting in everything all of the time, directing everything. It is not directing it in the sense of "do this, do that," but directing it by making it happen. It is the intelligence that, by its manifestation, brings out life, brings out appearance, brings out all kinds of things.

I think it is this intelligence, this Brilliancy—this core of all life, all existence—that is responsible for what we call evolution and development. I believe in evolution, that the species happened, that man evolved, and so forth. But the way I see it is that there is intelligence at the core of the underlying movement. Intelligence is manifesting itself so that in time it will show itself completely, consciously. So it is not like there is a set plan, a plan that God had: You are going to go do this, then that; first there will be crocodiles, then apes, then man. It's not like that. It is more like there is an ocean of intelligence that is moving and coming out. It goes in one direction that either works or doesn't work, and if one direction doesn't work it weaves around in some other direction that does work. There is an intelligence that guides the movement, so in time the intelligence comes out in more intelligent life, a more intelligent existence. And people could call that God's will. That is why Brilliancy is frequently related to God's will.

This dimension of Brilliancy is the connection to the Point, which some people might start experiencing. The Point is a brilliant presence that is who you are, your true self. We can say it is part of the living ocean of Brilliancy, one of its atoms. Brilliancy is not a point, not a concentration of presence. The more you experience it, the more it is in the room, the more it expands and fills the room. It has no specific shape or form. Also, the more it expands, the more you feel the sense of cleanness. Everything is clean, which is what I meant by elegant; everything is very sharply, smoothly, and elegantly delineated. There is no dullness on the edges. Everything is bright, clean, and pure. Everything is washed with some kind of pure oil. That is the sense of clarity and brightness you are experiencing as you regain your own eyes through integrating Brilliancy.

After a pause, another student begins working.

S: Since yesterday I've had a change in vision. It seems really physical.

AH: What do you mean?

S: I think that in the last five or six years my vision has deteriorated. I mean I don't need glasses, but more distant signs are sort of fuzzy. Occasionally, especially after an individual session, my vision will clear up and get very sharp. But I have never had it last for more than a couple of hours. This morning I was surprised to see the colors very sharp and clear.

AH: Very sharp and clear. That is what happens as Brilliancy pervades the eyes. It is the effect you see if you look at your eyes. You could see the eye itself is shining. The more Brilliancy there is in your eyes, the more there is a luminousness emanating from them. When you are cut off from that aspect, your eyes don't have that cleanness, that sharpness, that brightness to them. And the disconnection may affect physical seeing, as a direct result. In addition, the psychological issues of not seeing oneself and of not being seen by one's father also could create a blockage in the eyes.

The true essential quality of Brilliancy is a living quality to the consciousness that is aware and present. It has a sense of a luminous kind of intelligence that will affect our capacities in terms of seeing, perceiving, and also understanding and apprehending. The effect on the aesthetic sense—the elegance and the purity—is just beautiful. It makes us, our sense of presence, our life, and the environment, have a quality that is spiritual. It is actually more real than just calling it divine or spiritual. It attains an immaculate quality. Everything becomes more itself in a very pure, radiant way.

Another student begins working.

S: I realized something yesterday, last night, and this morning, something I hadn't seen before.

AH: Yes.

S: For a long time I have focused on all the negative things about my father, and there are a lot of them. This morning especially, doing the exercise,

I realized that there were some positive things I got from him. This just makes it hard to let go of him. It is almost like an enticement, those things that I got. He was this real negative show, most of the time, but sometimes he would take me into a private place and would open up.

AH: Secretly, you mean?

S: Yeah. Very secretly. One on one.

AH: He would become more open emotionally, you mean?

S: No . . . well . . . It is hard to tell. He would become more affectionate, more compassionate.

AH: So who was it secret from?

S: My mother.

AH: I see.

S: She had so many deficiencies, and he would try to fill her. He went through a period of about five years where he was really embarrassed that she wouldn't cook us breakfast, so he would get up and cook us all breakfast. And that was an attempt to fill in. But then he would single me out and give me things that he didn't give my siblings.

AH: How did that make you feel?

S: Special. Guilty.

AH: So it made you feel guilty, and at the same time it made you feel special. That is very confusing, right? You probably liked the attention, but you felt guilty that he didn't give it to other people, that it was secret. So you had a secret relationship with your father.

S: And I can feel how I don't want to let go of him because of that.

AH: Well, it seems to be the only goody you got from him. Why would you want to let go of that? Imagine a little kid getting some goodies from daddy, in a very secret way. You will cherish that very deeply. How do you feel now as you are seeing this?

S: I feel real shaken and sad.

AH: Do you know what you are sad about?

S: Just realizing that I have to let him go.

AH: Who said you have to?

S: Well, it just doesn't work to hold on to him.

AH: Maybe. But remember last night what I said about letting go? You don't try to let go, the letting go happens on its own if you understand the situation. But here you feel as if there is a pressure on you to let go. Maybe that's what your mother would like; maybe it is the guilt you mentioned. You feel guilty about having it. No? So now you feel, "Better let go of him. What is my mother going to feel? What are my siblings going to feel?" You see? You are taking that to mean that you should let go.

S: It's a lot of guilt.

AH: Are you aware of the guilt, right now?

S: Very much.

AH: What does it feel like when you are aware of the guilt?

S: It's like a bombardment of judgments from my superego: "I should treat you this way and not that way," and so on.

AH: What's the judgment?

S: Well, that somehow it's just really not fair. I can also feel how I've modeled myself after him in so many ways.

AH: Well, if you got some secret goodies from him, of course that would make you want to identify with him. That's one thing we can say about identification. Frequently we identify with a parent not just because we can't have him, or because we want him, but sometimes because we love him. Identification partly comes out of love. When you love someone you frequently want to be more like him. Are you aware of that?

S: Um-hmm. Yeah. It's like love-hate. Two extremes.

AH: Mm-hmm. I see.

S: Two extremes.

AH: So you are aware of both, two extremes.

S: There is so much pain, too. I got goodies, but it's almost like I got those if I could endure the pain. You see, he never protected me. He let my brother abuse me constantly, physically.

AH: So he was two fathers really.

S: Yeah. He was.

AH: In the open he was a certain kind of father; in secret he was a different kind of father.

S: Yeah. It just really seems confusing.

AH: Yes. Still feel the shaking?

S: Yeah.

AH: Let the shaking and the confusion happen. Don't fight it. See if you can just let it be, and we will see where that will take us.

S: [*Laughing*] I have this image of an old barn, and if it blows too hard it will just crumble.

AH: Um-hum. So maybe that's partly what you are afraid of—you might crumble.

S: Crumble.

AH: So let's see what "crumble" means.

[*Pause*]

S: During the meditation there was confusion too. All these things were crawling in and out, tangled and twisted.

AH: Yeah, well it was a confusing situation. In some situations he was a certain way; in others he was another way. That would have confused the hell out of any kid—besides the guilt and all that stuff, and mother and so on.

S: I think I might have even fulfilled for him the things that my mother didn't.

AH: Ah-huh.

S: When I was a teenager and my mother would go out, he used to take me out with him.

AH: So you sort of took her place with him sometimes.

S: Yeah, yeah.

AH: So that must have made you feel guilty, too. No?

S: Um-hum. My mother's really frigid.

AH: Yes. And how do you feel that related to the guilt and specialness?

S: When he did that it was just so awful, but it also felt good too. Because he'd take me out when I wasn't getting dates.

AH: Mm-hum. How are you feeling now?

S: Real shaky, especially in my thighs.

AH: Yeah. Now move your knees. [*Pause*] How about now? How do you feel?

S: Feels like it's tense in my lower body.

AH: What do you feel in the belly or the pelvis? I'm wondering why you're holding there.

S: There is a sense of heaviness.

AH: Ah-huh.

S: Heavy fear.

AH: You're aware of the fear now?

S: Yeah.

AH: Feel the fear. Let's see what it's about. Roll your eyes now. [*Pause*] What are you feeling now?

S: Nauseous. I'm getting a sense of a lot of ambiguity. He was giving me some nurturing when I was real little that I needed.

AH: Um-hum. So that's part of the secret relationship. You have some kind of nurturing relation. Anything else in that secret relationship?

S: I don't know. I cannot tell.

AH: Yes. [*Pause*] Now what do you think of your father? What do you feel?

S: I have mixed feelings, too.

AH: OK. We want to see what they are. Do you still feel the shaking in the legs, or has it stopped?

S: It feels quieter. I feel my pelvis getting fuller.

AH: Um-hum. See what happens when you get full in that area.

S: My pelvis and legs get tight. I think there is fear in the area.

AH: Do you know what the fear is about?

S: I can feel longing.

AH: Ah-huh, so you feel the longing in that area?

S: Yeah.

AH: So there's a longing for your father in that area. Okay, let that longing happen, let's see what it's about. [*Pause*] Is it OK to feel the longing there?

S: There is some kind of judgment. Superego says it is bad.

AH: Um-hum. Right, superego. Who's your superego in this case?

S: Oh, the Catholic Church. [*Laughing*]

AH: The Catholic Church, that's a big superego. So what is it that the Catholic Church is saying it is bad to feel?

S: Sexual feelings.

AH: Um-humm.

S: For father.

AH: Yes, it's understandable that you have those feelings in that kind of situation. It seems like it is something he encouraged.

S: Yeah.

AH: By having this secret kind of connection he made you more like his wife, instead of his real wife. So the longing is a sexual longing, a sexual feeling. So when you allow it to happen, how do you feel then in the genitals and the pelvis?

S: Calm.

AH: Do you feel comfortable then with these sexual feelings?

S: It is fine, they actually feel good.

AH: Does anything come up regarding them, other feelings or memories?

S: I just feel full and calm in the area.

AH: Calm. So it seems the guilt has to do mostly with the sexual feelings and longing. There is guilt, not just because he gave you something good that he didn't give other people, but also for the sexual part of it. It had sexual connotations, which I'm sure your mommy wouldn't like, the Catholic Church wouldn't like. Probably that made you a competitor with your mommy, huh?

S: She called him "Daddy."

AH: She did?

S: She didn't have a father.

AH: Yeah. Was she aware of that secret relationship you had with your daddy?

S: I think she was, on some level. There was a lot of jealousy.

AH: I see. So the shaking now is quiet?

S: Yeah. But it feels full in there, too; it feels pleasurable. I feel present, especially in my pelvis. The presence is like an energetic fullness that feels alive, vital, and wonderfully pleasant.

AH: Yes. So then there's more of a sense of fullness, and all the feelings that come with it. Not being able to feel sexual feelings without conflicts creates some kind of emptiness in the pelvis because you cannot be present there. To be present in any region of the body means you are in touch with any feelings that are there. So if there is anxiety or guilt, for instance, then that is what you will first encounter; and not being present becomes the consequence of not wanting to feel those feelings. In other words, the region needs to be empty of issues for the presence of Essence to pervade it.

Everybody is bringing up issues before I talk about them, which indicates for me the truth and organic order in the knowledge we are working with. Dealing with guilt and sexual longing is the next aspect of the relationship to father that I was planning to talk about. So let's look at the oedipal situation. We've talked so far about the separation and individuation part of the relationship with father. When the child reaches the ages of four to seven or so, sexual connotations start arising. Development in this area is generally different for boys and girls.

The girl usually will turn to her father as a sexual object—as a man instead of just a dad. So the relationship with father will have sexual connotations, and of course there's sexual longing and fantasies involved. I do not believe that the oedipal stage necessarily means the girl wants to have intercourse with her father and wants to kill her mother—not even in fantasy as Freud believed. My findings indicate that by this stage of the girl's development her sense of self starts including loving and passionate feelings that have some sensual and sexual overtones. The sexual feelings are usually not specific desires for sex. Rather, they are related to loving and passionate feelings that are present in the sense of self, which at the time is starting to include gender in its identity. As the child begins to experience herself specifically as a girl, she will experience passionate and gender-determined feelings arising in her affectionate relationship with her father. She starts to admire him as a man, liking his masculine presence. How much these feelings become specific sexual desires for father, or manifest as sexual fantasies, will depend not only on the girl, but also on the attitudes and responses of both parents to her developing gender identity and its related feelings.

The more that both parents regard this development to be normal and positive, and respond to it appropriately by treating her as a developing female, the more these feelings will be conscious and will become integrated as a positive investment in the child's developing gender identity. Inappropriate responses will affect such development and distort it. If the parents, due to their own discomfort with their love, passion, and gender, respond to their child's development as if it were sexual in the adult sense, the child will most likely view it as such. This inappropriate response can be either suppressive or seductive. The first will tend to push the girl's development toward oedipal feelings in the classical sense, resulting in the neurosis that Freud described. The second can also do that, but frequently involves situations of sexual abuse as well. Sexual abuse, as we know, can lead to more severe conditions. If either suppression or seduction is present, childhood sexual feelings—the normal gender-determined feelings of love, passion, and attraction—prematurely take on the lusty quality characteristic of adult sexuality.

Because the great majority of parents are uncomfortable with the child's developing sexuality, most girls develop with an Oedipus complex, where the normal gender-determined feelings of childhood become sexualized and exaggerated. When we view the situation this way, we see that Freud's findings about the relationship of the Oedipus complex to neurosis contain a great deal of truth, without us having to accept his theory that the Oedipus complex is a necessary and normal stage that occurs in everyone's development.

So, for the girl, the relationship with the father becomes connected with attraction, pleasure, sex—and not just with love. This development is also reflected in a competitive relationship with the mother—thus the triadic situation found in the Oedipus complex. And the triadic situation raises other barriers to having father, besides the rivalry itself: fear of loss of mother's love, fear of her disapproval, and guilt if the girl were actually to have father. Many qualities and issues arise that weren't present when we were just dealing with father as a protector and a support.

And for the boys, the situation is the other way around. In the oedipal situation the boy is more interested in the mother as the sexual object, or more accurately as the object of his gender-related feelings. The father becomes a competitor. So there is a competition with father and the related feelings: fear of his disapproval, fear of losing him or his love, and the fear of castration by him.

This means that for both boys and girls, the Oedipus complex, with its various feelings and conflicts, becomes one of the barriers against the integration of Brilliancy. In other words, the oedipal relationship to the father becomes a barrier against the direct experience of Brilliancy because the father stands for Brilliancy in one's unconscious. The more intense the oedipal feelings—that is, the more that the childhood gender-related feelings were disturbed—the deeper and larger is this barrier.

Of course, both girls and boys resolve this issue. In order to deal with the whole oedipal situation, the girl generally becomes more identified with her mother, becomes friends with her, and the boy becomes more identified with his father, becomes friends with him. But different people resolve this issue in different ways depending on their personal history. There are also resolutions that result from same-gender sexual preferences. These homosexual resolutions are more complicated, and may have other roots, some earlier than the oedipal phase, which could then affect the feelings and choices in that phase.

So we want to do an exercise now to explore this whole constellation. Basically you want to explore your oedipal relationship with father.

An exercise is given to explore the students' experience of father in light of the oedipal situation. Students inquire into their passionate feelings, whether desire and longing, hatred and competition, or fear and guilt, in relation to father as love object or competitor. The relationship to mother can also be included. After the exercise the students reassemble.

AH: So, questions or comments?

S: The exercise brought up memories and perspectives that I didn't have before doing it—all kinds of realizations about the contest that was going on that I wasn't consciously aware of. I saw how smoothly, and sometimes overtly, fathers can castrate their sons, or sabotage in some real smooth, subtle way the relationship between mother and son.

AH: Um-hum. So that's the kind of thing you saw? And what did it do to you to see that?

S: Ahhh . . . it's like going someplace, and you are with a horse trader who is better at trading than you are. It's only when you've gotten away, a long ways away, with some really bad horses, that you realize you've been screwed. And you say, "Why, son of a bitch." Well, you know, it's after the fact, it's already happened, but you just look at it and say, "Well, yeah," and you see the anatomy of the whole thing. I didn't realize I'd been had like that, and there was a sort of surprise, a certain shock, anger, fear—some rage, sadness.

AH: So that realization brings up lots of feelings.

S: Yeah.

AH: Did you find out what it is that made you not see it before? What was the unconsciousness about?

S: Well, I knew my father was a smooth operator, but I hadn't carried it all the way to the bottom to find out how smooth he really was, and how many more different ways he was smooth than I had realized—probably still haven't. What it brings up for me is just the fear that when you think you've really got a handle on the situation, when you really know it, then all of a sudden something crops up that you completely missed. What it does for me is bring up the fear that says, "Well, if I missed that then how many more things have I missed?"

AH: Well, it sounds to me like you're saying that the reason why you didn't see was because your father was smooth in his operation.

S: Yeah, either that or I was not very discerning in mine.

AH: I see. So you are saying he was smooth and you weren't discerning, right?

S: Right.

AH: Which means he had Brilliancy and you didn't.

S: Right.

AH: Remember, smoothness and discernment are qualities of Brilliancy. And you are saying that you yourself had no reason for not seeing it except that he had those qualities and you didn't.

S: Well, I probably had a reason; I wasn't looking, and maybe I wasn't looking as hard as I thought I was.

AH: So maybe you gave up your discernment for some kind of defensive reasons. Maybe it's important for you to see that he had smoothness and you didn't have discernment.

S: Well, what happens is that I lose him if I am discerning. You might say it was arranged that I rather hated my mother for being somewhat castrating. And so the catch-22 I am seeing is that I sometimes get more discerning and I catch one of his smooth, manipulating maneuvers. It's like, "Ah, caught you, you son of a bitch," and then I end up being the same castrating person that I didn't like. So there's that, and there's the sense of feeling guilty.

AH: I see.

S: You know, it's like "Okay, Dad, gotcha, I caught you at it," and in so doing I castrate him. So I feel sad about losing him.

AH: So you feel you lose him.

S: And I also feel guilty.

AH: Are you saying that if you see the situation as it is, you lose your father?

S: That's it, that's the point.

AH: So maybe that's your reason for not being discerning.

S: Yeah, part of me is like that.

AH: At least.

S: Part of me that doesn't want to catch it. And part of me would like to just continue to idealize him.

AH: Right. So seeing the situation as it is means you will lose the idealized father, the smooth operator, the discerning father, right?

S: Right.

AH: If you see how it is and how you feel about it, you won't idealize him, which means you will lose the support of the idealized father.

S: Yeah, I think that began to crumble after I started doing the work.

AH: Um-hum. So how do you feel now when you see all of these things?

S: Sort of desolate.

AH: Desolate.

S: Yeah. Desolate that that is the person that I always idealized and felt comforted by.

AH: I see.

S: It feels like everything is gone. And, you know, it was easier to be comforted by him when I saw him as this idealized father.

AH: Right.

S: You know, big, good-looking, soft, wonderful man. But now when I see him as sort of a sneaky little bastard, things change.

AH: So you lose the comfort.

S: It's harder for me to accept comforting from him when I see him as he is.

AH: So you saw him as comforting by projecting Brilliancy on him.

S: Yes.

AH: See, when you realize he isn't really like that you don't just lose him, you lose the comfort of that part.

S: He was brilliant enough to be pretty manipulative, but not brilliant enough that he could use his Brilliancy in a really healthy way.

AH: Right. There's a difference between fake Brilliancy and real Brilliancy. So when you say you feel desolate, what is that like?

S: Ah, like there's no safe place anymore.

AH: So you lose the sense of safety.

S: Right. It's like before I was trusting that there was a safe place, and that had something to do with him. And now, the sense is that there is no safe place. You know, the entire universe is now just a combat zone. There's no hope.

AH: Right. So how does that feel? Scary, uncomfortable, insecure, or what?

S: It brings up the same desolation that I've probably felt since I was about three years old. It's just the thing that there was always a lot of battlegrounds, but no safe place to go to. I mean, you know, it's like there's no place where you can take your guard off at all. So it makes me feel real sad, hopeless, desolate. I guess that's it, sad and hopeless, and the sense that I have to stay real sharp and real awake at all times.

AH: I see, you have be on your guard.

S: Right. And then the next thing is a feeling that says, "Well, God, if I have to live like that, to hell with it, I don't even want it."

AH: Um-hum.

S: And so it's this thing that says, "God, I can go out and do the battles and be like that. It's worth it if I have a safe place to go back to, to that protector or whatever."

AH: Like it's always not safe.

S: Right. But if there's no place to go back to then to hell with it, why fight it?

AH: I see.

S: And I get real tearful at that point. Real high desire to die, high death wish.

AH: What are you experiencing now, when you feel this deep desire to die?

S: Oh, a sense of calmness, with a certain rebellious background to it, a sense that "Well, it's fine, I don't have to worry about winning the war or fighting anymore because Dad is going to be real OK." Sort of like a "To hell with you, world" kind of thing.

AH: What else?

S: Mostly a sense of a closed heart and a sadness about it, and basically a sort of sick sense, right here. I'm feeling kind of sick in my solar plexus.

AH: Yeah.

S: It's like there's some sort of emptiness. I'm not sure if it's emptiness or sort of something that's like the substance of a dark rotten apple, or some rotten piece of fruit that maybe I should vomit.
AH: So if you just sense that feeling and let it happen, let it reveal itself.
S: It makes me feel tearful, and the sick feeling expands all over the rest of my body. Expands up into my head, and through pretty much all of me.
AH: Includes all of you?
S: Yes, and it becomes real dark; everything starts going black, starts going real dark, kind of closes in on me, and I feel like crying.
AH: What's the feeling of the darkness, that makes you want to cry?
S: A sense that I've had for a long time, which is like standing on a mountain all alone in an impending storm.
AH: So you are feeling alone.
S: Yeah, alone, and it's like it's not Brilliancy that's coming to the horizon; it's rather an impending storm as I'm standing there.
AH: So there's danger, dark danger, and you're alone.
S: Yeah.
AH: Okay. So there's a sense of aloneness and some danger there. The sadness probably is because of the aloneness then—you are all by yourself.
S: Yeah. And it's knowing perfectly well that if I really push it I can be impeccable enough to make it through, but really having a sense that I no longer have the motivation to do it.
AH: Maybe it is possible for you now to just stay with that feeling of darkness and aloneness and not think of it as good or bad, and not do anything about it one way or another; just be there and be aware of it.
[*Pause*]
S: It makes me long for somebody that really loves me.
AH: Um-hum, makes sense. So longing for love, a loving person.
S: A loving mother.
AH: A loving mother. I see, both parents are gone then, in that aloneness. So let that longing happen, let yourself feel that longing for loving parents. So that's what's in the heart, the longing. Let's see what happens if you stay with the longing—go with it, flow with it— let's see what more it tells us.

S: I don't think I can really verbalize it—just tears.

AH: Tears, that's okay. Just stay there for a while. So as you see the loss of father, or the idealizing of the father, it brings aloneness, longing, tears.

S: Yeah, I feel real caught in my throat.

AH: So stay with the tears, the longing; there's nothing you need to do about it. That is what you feel about the situation, that is where you're at.

S: Yeah, I feel like I've been stuck in this place for a long time.

AH: What place, the tears?

S: Yeah, the longing.

AH: Longing? So you felt the longing before?

S: For both the mother and father.

AH: Um-hum. So let's see what happens to it now if you just stay with it, and not think of it as good or bad, not think of it in terms of whether you are going to be stuck with it or be free from it. Just be there with it, without doing anything. Let's see what happens if you don't have any attitude about that longing or that sadness.

AH comments: *The point we are making is, if this person takes any attitude or action regarding the state he is experiencing, if he takes any position in relation to it, he will interfere with that experience and change its qualities, and that would make it impossible for him to see his experience as it is, which would preclude his accurate understanding of that experience. Note that this does not mean resisting a position or inner action that arises from the inquiry; doing so would itself be taking a prejudiced position. The intention is that he notice his positions and attitudes and that by doing so he stop siding with them, which will allow his experience to unfold spontaneously. Understanding will then be a natural and spontaneous comprehension of, or insight into, his experience. This approach allows the understanding to arise as a response to an inquiry that is motivated only by the intention to see the truth.*

It will be necessary for him to be open and impartial toward whatever experience arises in order to expose whatever resistances and defenses he has against what is unfolding and the underlying fixed positions he happens to identify with. This is a continuous process of experience revealing its truth wherein the teacher is the guide who as-

sumes the voice of open-ended and motiveless inquiry. The process is not directed toward or aimed at achieving any particular end or state because that too would reflect adherence to a position, which in turn would automatically influence or interfere with the natural and spontaneous unfoldment of experience. Experience unfolds as a response to an open-ended inquiry that is only interested in seeing and comprehending the experience itself. Inquiry invites understanding, which in turn transforms the experience as it unfolds the potential of the individual.

So we continue now with our investigation of his experience.

S: Sort of just accepting it as part of my state.

AH: Right. Exactly. Not even accepting it. You don't have to accept it; you don't have to reject it. Simply not to have any ideas about it—to really leave that state alone, completely. But this does not mean rejecting or resisting your ideas and attitudes about it; rather, it means you need to see what ideas and attitudes you have about it, to be able to let it be. So why not? Why not leave it alone? Why do you have to do something about it?

S: I can see my resistance.

AH: Yeah, so that is what happens when you become interested in not taking an attitude about your experience. So what is the resistance about?

S: The resistance is . . . to do that would be truthful; and if I really do that and I'm honest and truthful about it, Essence will give me what I really want.

AH: Okay, and?

S: And I'm really afraid to have what I really want or anything that really turns me on because I think it would hurt so bad to lose it.

AH: I see. It's better just to long for it. Are you saying you're afraid of getting that love because if you get it you might lose it and you might feel hurt?

S: And I would lose my identification as a desolate and rejecting person.

AH: What will happen if you lose that, feeling desolate and being rejected and not loved?

S: Well, maybe I would become a lovable and desolate accepting person.

AH: I see, it seems the longing is a way not to stay in the aloneness, is a way of having a relationship again. If I understand what you are saying, you will lose your relationship of not having the love of a person if you let the longing be, which means aloneness.

S: That's right. But that would be really honest about my interests. You know, not being manipulative about my experience at all is difficult. In fact, I'm well aware that that's the best prayer there is.

AH: How about now? What do you feel?

S: A lot of self-doubt. A lot of unworthiness. Sort of like if I go with that honest longing, that honest emptiness, knowing that it's the only prayer in this situation and, letting Essence fill that space, there's a fear that I will be unworthy to be it.

AH: I see.

S: That brings up more tears.

AH: I see. So the possibility of having the love brings the unworthiness. So you hold on to the longing.

S: Yeah. I fear that I'll be unworthy. What I would hate worst in myself in any situation is to find myself unworthy.

AH: If you're afraid of that, the feeling of unworthiness, it means part of you probably believes it.

S: Yeah. I guess that that's probably the closest I come to indulging in guilt.

AH: Um-hum. Is that what you feel now?

S: I feel a little caught. I'm wondering what I could do to make myself feel more worthy.

AH: OK, I'll tell you: The way you can make yourself feel more worthy is by allowing yourself to experience, without rejection, the feeling of unworthiness. It's a foolproof method; it always works.

S: Yeah, that figures. [*Laughter*] The nonresistance method. It's very good.

AH: Do you notice that every time you experience a certain feeling you right away want to do something about it instead of just experiencing it?

S: It seems to happen automatically.

AH: Right. Seeing that and staying with your experience now, what do you feel?

S: What I get in the body is this real dark space. It's like walking into a house at twilight—it's not completely dark, but it's kind of gray. It's not murky gray. The space is there but you can't see very well in it.

AH: What happens when you just stay with the space, when you feel the emptiness itself, the darkness?

S: Yeah, I already feel it. It's pretty engulfing.

AH: And what's the emotional content to it? What does it feel like?

S: There's a sense that there isn't much brilliance there. But it's okay; it has potential.

AH: The idea is to experience and be with whatever happens in terms of your experience. It doesn't matter what's in it or what's not in it, right? We don't know what's supposed to be there really—maybe Brilliancy, maybe something else. Who knows?

S: Yeah, but with bright space I'd feel like it was brilliant, but right now it isn't. What I do feel about it is that sense that there is more availability.

AH: More potential, as you said.

S: Yes, that anything could fill up that space. It's kind of what I feel about myself, that there's not much brilliance right there now, but there's potential.

AH: Potential, I see.

S: Thanks. It's almost a kind of a feeling that you get if you wake up just before sunrise and there's that, not a sense of urgency, but a sense of just being keyed to see what's going to happen: What will the day bring? And it could bring anything; it could bring a cloudy day, a foggy day, a sunny day.

AH: Right.

S: And like, when you wake up and you haven't even opened the curtains yet, but you have a certain curiosity, a certain pique of curiosity, really watching to see what's going to fill it.

AH: Um-hum, very good. So we'll see what the day will bring?

S: What's really weird is that I won't know what's going to fill it.

AH: Right. Isn't that exciting?

S: Yeah! And there is a real excitement to it. It's like I can't go back to sleep.

AH: Right. Daybreak.

S: Yeah, that's what it is.

AH: Um-hum, very good.
    So time for lunch now.

AH comments: *This student obviously did not proceed to further exploration of his relationship with his father. The work focused on his resistance to his experience in general, which took the form of wanting to do something about it instead of experiencing it fully. His resistance became the focus of the work by the mere observation that he would not leave his experience of longing alone. Finally he arrived at a state where curiosity about, and lack of manipulation of, his experience became the experience. He learned something useful about how to relate to his experience, which was exciting to him. That excitement, which frequently becomes an unalloyed joy, usually accompanies the process of free inquiry and exploration. The exploration of one's experience may become a thrilling adventure, if we learn to inquire truly, if we find our love of Truth.*

10

Meeting Five

☙

We have explored what Brilliancy is and its relationship to father and to the father image. We discussed what father means: the function of father, and the father's roles of providing protection, safety, security, guidance—of being the guiding intelligence—and support for functioning. We found that the more we explore both what kind of father you had and what the real father is, the more you become aware of the essence of the kind of father that you didn't have, or didn't have enough of. This exploration showed us that all the identifications with your father, all the longing or the hurt and anger, is a natural desperate desire, a need for the father that represents all these things. And as we saw in the last exercise, father can be a source of comfort, love, pleasure, and joy.

So there is in every person a very deep, powerful, and perhaps biological need to have those qualities or functions in one's life and one's mind. In other words, father doesn't represent just the physical body that we call father. We are seeing that father stands for a certain reality that is needed by all human beings as they grow up. We are also seeing that the fathering role and function is distinct from the mothering function. The father role might not be attached to a man—sometimes a woman might take on that role—but it stays the father role regardless of who takes it on. The father role and the mother role, those two realities, complement each other. They are both needed for human survival, development, and maturity.

So we want to explore the need itself for father. The fact that the need persists and has not been satisfied indicates that there is still a gap, a hole, an absence—that father, or the reality that the father represents, is still not there. There is a sense of loss, a sense of absence, in a very deep place. Otherwise, if you didn't have the sense that something was missing, you wouldn't have any of the issues about father that you have been seeing; you wouldn't have any of the longing or identification, the fear or the anger, or any of that. So we're going to do an exercise now to explore this part of our work here.

The students are asked to identify and explore the need for the qualities and functions of the father they didn't have or didn't have enough of, the father that was really needed. The focus of the inquiry is specifically into the experience of lacking the good father and how that has impacted the student's life. After the exercise, the students reassemble.

AH: Any questions or comments?

S: I feel a sense of desolation as a result of doing the exercise.

AH: What do you mean by "desolation"?

S: I feel sort of dry.

AH: So that's how it feels now?

S: Right.

AH: Dry, desolate.

S: Dry and empty.

AH: So what's it like when you feel that emptiness?

S: Some fear about it. I feel I want to hold on to the fear of the emptiness not ending, going on endlessly. I guess I think that at some point, I am going to be gone.

AH: So if there is an ending, the ending will define the self?

S: Yeah. I had some ideas of who I was.

AH: So you feel now there's no idea of who you are?

S: No idea.

AH: Mm-hmm. I wonder if it is possible for you to let that be, to just stay with that—the feeling of no idea of who you are.

[*Pause*]

S: I give up. There is fear.

AH: Well, it's understandable. You're afraid you don't know who you are. It's a scary condition. How about now, Donald, what do you feel?

S: Small, tiny.

AH: How do you feel emotionally?

S: I know myself.

AH: Mm-hmm, that's it. So how do you know yourself now? What is it that you know?

S: I know myself as the child I was.

AH: I see, uh-huh.

S: I feel alone in this big emptiness, and I miss my daddy.

AH: What is it like to stay with this missing?

S: I feel sad and empty and alone.

AH: What does the emptiness feel like?

S: It is related somehow to the loneliness and aloneness; I feel a great deal of grief for not having had the father I needed.

AH: What happens when you stay with the grief and emptiness?

S: I just feel hollow now, with a feeling of something missing.

AH: What do you feel is missing?

S: Something related to father, something I wanted from him.

AH: Is it possible to stay with this feeling that something is missing, without trying to do anything about it?

S: I feel it is happening anyway. I actually feel curious about this. But I feel this deep longing for father, or something I wanted from him. The more I feel this, the more I feel the hollowness. I feel hollow, especially in the lower part of my chest. It is expanding. I feel hollow almost everywhere.

AH: What happens now, as you stay with the hollowness?

S: It changes. The grief and longing are gone.

AH: That is interesting. And what do you feel now at the lower part of your chest?

S: I feel something pushing out, as if some kind of energy is trying to come through. It is starting to look bright. Amazing . . . I feel a fullness with brightness at the lower chest. I feel strong and solid there.

AH: How is that related to your earlier feeling of missing father?

S: That feeling is all gone now. I don't feel I need my father now. I actually feel I have what I need.

AH: What do you mean? What is it you feel you have?

S: Some kind of solidity that makes me feel unusually safe and secure. I feel alive and joyous.

AH: And what else?

S: Some kind of expansion. I feel more grown up.

AH: Yeah. Now, what's the feeling toward the small, lively you?

S: I feel that I want to protect and guide him. I feel I can do that now. Amazing. I feel just what I wanted father to give me. I didn't think that was possible.

AH: That's nice. I mean, feeling joyous and lively definitely beats being gloomy. No?

When we realize we didn't have the father we thought we had, we might get pretty gloomy and depressed; it might start seeming to be the end of the world. We forget that what we need is not exactly father but what father represents. You are knowing yourself by recognizing yourself at that age. So, as you recognize that part of yourself, it grows, gets bigger and stronger. To really be the father toward yourself is to protect and guide your inner child. So integrating Brilliancy means, among other things, to be the right kind of father to the child within you.

You need to see that you wanted the good father; but this longing reveals a hollowness that gets replaced by the brilliant presence, which you then recognize as exactly what you wanted from your father. In other words, by longing for the good father you are actually longing for Brilliancy. This association between father and Brilliancy is universal.

In contacting the longing for father, you find your soul the way it was when its development was arrested. This is what I call the Soul Child. When you integrate the Brilliancy by working through the relationship with your father, you become the needed protective or guiding father for yourself, the father you never had. More accurately, Essence becomes the protecting and guiding father for the soul. As the soul grows and matures, it attains the qualities and capacities of Brilliancy. In this way, the soul becomes whole, integrated, and inseparable from the qualities and capacities of Brilliancy.

One more thing I wanted to say. The absence of Brilliancy manifested in the lower chest, and staying with this area allowed this bright presence to arise there. This place at the sternum is the center of this aspect, the center I call the mobius.

After a pause, another student begins to work.

S: What I was going through is similar to what Donald was saying, except that it started from a sense of the aliveness that left when my father—you know, the oedipal father—left.

AH: I see.

S: And then what I was able to see from that is that I never had a self.

AH: Mm-hmm.

S: I never had a tangible sense of self. I mean, that feels like a big, big loss.

AH: So you don't just lose your father, you lose yourself too as you lose him.

S: Yeah.

AH: And what does that feel like, that you don't have a self?

S: It just feels empty. It feels black.

AH: Is it difficult to feel that?

S: No, but there's a lot of pain in it, a lot of sadness, grief—a lot of feelings. It felt, when I first got into it, like I was always looking for a father who would find me. So it was like a sense of being lost.

AH: Yeah.

S: In a way, it's interesting because it's like seeing that I never had a self to value. So the value was always in the wrong place, and everything I had or everything I took to be myself didn't have any life in it. So it's like that is gone. Now it is just being emptiness. Empty.

AH: Do you feel that you don't have a self, or do you feel you have an empty self?

S: I feel like I've never really had a self.

AH: So you didn't have a self at all; it's not like the self is empty.

S: Feels more like no-self.

AH: No-self, okay.

S: Yeah, it's like I know what I feel like when I feel a sense of self, but this is like no-self. And that's empty too, in another sense.

AH: Yes. So let's explore more this state of emptiness and no-self. If you just sense that emptiness, what does it tell you? What is it like, what is it about?

S: Well, there's a feeling in my head as if there's a sense of something being lost. But it feels like in my chest it's just black. It feels like black space.

AH: And that black space, what's the feeling of it? Is it painful, or desolate? Is it quiet?

S: It's okay.

AH: Uh-huh, so that's your sense or feeling of it—is it just quiet, peaceful space?

S: Yes.

AH: But your head says—or rather, misses the self in that?

S: Yeah.

AH: That space says there's no self.

S: Yeah, but actually if I feel the space, there's not really a feeling of lack.

AH: Yeah, there isn't a lack.

S: Yeah.

AH: Right. So the lack comes from your mind putting the lack on the black space that feels peaceful in your chest.

S: Yeah. You know, it makes me look tragic.

AH: Tragic?

S: Traumatic. So if I leave my mind alone, then my head feels somewhat peaceful.

AH: I see.

S: It's nice.

AH: Black space goes into the mind, makes it quieter—the mind that is so full of those ideas about self and no-self and all of that, right? Who says there has to be a self?

S: That's true! It even makes me wonder what a self really is.

AH: Right! What's it for and all of that.

S: Yeah.

AH: So when black space goes into the head, the head itself becomes quiet and peaceful. So let's see if you just let that quietness and peacefulness be there, let it pervade you—what happens? Where does that peaceful space go, what does it do?

S: In a sense it's restful, and in another sense it's like it doesn't matter if there's a self or not a self, or anything else.

AH: Right, because basically in itself it's complete, right? There's no sense of something missing in it, no?

S: No.

AH: It is what it is and that's it.
S: Yeah, it's enough in itself.
AH: It doesn't have a lack in it.
[*Pause*]
S: It's almost as if there's not anything to say about it.
AH: Mm-hmm. [*Chuckles*] Well, isn't that nice?
S: I like it.
AH: Sure. No drama?
S: No drama.
AH: No drama, no tragedy.
S: No drama, no tragedy.

AH comments: *In this student's case, the experience of the loss of father led her to experience the loss of her inner sense of self. She felt that loss as a deficient emptiness, an emptiness that was characterized by feeling a lack of the sense of self. As this emptiness is accepted and allowed, it shows its inner truth, its essence, which is a peaceful, black, spacious emptiness that has no sense of self, but also has no feeling of lack or deficiency. There is just a contented, peaceful, and expanded spaciousness. So deficiency transforms to abundance when it is allowed and understood. And the deficient sense of self, when allowed, transforms into the peaceful spaciousness of no-self.*

AH: No problems, just quiet. So, what are you going to do with your life now?
S: I'm going to take it easy. [*Laughter*]
AH: That sounds good. [*Chuckles*]
S: Sounds good to me, too.
AH: Take it easy . . . have a nice rest.
S: A nice, peaceful life.
AH: And good sleep.
S: Yeah, I didn't sleep at all last night. [*Laughter*]
AH: Tonight it will be good sleep.
[*Pause*]
S: It is—it's like putting all that to rest.

AH: You see, the beauty of working with Essence is that there's no place that you can get to emotionally that doesn't turn out to be fine if you just stay with it.

When you work with something—in this case, the absence of the needed father—you may lose yourself at any step of the way, and then you have all your emotions about losing yourself. But if you stay with your experience, you realize that even losing yourself is wonderful. You might get to another state, and suddenly you will have a self, and having a self can feel wonderful. It doesn't matter what steps you go through; Essence manifests in all kinds of ways, and each one of them is fine. So there's no bad place that you can get to on the essential level. Essence can manifest as self or as no-self, or as neither, and there is really no need to worry which way it is going to go. Inquiry and exploration, if carried deep enough, are bound to manifest Essence in one way or another.

S: It's like seeing the fluidity of this process versus the stagnation and crystallization of what the mind thinks should be. The mind takes a position: It's either this one or the other one, or something else. This is a lot looser and freer.

AH: A lot looser. Things are always changing: Sometimes there is a self, sometimes there isn't a self, sometimes there is this, sometimes there is that. How can you control this? This is one of the Four Noble Truths. Do you know the Four Noble Truths that the Buddha taught?

S: Suffering.

[*Pause*]

AH: Second Noble Truth?

S: There's a path ...

AH: No, the Second Noble Truth states why there is suffering: the fact of transitoriness.

S: What?

AH: That everything is transitory. Nothing stays the same; and if you try to hold on to anything, that causes suffering. So the end of suffering comes by not trying to hold on to anything, not even trying to hold on to no-self.

S: Don't even do that; just don't hold on.

AH: It always happens the way it wants to anyway. Things just keep on arising and changing, regardless of what we like or don't like. The moment we quit bothering with it, things are fine. But we usually don't leave it alone; we always want to change our inner state.

After a brief pause, another student begins to work.

S: I find that kind of difficult, because the one thing that seems to come that's the most difficult to really deal with is the terror that is there.
AH: The terror there?
S: Yeah, that there is a self.
AH: Oh! The terror that there is a self?
S: Yeah. It seems like everything is fine as long as there is no self.
AH: Mm-hmm.
S: And as soon as there is a self or a recognition of a self, then there is terror. And one thing I've found in working on these issues is that it goes back to the fact that my father was very brutal with me when I was an infant.
AH: I see. Yes?
S: And being a self brings up an awful lot of fear, because whenever I was myself, that was when I was beaten.
AH: Mm-hmm.
S: So when I look at what I would feel like if I had had a real father, I see that I would not be living a life in terror.
AH: Essentially, you are afraid of your father.
S: Yeah.
AH: You are scared of the father you had. So if you are present, you are yourself, and your father is there, you'd be scared.
S: And by staying with that, I'm able to feel . . . I get really angry about it.
AH: Mm-hmm.
S: And if I get really angry about it, then I get really hurt about it. And if I get really hurt, or I really feel the hurt—which is difficult because feeling the hurt was also bad and being angry was bad . . .
AH: I understand.
S: . . . then sometimes I allow—or something allows—a little bit of compassion there for me.
AH: So when you feel your hurt and stay with it, compassion arises for yourself.

S: And with that I become more solid and grounded and I have a self and I feel . . . I have confidence, I have will, I have strength, but I have to go through . . .

AH: All of that.

S: . . . this routine . . .

AH: I see.

S: . . . of recognizing all these things.

AH: That makes sense—that's what everybody has to go through.

S: Yeah, and just saying, "Okay, I'm terrified and I'm really pissed because it's always this way," and then I feel the hurt, and compassion arises. But because things change all the time, there's just kind of a constant battle.

AH: How do you feel now, though?

S: Well, I feel pissed about it, you know; I feel really pissed about it.

AH: Pissed about what?

S: About having to go through all of that, about the way things were.

AH: I see.

S: That puts me in a position where I have to face this struggle every day; and it pushes really accomplishing something, and I feel that I need to do something.

AH: Mm-hmm.

S: It is such a battle; I mean, I have to go through it over and over again.

AH: Mm-hmm.

S: It's not like I can just see that it has to be done and do what has to be done.

AH: Mm-hmm.

S: Everything comes up . . . and then I feel I should be able to really do this. That brings in a superego thing where in order to do this, I feel I have to be like my father—forceful, with will. But he had a false will. I don't get it.

AH: I have a suspicion of something tricky here: You say you're angry at your father, that your father treated you that way—cruelly—and you had to go through all of that, right? That he scared you.

S: Yeah.

AH: There is something I need to understand in what you are saying, because I am getting confused. Let's see. Now, when feeling scared, how do you see your father at this moment?

S: I see my father as big, ominous, heavy.

AH: Heavy, mm-hmm. And how do you experience yourself then?

S: Small, weak.

AH: Mm-hmm.

S: Like a person who needs to really battle in order to get out of that, or needs to fight him—a little person who needs to fight.

AH: I see. So you're small and weak and scared, and the father is big and strong and ominous. Now the tricky thing here is the fact that your father is big and ominous and strong and all of that. But first, are you telling me that you never feel that way yourself—you never feel big and ominous and strong?

S: I do.

AH: Oh, you do feel that way sometimes?

S: I do, yeah, but after the routine, I mean, it's not a spontaneous thing.

AH: You don't feel strong, the way he is?

S: I feel that now because I'm TALKING [*angry tone*], leading up to saying something. I had to feel little, and I had to get big, and the more I talked, the more I felt angry.

AH: You become aggressive like him, angry, and all of that, right? But that's not exactly the same thing as just having a self, or having confidence. We're talking about being like your father here, right?

S: Yeah.

AH: Okay. So we're seeing that sometimes you are the small, scared one and sometimes you are like your father—the big, angry, ominous one—right? Your relationship with him is that you are the small one and he is the big one. So what we are seeing here is the whole object relation that you have internalized, no? The object relation here consists of the object, the aggressive big father; the self, the small and scared kid; and the feelings between the two. Sometimes you are at one end of it, and sometimes you are at the other end of it. When you are the small one, then your daddy is the big one, or somebody else is the big and scary one; but sometimes you're the big and scary one. Right?

S: Yeah.

AH: And the little one becomes somebody else, or a part of you, that you judge and beat up? No? So that leads me to believe that the important thing here is not the fear. The important thing here is the totality of that object relation. Does that make sense? Because sometimes you are afraid, sometimes you are angry.

S: Right.

AH: You go back and forth. That's what is always continuous here. What doesn't change is the presence of that object relation. No? Which end you are at changes, but the constant is the totality of that object relation. This leads me to believe that there is a holding on or attachment to that object relation, which means attachment to your relationship with your father. Does that make sense?

S: Yeah.

AH: Now you are aware that the whole object relation is there, that there are two ends to it?

S: Right.

AH: Sometimes you are this end, sometimes the other, but now we see that the totality of the object relation is part of your mind. Now, can you be aware of that object relation as a totality, on its own? Whether it is acted out with your father or it is all inside, it is the same object relation, which is a whole structure within your mind. What happens then, when you see the totality of this object relation instead of seeing only one pole of it? How do you experience things?

S: I experience it as foreign. This whole thing, this whole object relation feels foreign. I do not feel as part of it.

AH: And how do you feel when you see that it is foreign?

S: I feel empty. It's like it just went "poof!" over here.

AH: Right! And then all of a sudden, you start feeling empty. So that means that the terror and the anger keep coming back so that you do not feel empty, you see? The terror and the fear is a way of hanging on; that's why you keep having to be at one end or the other of the object relation over and over again. You didn't see that you need to have that whole object relation.

S: I never saw that it was all one thing. It was always a battle.

AH: Right, it was always a battle. But the battle is just the content of that object relation, you see? The moment that you see it as a whole object relation, you start feeling empty. Now what's it like to feel empty that way?

S: It's very spacious.

AH: Very spacious, mm-hmm.

S: Without any fear.
AH: Interesting, huh?
S: That's too easy. [*Laughter*]
AH: You have to battle, you mean? You have to bring this back again?
S: Let's go back. [*Laughter*]
AH: Saying "too easy" means that there is something about this emptiness that you still object to. So you want to have the struggle.
S: That's right; the struggle is part of the object relation with my father.
AH: So what is it about this emptiness that is somewhat uncomfortable?
S: It's a nice emptiness, but it is kind of a desolate type of emptiness. It's like it doesn't have something happening. Like there should be something there, something happening.
AH: Does that mean that something is missing?
S: Yes, missing something.
AH: Okay, good. Let's be aware of that sense that it is missing something. Isn't that interesting? What you first got was peaceful, but then you think it's too easy. But really it's tricky stuff here.
S: Very tricky. Emptiness with something missing.
AH: Very tricky, yes. So let's see what it feels like when you feel that sense of something's missing. Do you feel it's something specific missing? Or it's just a general sense that something is missing?
S: Well, it's a sense of a lack of something, like a part of something, like a piece of something.
AH: A piece of something is missing, mm-hmm. What does that lack feel like?
S: It feels like a hole.
AH: Like a hole . . . I see.
S: It feels like there's a hole in the emptiness.
AH: Where do you feel the hole?
S: In my belly.
AH: In the belly, okay. So it's an emptiness with a hole in it.
S: Yeah.
AH: Interesting. So feel the emptiness that is in the hole. What is that like?
S: The emptiness that's in the hole?
AH: Yeah. See if you can feel inside the hole.
S: The emptiness that's in the hole feels dark first, but then it changes.

AH: What is it that you feel? How does it change, or what does it change to?

S: It's like space.

AH: Space, yes. I see.

S: More space, and like I'm breathing space. Feels fresh.

AH: Freshness, uh-huh. Interesting.

S: But it still feels like there's something there.

AH: Something in the space?

S: Yeah, but it's more like something's flowing. There's flowing there.

AH: There's a flow in that space.

S: A flow.

AH: Feel that flow, let that flow happen, let it come out, let it expand. Now, what does that flow feel like?

S: It seems that the flow is into my heart.

AH: Into the heart. What does it make you feel when that happens?

S: It's kind of a sadness. It feels like sadness. It has a flavor of emotional warmth, something like compassion.

AH: Sadness. So the flow is the flow of compassion.

S: But I'm still very clear.

AH: And there's a clarity, a space to it too.

S: Yeah, and it's not necessarily bad. It's more like a feeling of compassion for sadness.

AH: Seems to me that the compassion is what you didn't have with your father. No? He was cruel, brutal, instead of compassionate. Compassion is what was missing in your relation with him. Hence it is absent in that object relation.

S: I feel a lot more human. A little more of a person, but I feel real spacious.

AH: So, spaciousness with humanness. Does the sadness seem to be about anything in particular? Or just a sadness?

S: I think it's more of a compassion for myself, or for my sadness and pain.

AH: Right.

S: And there's in it a kind of an acceptance of suffering; there's that there. But there's not a real judgment in that.

AH: There is that suffering. And there is the compassion for the suffering. Are you aware of the substance of the compassion, the flow itself?

S: One thing I really felt—I mean it feels like there is a network there. And there's a sweet taste in my mouth. But this flow is kind of like an emerald flow.

AH: An emerald flow. Interesting.

S: You know, like Bruce was saying.

AH: Right. You recognize the compassion more when you see the emerald flow. It's a pretty color.

S: Wonderful experience.

AH: Yes. [*Pause*] So there's a compassionate presence instead of the struggle. There is the presence of compassion that is for the struggle, for the suffering.

S: It still amazes me how fast the object relation disappeared—I mean, it was like something inside of me just stepped out.

AH: Yeah, the moment you recognize that it is an object relation, it just evaporates.

If you believe that it is reality, it becomes reality and it stays; it envelops you and you are in the middle of it, and it is reality. The moment you see it, you step out of it; and the stepping out of it is the same as the arising of the aspect of Being that is space. This is the openness and spaciousness of Being. Space takes the place of the object relation because this object relation is part of the ego structure. Space here means that part of the mental structure is not here anymore. Then Essence arises in the space, in the openness of Being. You see, that's essential work, but it's done using the knowledge developed by object relations people. Isn't that interesting? [*Pause*]

Sometimes we deal with the father, sometimes we deal with the self, and sometimes we deal with the whole totality of the object relation. Each will lead to a different place. If you deal with the object, which is father in this case, you will have a certain experience; if you deal with the self, you will have a different experience; and if you deal with the totality of the object relation, you will have yet a different kind of experience. In this case, obviously you dealt with both the object and the self, because the mind was holding on to the whole object relation. When you have worked through a whole unit of an object relation, the essential state that arises is that quality of the Personal Essence that is missing in the object relation. The aspect missing in your case was compassion. Therefore, the Personal Essence manifests in the feeling of being human, and more of a person, as you felt, but with the warmth of compassion or kindness.

After a pause, another student starts working.

S: Ever since I did the exercise, I've been really confused. The last exercise was really hard for me to feel.
AH: Still feel that way?
S: Yeah.
AH: Head stuck. What happened in the monologue?
S: I started talking about the way I saw my oedipal cycle, which seemed really reversed from most women. I totally denied my sexuality and being a girl, and ended up feeling a complete sense of loss, actually being really lost, really confused. And I really didn't have any memory of the early sexual or erotic feelings, or of relating to my father that way. It's repulsive. And the two people that were in the exercise with me came out and said exactly the opposite of what I was talking about and what I was expecting to hear from them. They were saying that I was very feminine and I must have loved my father a whole lot. And just right then and there, this cloud came over me. My head got really heavy and really confused.
AH: So maybe you don't love your father a lot. What do you think?
S: Right now I love my father a lot.
AH: Oh, you do? Well, what's the confusion about then? [*Laughter*]
S: Well, when I was young, I hated my father's guts.
AH: Oh, I see, you are confused about then and now.
S: Yeah, because when the oedipal thing was not seen, I kind of carried that nonsexuality throughout my life, up until now. But now I don't know.
AH: So that's the main part of the confusion?
S: Yeah.
AH: Whether you are feminine or not? Because people give you the feedback that you are feminine, but you don't believe it?
S: Yeah.
AH: How about now? How do you feel?
S: I feel a lot of tension around my head.

AH: Now roll your eyes. [*Pause*] How about now? What are you experiencing?

S: I feel a combination of a lot of sadness and hurt and loss.

AH: Do you know what the sadness and hurt are about?

S: Feels like . . . um . . . I miss something deep in me.

AH: Oh, you feel you lost a deep part of yourself.

S: Yeah.

AH: What do you feel in your chest?

S: Like a void or a hole there.

AH: I see. So feel that void and the hole. Let it happen. Maybe that's where the sense of loss comes from.

[*Pause*]

S: It feels empty deep inside the chest. But there is something else in that emptiness.

AH: So what does it feel like down there?

S: Feels . . . umm . . . feels vulnerable. And expectant—expecting to get hurt.

AH: I see, by whom?

S: By my dad.

AH: So it sounds like you felt hurt by him.

S: Yeah.

[*Pause*]

AH: You still feel the emptiness in the chest?

S: Yeah. It still feels . . . umm . . . like something was ripped out of there.

AH: What do you feel was ripped out of there? What do you feel is missing?

S: Feels like, um, father and compassion.

AH: Father and compassion.

S: And softness.

AH: So softness was taken out of there. So feel the emptiness there, sense the voidness of it.

[*Pause*]

S: It's hard to get into it.

AH: Do you know what the difficulty is?

S: Umm . . . fear of seeing.

AH: Fear of seeing. So there's fear. You are aware of your fear?

[*Student is nodding head "yes."*]

That's good. Feel the fear then. See what happens when you just let yourself feel the fear.

[*Pause*]

S: It's a childhood fear.

[*Long pause*]

AH: How about now—what do you feel?

S: The void seems to be opening up now. It's opening backward.

AH: Mm-hmm. That's fine. Let's see what happens; what does it reveal as it opens up? Maybe it wants to reveal something to us.

[*Long pause*]

S: I feel there's something really simple, really precious, and I can't quite get to it.

AH: Well, don't try to get to it. Just be aware that there is something like that.

S: Feeling that I want it.

AH: Just be aware that you want it. Something simple and precious that you want, that you perceive there. What does it look like?

S: It's soft, and warm.

AH: So as you see it and feel it, how does it make you feel?

S: It makes me feel compassionate, and really peaceful.

AH: Peaceful. What happened to the voidness in the chest?

S: It kind of turned inside out.

AH: Inside out. I see.

S: Instead of a black hole, it's more white.

AH: More white, uh-huh. Move your knees now.

AH comments: *I became aware while she was working that there was tension in that part of her body. And since defenses and resistance sometimes arise in the form of physical tensions, a physical exercise will confront the defense, expose it, and may even release it.*

AH: How are you feeling now?
S: I feel the presence.
AH: Presence, mm-hmm.

S: It is white.
AH: So you say you feel the whiteness. You see whiteness in the chest, right?
S: Yeah.
AH: Subtle. Does that go down to the belly or not?
S: Yeah, it goes down to my genitals.
AH: Ah-huh, okay. So it goes down all the way to the genitals. How do you feel there in the pelvis, or the genitals?
S: Um, kind of open and warm.
AH: Open, warm. So it's a pleasant feeling, then?
S: Yeah.
AH: Mm-hmm. [*Pause*] So it seems that softness is now present there.
S: Yeah.
AH: So let's go back now and talk about your father. What's the sense now about your father, what's the feeling?
S: I realize that I did really love him a whole lot, a lot more than I thought, but I tore it out of my chest.
AH: Do you know why you had to do that?
S: So he wouldn't hurt me anymore.
AH: I see. It was because of the hurt that you stopped feeling the love. So you feel more present here? You feel more yourself?
S: Yeah.
AH: Presence and warmth and compassion. It seems that the softness is the love. It is back in your chest now. The white presence is the Personal Essence. So you are present now to your love for your father—or more accurately, your relation to him now, as you are present and feeling personal with him, is that you love him.
S: That's right. I feel personally present. It is me, and my real relation to my father is soft and loving.

A student indicates that he wants to work.

AH: Hi, Stewart. What's happening?
S: I've been trying to get this out for three days and I can't.
AH: So, you're huffing and puffing. [*Laughter*]

S: My situation seems like there is a hook in it. There isn't a relationship. When you described this morning what a real father is all about, that was a description of the way I saw my father at a very early age. He was the protector, the support. It wasn't until the oedipal thing happened that it began to shut down—or at least I wasn't aware of it.

AH: Yeah.

S: So the hook is that in my earliest conscious memories, he was not only the provider and the protector and the security, but he also set the tone of the relationship within the house with my mother. He provided the tranquility. He was the knight on the white horse that went out at eight o'clock in the morning and came back at five at night.

AH: So you're saying that in your experience, you feel that as a child you had a father you loved.

S: Yeah, and the reason that is a hook is that I want to hang on to that.

AH: Hang on to what, which one?

S: Hang on to the image that I had of him when I was a small, small boy.

AH: I see. So you are aware of that feeling, that image?

S: Yeah. I've been aware of it all day and most of yesterday.

AH: You are aware of the feeling of your father as a protector.

S: Yeah, absolutely. And the confusion came in when I started thinking, "Well, now, hold it. This isn't the way it was later."

AH: Mm-hmm.

S: And then I thought, "Well, maybe you're kidding yourself, you really didn't see him in a real light." And that could be, but there was that element about him. Maybe I don't want to let go of that element about him.

AH: Well, who said you have to let go of it?

S: That's a good point. But the frustration comes in when that isn't the way he was later.

AH: I see. How was he later?

S: Oh, he was zoned out. I may be imagining it, but when the oedipal thing happened, there was a split in the relationship. I began to see him, perhaps, the way he was.

AH: How was that?

S: Oh, he would come home from work at night and sit down and read the newspaper. We made a game out of this. You could talk to him while he was reading the newspaper and he literally couldn't hear you. I mean, you could fire a gun in the living room and he wouldn't hear anything. [*Laughter*] He was just, ah, he was there but he wasn't there. And it got kind of scary because I thought, "If the outside world is that tough, that people come home at night in this kind of state . . ." I think, frankly, that's what led to my hyperactivity, as a defense against seeing him zoned out and in slow motion all the time.

AH: Mm-hmm. So he wasn't available although he was there physically?

S: Right.

AH: So, in the beginning, when you were younger, was he actually more available?

S: Well, it seemed like he was.

AH: Or maybe you didn't need him to be available that way.

S: Yeah, that's right. Or I was spending more time, obviously, with my mother.

AH: Ah-huh. So you felt he was around.

S: Oh, yeah.

AH: And that's all you needed at the beginning?

S: That's right.

AH: And maybe as you got older, you needed more personal contact with him, and he wasn't there for it.

S: Right.

AH: He will continue being the protector and provider, right?

S: Right.

AH: But the personal quality wasn't there, see?

S: Exactly. So the defense to that was, I made him my friend, made him my best friend. Great buddies.

AH: So you became good buddies.

S: Yeah. That was in defense of the castration, also.

AH: So you saw him as a certain aspect of father, which is the provider and protector; but you didn't see him in another sense, which is more the personal sense, of contact, guidance, and all of that.

S: Right. The guidance was admonition, and was not personal to me.

AH: That was the part you missed: the sense of more personal interaction.

You needed him to be there in a personal way, to have contact with him. That's what was missing. Is that how you feel he was missing?

S: Right. And that contact didn't appear until I was in college, and then of course it increased quite a bit. I mean, it was almost unbelievably there, until I did some kind of a psychological process, and then the relationship changed.

AH: Mm-hmm. How are you feeling now?

S: I've got a big hole in my solar plexus.

AH: Solar plexus? Interesting. What's the feeling there?

S: And in my stomach. Just lack of support, emptiness, like a negative harsh feeling in my belly.

AH: Mm-hmm, yes. Feel that emptiness, that sense of lack of support. Just sense that, be aware of that. Let's see what that's going to tell us.

S: Fear.

AH: So there's fear. What's the fear about?

S: Fear of, ah, not knowing who I am?

AH: Mm-hmm. [*Pause*] So if you feel that emptiness, you won't know who you are then.

S: Yeah, but the emptiness is moving, expanding.

AH: Mm-hmm. Yeah. So as it moves, as it expands, just sense it.

S: It's very spacious.

AH: More spacious. When you recognized what the fear is, the emptiness got freed.

S: Now it seems there's a contraction of the spaciousness in my solar plexus.

AH: Solar plexus, yeah. Now move your knees. [*Pause*] What about now?

S: Feels like it's growing into my sacrum . . . the whole pelvic area is just filling up.

AH: So it's not getting empty, it's filling up.

S: I don't know what it's filling up with.

AH: How do you feel as it fills up?

S: Feels good.

AH: [*Chuckles*] A little pleasure.

S: Yeah.

AH: What else? Sacrum feeling—well, it's a very rare experience.

S: Why is it rare?

AH: Well, most people don't know what the sacrum feels like anyway. For it to feel good, that's unusual.

S: Well, it feels like it's open—there's warmth to it, there's a groundedness. I feel connected from here [*indicating solar plexus*] down. Ocularly, it seems to be clear.

AH: Clear, ah-huh. So now you are getting the support that you felt you were missing. So it is a definite sense of groundedness and connectedness.

S: Right.

AH: When you sense that support, how do you describe it, what does it feel like?

S: Liquid, like a column of oil.

AH: Interesting.

S: Fluid, movable, flexible. But there's still the hole in my solar plexus.

AH: So there's a hole in the solar plexus now?

S: Yeah.

AH: Good. Feel the hole in the solar plexus. Feel inside the hole. What does it feel like inside the hole?

S: Feels like a wound.

AH: A wound, yes.

S: A lot of hurt.

AH: Yeah. What's it about, Stewart?

S: Not being seen, being devalued, the tendency to want to get angry.

AH: So you talk about your father—not being seen by your father, particularly?

S: Yeah, no matter what I did.

AH: So that's the feeling you got when he was reading his paper.

S: Yeah, like how can you be seen by a blind man?

AH: Right. [*Pause*] What does the hurt reveal?

S: It's like injustice.

AH: Yeah. It was unfair. [*Pause*] What else?

S: The toughest part of it is that, ah, I love him, and that's what makes the hurt.

AH: Mm-hmm. You loved him, but he didn't see you, and that's really painful.

S: Right.

AH: Mm-hmm. [*Pause*] So that hurts. So, let's see: When you feel that hurt, you loved him and he didn't see you. How about now? How do you feel?

S: A lot of hurt.

AH: Where do you feel the hurt?

S: Feel it all the way through my back.

AH: All the way through the back. Follow it all the way through the back; see what's there. It's taking us to the back—let's see, where is it taking us?

S: It's taking us right to my spinal cord.

AH: Yeah. What's there?

S: No support.

AH: Feel that there. So at the spinal cord, you feel no support. So what's it feel like? Is it empty or weak or what?

S: Like it's broken.

AH: Broken?

S: Like my back is broken.

AH: Broken. Be aware of that without doing anything to it. [*Pause*] What does that thing in the back reveal when you stay with it?

S: I don't know—it feels like a rod.

AH: Aha! Like a rod.

S: And it's going through right here [*indicating the solar plexus*].

AH: Ah-huh. What kind of rod?

S: Like a dowel, like a cylinder.

AH: Mm-hmm. So it goes all the way to the back. And what does that make you feel?

S: It makes me feel . . . it's like the dowel should stand upright instead of horizontal.

AH: Yeah.

S: It's like I've lost the feeling of hurt.

AH: Now roll your eyes. [*Pause*] What now?

S: Like I've got to avoid that hurt.

AH: That's how you feel?

S: I feel the hurt, but I can't tolerate it much.

AH: What about the hurt can't you tolerate?

S: Devastation.

AH: There's a sense of devastation?
S: Yeah.
AH: What's this devastation feel like?
S: Death.
AH: Like death. Do you feel that or is that what you think is going to happen?
S: No, I'll tell you—I feel hate right now.
AH: Hate.
S: I feel a lot of hate right now.
AH: That makes sense. Feel the hate. Let it come. When you feel the hate, what's it about?
S: The hate is about getting a bad deal. The hate is also the fact that that was a lot of his shit projected on me.
AH: Mm-hmm. So the hate is toward him.
S: Yeah. It's like I can feel the hurt and the hate simultaneously.
AH: Yeah. It sounds like the hate is because of the hurt, no? If there is a hurt, there might also be a reaction of hate. When you feel the hate, what do you feel that you want to do?
S: Punch him out.
AH: See yourself do that; see what happens.
S: Guilt.
AH: I see.
S: A lot of guilt there.
AH: Because of the hurt and hate?
S: I don't know. I just really felt bad about it, and that continued on until today.
AH: So what do you feel the guilt about now?
S: I basically got what he wanted and couldn't get for himself, and I made sure he knew about it. He was my best friend, but he pissed me off.
AH: It sounds to me like you feel that because he was your best friend, and you loved him, you shouldn't hate him.
S: Yeah. But you see, all my accomplishments were a way of getting his attention, which I never got. And when I got it—it was like when I beat him arm wrestling—it's like now I'm the daddy and you're the son. It's almost turned to that point. He calls me for advice.
AH: So you're giving him support now.

S: Yeah!

AH: While before, when you wanted it from him, he didn't give it to you.

S: Exactly.

AH: So that's a bad deal.

S: You bet.

AH: So you're pissed about that.

S: Yup.

AH: Sounds like you are feeling shortchanged.

S: I feel hurt.

AH: Right. Feel the hurt. Let it happen. Now you're giving him what you needed from him that he didn't give you. [*Pause*] Is it okay to feel that hurt?

S: To a point.

AH: Okay. What stops it then? What determines the point where it stops?

S: It's like weakness determines the point.

AH: Weakness. What do you mean?

S: It's to a point where I feel that hurt so deeply that it's like I'm breaking down.

AH: What's bad about breaking down?

S: It's weak.

AH: What's bad about being weak?

S: I don't know.

AH: Let's find out. Maybe all this time, you think it's bad to feel weak, but who knows? We want to see that state without judgment and find out what it's about. You feel the hurt, and let's see where it really takes us. Maybe it's something different than you think. You think it means weakness. Maybe and maybe not—let's find out. [*Pause*] What's happening?

S: I feel a lot of hurt in my heart, and this brings a sense of weakness. I see— I somehow associate feeling hurt with being vulnerable, and I usually feel that to be vulnerable means to be weak.

AH: What happens when you have this insight?

S: The hurt deepens, and there are tears coming to the surface.

AH: So it seems like there was a lot of hurt in that relationship. [*Pause*] What happens when you feel the hurt?

S: It goes back to the emptiness.

AH: Okay. And what does the emptiness feel like?

S: It's really nice.

AH: Oh, it's a nice kind of emptiness. Interesting. You thought the hurt would take you to weakness, but it took you to a nice emptiness. [*Pause*] In what way is it nice to you?

S: It's staying the same, except I notice I feel that strength and aliveness is starting to come, and the support; and the black thing goes out of my eyes.

AH: What do you feel in the chest?

S: Something's there. It's an aliveness there.

AH: Right.

S: I feel my heart.

AH: How does that feel?

S: Different.

AH: Different from what?

S: From what I normally feel.

AH: Oh, I see. What does it feel like when it is different?

S: Here comes the hurt again . . . but there is also sweetness.

AH: Because the hurt is connected with the love, remember?

S: Yeah.

AH: What do you feel in your head?

S: It's like I'm more below my neck than above my neck.

AH: Yeah. It's more of a heart and support. So it seems that by him not recognizing your love, you felt he didn't support it.

S: Right.

AH: And as a result, you lost the love—the heart—and the support, and now you are feeling them both again. [*Pause*] So now when you think of your father, how do you feel?

S: Oh, a kind of compassion, and there's an understanding to it. Still a hurt.

AH: That's fast! Understanding, eh? I mean, five minutes ago you hated his guts. Isn't that amazing? [*Laughter*]

S: Yeah.

AH: Talk about feeling different!

S: Yeah.

AH: What's the understanding?

S: The understanding is that he did do something for me. He didn't do a lot of things, and he didn't really see the love.

AH: But you feel that he did something.

S: You bet. He did give me some love.

AH: So you're seeing him more objectively, instead of making him all bad or all good.

S: Oh, yeah. That's what's been so difficult in this.

AH: Right, you had to go back and forth. Now we're seeing it more, the reality of it . . .

S: Yeah.

AH: . . . that there were some things that were good in the relationship, but some things were not. What do you feel in your forehead?

S: I'm not aware of . . . in my forehead? [*Pause*] It's like I can feel from the back of my head to the forehead.

AH: And what do you feel in the back of the head?

S: There's a connection between the back of my head and my forehead, just like there was here [*points to chest*].

AH: How does that affect you?

S: It's like, ah, I can see better.

AH: Right.

S: My perception is changing.

AH: Yeah. In what way . . . how is it changed?

S: There is a calmness to it when looking around.

AH: What do you feel right here [*points to middle of forehead*]? Are you aware of that area?

AH comments: *I was aware of a growing tension in his forehead and around the head in general, although he was not paying attention to it. My question was a way of drawing his attention to that part of his experience. This blockage started occurring the moment he mentioned his understanding of the situation.*

S: It's more coming from the back than anything.

AH: Yeah. Roll your eyes again.

S: Feels blocked, like a knot.

AH: Sense gently that knot. [*Pause*] Sense it gently there. See what comes out of it.

[*Pause*]

S: It's like my whole head is open, and my whole face is open. My vision is peripheral. It's like I can see things wide-angle.

AH: So when the head and the face open up, how do you feel?

S: Light.

AH: A lightness there.

S: Brilliant, more brilliant.

AH: And how do you feel at the area of the forehead now?

S: It just feels like panels have been taken away, opened up.

AH: Does it feel opened, empty, clear?

S: Feels empty, and there's a clarity—but it's primarily spaciousness.

AH: Spaciousness. So, when you feel the spaciousness and the clarity there, how do you now see your relationship with your father?

S: He did the best he could. It wasn't enough for what I wanted and needed as a child. What I wanted as a child was not that—I wanted something more—I wanted something he couldn't give me as a child.

AH: And what was that?

S: Love. [*Pause*] I mean, his total love, not just a little bit.

AH: How do you feel in general at this point?

S: Still got a lot of hurt.

AH: So more hurt comes.

S: Yeah.

AH: So you recognize more specifically that you needed that total love.

S: Because he gave me the taste of it.

AH: Okay, I see—which probably made you want it more.

S: Yeah.

AH: Okay, you got some of the love, but you wanted it more, more fully, right? Now how do you feel in the chest?

S: Oh, it hurts.

AH: Hurts? Lots of hurt!

S: Right.

AH: Lots of hurt. Follow the hurt. Go deeper into it. Let it take you to its depth.

S: Now it just opens up again.

AH: Again to a space.

S: Yeah. It just contracts and then it just opens up.

AH: As it opens up, how does it feel now?

S: I feel very clear.

AH: Very clear.

S: Yeah, like my head clears up. I feel a contraction in my heart, and I go through that and then my head clears up and the chest clears up.

AH: Yes. It seems that what closed the heart is your not seeing clearly what the situation was. So the more the head clears up, the more you get clear about the situation, and the more that opens the heart.

S: That's true. I didn't know what it was all day today. I considered love as a possibility, but it didn't click then.

AH: You had to see more specifically that it wasn't just love; there was love, but just a little bit, enough to titillate you. This is the case most of the time with parents. The situation is mostly that there is a little bit of love, and it makes you feel and know that it exists, but then of course you want it—you realize that's what you need—when most of the time it's not there. And that exactness of understanding, the specificity in seeing the situation, has a lot to do with clarity in the head. The more there is clarity in the head, the more you see things specifically. And then the heart and the head can both be open, and there will be heart openness—but with clarity, right?

S: I never felt this before, not like this.

AH: Yeah. So what does it feel like when both the heart and head are open?

S: My heart isn't completely open, but it's like it's directed. It's like the love has intelligence, in some sense.

AH: Yeah, directed. Interesting.

S: I mean, there seems to be a direction to it.

AH: What's the feeling of the love, the sense of it?

S: It's in a pure form. It's more objective like.

AH: And when you sense that, what's the texture of it?

S: It's more satiny, more slick.

AH: So the love itself has clarity?

S: Yes.

AH: So you see that when the head opens with the heart, the two get connected and the heart itself becomes objective and clear. That seems to be what you needed to find out here. You needed to become objective about the issue of love with your father. You needed to be clear about it, not just feel that love. You are understanding, in your relation to your father, the real story behind your feelings. And as you are seeing, love then attains different dimensions. Now you feel that it is more clear, more precise, purer.

S: It's amazing.

AH: You are seeing how Essence transforms, depending on the understanding. The more facets of an issue you understand, the more the aspects of Essence transform, change, and attain more facets. In this case, love becomes purer, more itself, more objective—it reveals itself as the essential aspect of Love. What do you feel now in the heart?

S: Like there's still hurt there, still a contraction, yet I can feel the Love.

AH: Where do you feel the Love?

S: It's like it's through here, it isn't just in here [*points to chest from back to front*].

AH: Right. Does it have a shape? Does it have form?

S: I don't know.

AH: Does it feel liquid or not liquid?

S: It feels more liquid, but it isn't liquid and it's not like air. It's clear.

AH: So you mean it is not liquid, but then there's a slight flow to it?

S: Yeah. I guess it is more like liquid. But it's not like a heavy, sticky liquid; there is more clarity.

AH: More clarity.

S: Crystal liquid.

AH: I see now. It's what I usually call diamond liquid. A manifestation of Essence, like Love, attains the diamond quality at some point. When it becomes clear and objective, the essential aspect becomes diamondized. The crystalline quality in the presence of Love means it has become objective—but it is still Love.

S: And it's so pure.

AH: That makes it more pure then, yes. That's the kind of Love that's not known very well. On the diamond level, Love is more objective and clear. Most of us don't recognize such purity of Love because of its clarity and objectivity. Love usually has to be somewhat sticky and mushy, otherwise people don't recognize it. Right?

S: Yeah. I mean, that's why it didn't feel like Love. It wasn't the cotton-candy kind that I felt and knew before.

AH: No, it doesn't feel like cotton candy; it's not like that. It's sweet and soft but pure at the same time. It gets purer but less recognizable as it attains the objectivity of the diamond level.

I think this is very instructive. As we work through the relationship with father, one thing we see here is that the underlying Love emerges. This example also demonstrates that when we want to understand a specific manifestation or issue, like our relationship with father, understanding needs to become precise, needs to become specific. When understanding becomes precise and specific, the whole experience goes to another level. For example, if we understand about Love and your father in a general way, after a while you may feel the Love. But if you get more precise—see the fine points about it, exactly what the situation was and how you felt exactly about love—the Love then appears again, but in a clearer, more crystalline way.

It is also important to see that our work is not a matter of working only on psychological issues. If it were, I would have stopped working with Stewart when he started feeling the sweetness of love; but I continued the exploration. So the exploration focused on the Love itself, which is an essential manifestation, a spiritual quality. By exploring Stewart's experience further, we got to see Love on the Diamond Dimension. The psychological issues will take us to the spiritual dimension of Essence, at which point our exploration then continues on in this new dimension. The exploration brings back the psychological issue, but takes it to another level, one of greater precision and specificity. As you see, the spiritual and the psychological are inseparable. The deeper investigation of how Stewart felt the Love, and the greater clarity about it, transformed the Love to the deeper and more objective dimension.

I am stressing this because I want you to see and learn the perspective of this work: It is not work on solving problems, but rather an adventure. It is an exploration of truth, regardless of where the truth takes us. And since the truth we explore is our own intimate experience, the exploration is bound to take us to various psychological issues. However, this does not mean that our interest is merely in solving issues. Issues may get solved this way, but that is not our motivation and not our orientation, which is always toward the truth.

Okay, we will resume after dinner.

AH comments: *We see here the experience of essential Love on at least two levels. On the first level, it feels like a sweet and fluffy presence, like cotton candy. There is sweetness and appreciation, lightness and pleasure. Then essential Love can move to the next level, the diamond level, when our understanding of Love and the issues around it becomes precise and specific. This gives Love itself a precision and an objectivity that then make it feel clear and crystalline. The cotton candy loses its fluffiness and is replaced by objectivity and clarity. It becomes a presence that has clear and crystalline qualities to it, but it still retains its sweetness, lightness, and appreciative quality. This can be felt as the purity of Love, as Stewart felt.*

This also points to the fact that Love is an expression of Being and is not merely an emotion. Stewart experienced it as having texture, taste, and viscosity, in addition to having an affect. This is because Essence is a presence, an ontological reality with its own phenomenological characteristics, which makes it almost like a physical substance. This shows the fundamental reality of Essence, as contrasted with the ephemeral nature of feelings and thoughts.

11

Meeting Six

☙

The meeting began with a short sitting meditation.

AH: So what's happening with people?

S: I've seen how much defense I've got against wanting and needing father. The defense is just really strong. I've been feeling that more this past week. This morning, I woke up to the image of a brick wall about two feet thick that had cracked and was just sort of shaking. And seeing that, I've been thinking I want value from my father, and I've been thinking that all day long: I want value from my father. And when the last person was working, I realized that the way my father showed his love was by giving me money—and here I was thinking that I wanted him to give me money, and that that was value. But I wanted my father to love me and value me, not just give me money.

AH: So you didn't think of it as an alternative. What does it make you feel to see that you never even thought of that as an alternative?

S: It hurts.

AH: So the hurt is about wanting love and not getting it?

S: I thought it was my fault that he didn't give me love. I believed I didn't deserve it.

AH: I see. So because you didn't get it, you took it to mean that you didn't deserve it. How about now? How do you feel?

S: Hurt.

AH: What comes up when you are present with the hurt?

S: Just seeing all the ways that he manipulated the relationship and how I became defensive.

AH: Do you know what exactly made you become defensive?

S: When he treated me the way he did.

AH: That made you close off?

S: I just get all uptight and tensed up.

AH: Do you feel that now or do you feel something else?

S: I'm feeling something shifting as I focus on the defensiveness. I am shaking. I feel this rage coming up.

AH: Is it okay to feel the rage?

S: I think I'm really angry at the capacity he had to manipulate.

AH: How did he manipulate?

S: I felt that he took advantage of me when I was twelve. My mother was pregnant with my sister, and he took me out when she was in the hospital. It made me feel at the time like a real woman.

AH: And how did that make you feel?

S: I felt alive. He encouraged me to feel that way.

AH: And how did you take it then?

S: That I was really worthwhile.

AH: So you valued it some.

S: I thought that I was important.

AH: And what happened? It wasn't true?

S: No, it was a lie.

AH: So you realized he was lying, it wasn't true? When did you realize it wasn't true?

S: When my sister and my mother came home.

AH: So it happened for a period of time. How was it before then, before you were twelve?

S: There were different, mixed messages. When I was three or four, sometimes I fell off the stairs, and I felt that he didn't accept me because of the way he treated me then. A couple of times, he told me to go away and actually picked me up and threw me down. And then he rejected a valentine I gave him that I made in school, and I just felt really hurt. I did love him. But he asked me why I loved him, and he said that he wasn't any good. I feel like I wanted him and needed him.

AH: So it seems you are saying that sometimes he was nice with you, sometimes he wasn't. Things didn't stay steady, they kept changing. And what did that do? What happened to you when things kept changing?

S: I don't know, exactly. I remember fantasizing why things were okay sometimes—"Daddy likes me"—then feeling him reject me at other times. But I tried to be what he wanted.

AH: I see, to get him to like you. So you feel you got something; but sometimes you wouldn't get it and you worked at getting it. [*Pause*] How are you feeling now?

S: I feel energy rising.

AH: How do you feel when you think of him now?

S: Feel like he's really screwed up.

AH: And how do you feel toward him?

S: I don't want to have any feelings toward him.

AH: Why not? What's objectionable about feelings?

S: Well, because I have feelings for him that I'd just rather not have. It is better this way.

AH: Well, you probably have feelings for him because you are a live human being, and he was your father. So there must be another reason why you don't want to have feelings. Is it like you are angry at him and you are saying, "I don't feel anything about you, I don't want to care about you"? Or is it something else? What is it?

S: It's more like I don't want to feel because I don't want to feel the pain.

AH: I see . . . if you feel, you feel the hurt. Okay, so you don't want to feel the hurt. What is it about the hurt that makes you not want to feel it?

S: It makes me feel vulnerable, shaky.

AH: That's how the hurt feels?

S: Feels like a real natural part of me has been wounded.

AH: And what does that feel like, to feel that part of you is wounded?

S: Some kind of tension.

AH: Uh-hum. Do you feel stiff?

S: Yeah. Before I started to feel stiff, I was shaking. I was really scared.

AH: So the stiffness might be related to the fear. What are you scared of?

S: I think I'm scared of wanting my father.
AH: What's scary about wanting him?
S: I won't get him.
AH: I see. So it won't feel good because you won't get him.
S: And I'll be used.
AH: And you'll be used on top of it.
[*Pause*]
S: I think that's what really hurts.
AH: So you have to close your feelings about wanting him, and all that, so that you don't expose yourself to being used and hurt. Still feel stiff?
S: A little more relaxed. It seems it's okay for me to want value from him, to want him to give me something material.
AH: Yeah. So what is it not okay to want?
S: It's not okay to want love.
AH: No?
S: Something that doesn't have substance.
AH: I see, because you won't get that, and you will also be used. [*Pause*] What's happening now?
S: I am shaking.
AH: All over?
S: Yeah.
AH: Is it okay to have this shaking?
S: Yeah.
AH: So what happens when you just allow the shakiness?
S: I see that wanting him to give me something of material value is sort of misplaced.
AH: Uh-huh. In what sense is it misplaced?
S: What I really wanted to get was his love.
AH: And you also wanted him to value you, in a real way, instead of just giving you something, right? Wanting value is not necessarily just wanting objects. There's a sense of being valued and appreciated, just like love.
S: I sense that he had love, though he was giving me material things.
AH: You're saying that's not what you want. You want something he feels.
S: Right.
AH: Now what do you feel in your chest?

S: Watery.

AH: What happens to the shaking when you feel the watery feeling?

S: It sort of dissolves. It's smoothed out.

AH: Uh-hum. [*Pause*] How do you feel now when you think about it?

S: I hate him.

AH: Okay, maybe that's part of what's there—hatred. Is it okay to be there?

S: Yes, but I also feel sweetness.

AH: I see. So you feel both at the same time now—both hate and love? Seems that's more accurate for the situation, no?

S: Uh-huh.

AH: Sometimes he was nice, sometimes he wasn't.

S: It seems like the hate was mixed up with the love because when he was nice, when he seemed to be loving, he used it.

AH: Yes. Did he do that even before you were twelve?

S: Yeah.

AH: How? How did he use being nice before?

S: When he wanted to get attention. Sometimes my mother wouldn't give him attention, so he would turn to me.

AH: So your relationship to him is both love and hate. That's how you feel about him—love him and hate him at the same time. How does it affect you when you feel that way?

S: Feel good and clear.

AH: More clarity.

S: And I feel like there's nothing to get from him.

AH: Just stay with that mixture of feelings and see where that takes you. It is better not to try to change it one way or another. You might also see the details of the ways that he used you. You mention him getting attention, but there might be more to it than that. To me, your hatred seems not sufficiently explained by that. You are feeling clear and more resolved because you see both the love and the hatred and have some understanding as to what they are about. This is good for now, but this does not mean there is nothing more to explore in this relationship.

After a short pause, another student begins to work.

S: I seem to be getting static from my friends about my relationship to my father. It makes me feel real nervous talking about it because there's a part of me that feels really needy and really wanting him. It feels sticky. And I'm just feeling really ashamed of that.

AH: I see.

S: I realized that what I wanted from him a lot of the time was expressed in trying to be brilliant for him because that's what he wanted. Then I keep getting waves of hurt. I'm really ashamed of that, of wanting and needing him.

AH: What's shameful about it?

S: Because I feel like I'm not living up to his expectations of me.

AH: Oh, I see: He doesn't want you to be that way.

S: No, he wants me to be a certain way.

AH: How does he want you to be?

S: Um, well, clear, all knowing, and not dependent on him.

AH: I see, so he doesn't want you to want him.

S: No, and there's a trick to that because there's another part of him that says it's okay for me to want him when he wants me.

AH: I see. So you can want him but on his own terms, not when you need him.

S: Right. [*Pause*] Frustrating.

AH: Sure it's frustrating.

S: Like I don't know the way out of this frustrating situation.

AH: Well, how about if you don't try to find the way out?

S: [*Laughs*]

AH: [*Chuckles*] You just feel what you feel: frustrated, sad, you want something, you're not able to have it, you feel ashamed about wanting it. All these things are what you feel about this relationship. What happens if you just let them be?

S: Well, I get a sense that I'm not with him.

AH: Ah, I see. I get it. It's one of those tricky things. You get attached to wanting him, so you won't just let yourself be.

S: Yeah.

AH: It's important for you to feel that you want him and you can't have him. That's the relationship.

S: Yeah. I feel that.

AH: Well, you believe it's true, it seems. You feel you want him—you can't have him. You are always trying to get him by being bright and all that.

Does that mean you believe that if you don't do anything you won't get him?

S: You got it. I feel that something is crumbling.

AH: Something starts crumbling if you just let the feelings be. [*Pause*] So what happens if you follow that crumbling feeling?

S: Hurt comes up. I feel separate. Something negative, like rejection.

AH: So maybe there is a sense of rejection and abandonment already there, which makes you always try to do something to make him love you.

S: Yeah, it's embarrassing that it is such a pattern. You know, I'm still playing it out so much in my life. I'm still waiting for the rejection, always.

AH: So what are you experiencing now?

S: I feel a lot of hurt. I feel shattered.

AH: Is it okay to feel that?

S: It's difficult.

AH: It is. Hurt is painful. And shattered is definitely a difficult condition.

S: If I let myself feel it, the whole relationship will shatter.

AH: I see. So you don't want the whole relationship to be shattered.

S: No, I don't know whether I'll like that. I'd rather feel rejected.

AH: Yes, so that you don't feel the absence of that relationship. So what is it about the absence of that relationship that you don't like?

S: I feel quite alone.

AH: Right. Is that painful? Is it okay to feel it?

S: No, not with all of these people looking at me. [*Laughs*]

AH: So how does it feel to be alone with all these people around? Should we turn off the light? [*Laughter*] So what does the aloneness feel like?

S: Well, there's a sharpness to it . . . a sharp object, like a burning—but it's like ice burning.

AH: Ice burning. Uh-huh. Cold burning. What's inside that burning?

S: Let me see. I almost want to say like a cut or wound.

AH: So the aloneness has a hurt in it. The aloneness means something in this case, maybe rejection. It seems it's not that you are just alone; you're alone because somebody doesn't want to be with you.

S: Right.

AH: An aloneness you haven't asked for—that's why it's hurtful.

S: That's exactly right.

AH: What's inside the cut?

S: Feels like pain and sadness. There is an ache.

AH: How deep does the ache, the wound, go? How deep does it go?

S: All the way to my back.

AH: All the way to the back. Real deep wound. Uh-huh.

S: Yeah, it feels like I really, really wanted to be with my dad.

AH: Yes, that's what it feels like. And you're deeply hurt that that didn't happen, because it didn't. [*Long pause*] How are you feeling now, Karen?

S: Still I feel cut off from him. Feel more relaxed though.

AH: So it's easier to accept when you know the situation and what it's like. It's more tolerable then.

[*Pause*]

S: I'm starting to feel the hurt more in my belly.

AH: Does it have a different quality when it gets to the belly?

S: Yeah. It's not like the cold burning, but something about it is the same.

AH: I see. Let's try to relax your pelvis and belly and see what feelings are there. Now, move your knees. [*Pause*] Okay, how is it now?

S: It feels really related to that issue of being alone, you know, of feeling rejected, and alone, alone because rejected. And that makes me feel ungrounded.

AH: Aha, I see.

S: But it is starting to change.

AH: I see. How do you feel in the pelvis now?

S: Well, I feel my *kath* is open; it's warm, I feel like a golden fire is there. I feel grounded.

> **AH comments**: Kath *is a name from the Western esoteric tradition that we use in the Diamond Approach for the belly center, what the Japanese call the* hara *and the Chinese call the* tan-t'ien. *It is this center of the inner physiology that is related to one's sense of grounding and being solidly on one's feet, embodied, and in the world.*

AH: Good. You say you are feeling grounded?

S: I felt ungrounded when I got in touch with the rejection.

AH: How do you feel now though, when you see the golden fire?

S: More present in the belly, more grounded.
AH: More grounded. So the golden fire is in the belly? What happens if the golden fire gets bigger?
S: It seems pretty easy.
AH: How does it feel when you sense in the belly?
S: Feels real grounded in relation to the truth. I feel I am really tired of bullshit.
AH: Right. You want the truth.
S: Yeah. And a relationship to it.
AH: I see. So the golden fire has to do with your relationship to truth.
S: I felt it like action.
AH: Action in what sense?
S: It is a sense of no more bullshit. It's a sense that I want to live in a real way. I want my actions to be toward the truth.
AH: Toward the truth, yes.
S: In a practical and honest way.
AH: Right, no more bullshit, eh? Getting down to business.
S: Well, I think of my relationship to my father—I feel my relationship's gotten so full of bullshit because I'm always trying to maneuver and pretend, and all this doesn't seem very straightforward when I'm in that golden fire.
AH: Well, now the kath is more oriented toward the truth, what's real.

Fire or flame usually indicates an aspiration toward something, but this aspiration is originating from the spontaneous depths of the soul and not from the mind. Gold is the color of truth on the dimension of essential experience. Golden flame is then an aspiration toward the truth, and golden fire is a strong aspiration and movement toward truth and away from falsehood and lies. This is a wonderful orientation. It is actually the specific orientation of our work. And we see that this orientation cannot come from the mind—it has to be real; it has to originate from the essential depths of our soul. The mind does not know what the soul needs to aspire to because the mind is influenced from outside. But the essential depths of the soul can be the source of true aspiration without the mind knowing what the aspiration is toward.

The flame can be of other colors, with each indicating different manifestations of Essence. The flame can be luminous black, for instance, indicating the aspiration toward peace and inner stillness; or it can be a brilliant flame, indicating the spontaneous aspiration of the soul toward the true intelligence of Being. The flame can manifest in any of the various inner centers. It can manifest in the heart, for example, indicating the aspiration of the heart and feelings. Or it can arise in the belly center—the kath, or hara—and in this way orient actions. It is the aspiration toward true action.

In our exploration, we have been seeing all the varieties of relationships to father and the feelings that go with them: the wanting and not wanting, the hurt and anger, the emptiness and aloneness. Remember, this started with exploring Brilliancy, an aspect of Essence, and how the father is related to it. I have talked about Brilliancy in terms of protection, intelligence, security, safety, magnificence, and majesty. But we're seeing that everything about father came up because the issues that prevent us from experiencing the Brilliancy are the conflicts in the relationship with father.

Usually, when you consider a certain aspect or manifestation of Essence, the specific psychological barriers against it arise as particular issues. And that's why the issues of father came up when we started with intelligence, which is one of the qualities of Brilliancy. So the barrier against experiencing and embodying the particular aspect of Brilliancy is the unmetabolized relationship with father, and the associated conflicts and vicissitudes.

We've seen many things about how we tend to project Brilliancy on father, or father on Brilliancy, and all the issues that arise from that—the hatred, the anger, the hurt, and so on. This means that the barrier can manifest in many ways. If you think unconsciously that father and Brilliancy are the same, then you will not be able to recognize Brilliancy as part of your natural endowment. That's one way. Another way is that you believe you can't have Brilliancy because you're afraid of your father. Or perhaps just the mere fact of projecting it stops you from having it. Maybe you feel you have to appease daddy, or agree with him—whatever it is that you do to please him—and that stands in the way of experiencing your Brilliancy.

Before, we explored your relationship with your father; now you want to see how that relationship prevents you from feeling that luminous part of your Essence, the actual presence of intelligence that is part of you.

In this exercise, the students explore how their own internalized and fixated relationship to father prevents the experience of Brilliancy. The students reassemble after the exercise.

AH: Does anybody want to work, or have a question or comment?
S: I noticed that there's been this block to my own Brilliancy, which is fear of my own self-expression. The whole time, I have been terrified to talk. The fear is that if I truly express my own feelings, it will push my father away; so I couldn't express myself. And it seems to be kind of a catch-22 situation, because at the very times that I would meet him with expression of my feelings, he would push me away.
AH: But why will that stop you from talking now, in here?
S: Well, I feel that way almost everywhere.
AH: The same as you have been feeling here?
S: It is more intense here. I am usually afraid of talking to you.
AH: I see. What is it about me that makes you feel this way?
S: I see now that I have been seeing you as a father figure, but I didn't know till now that it is the same fear that I have had with my father.
AH: So you have been feeling toward me what you felt toward your father?
S: It seems so. I realize I have been feeling that you will push me away if I try to express myself here. That is what I felt my father did.
AH: Your need to express yourself will make me push you away, just as he pushed you away.
S: Yeah.
AH: So what did you do? How did you handle it at that time? You just were quiet?
S: Stopped it.
AH: Stopped it?
S: Yeah. I would do other things—have a problem, for instance—so I could approach him. But these days it is different. We talk.
AH: So how do you feel now that you speak with him?
S: I'm glad.
AH: Oh, so you're not scared now.
S: Yeah, it's like I feel that self-expression is real important.
AH: So it feels good to do it.
S: Yeah...

AH: So you can do it now and feel glad instead of scared.

S: ... if I don't stuff the self-expression, as I did all my life.

AH: Okay, now that you are expressing yourself, do you feel you are losing something, pushing away anybody?

S: Not at the moment. Maybe it would be okay to express to him that I was happy. But if I felt sad or scared, then it gets more difficult.

AH: So what about in here?

S: Somewhat okay.

AH: Okay to say that you have fear?

S: It's more difficult to say that.

AH: ... than saying you are glad?

S: Right. I must still feel you are my father or something.

AH: Well, let's experiment with it. Say it a few times and see what happens.

S: Which?

AH: "I'm scared."

S: "I'm scared"?

AH: Yeah.

S: Ah, I'm scared ... I'm scared ... I'm scared.

AH: Okay.

S: There's still a fear. I feel that I'm still holding back, that if it were a real desperate need, it would be more possible.

AH: What's the desperate kind of need?

S: To express my fear.

AH: Are you holding that back now?

S: Somewhat.

AH: Yes? How would you feel if you didn't hold it back? If you don't hold it back, what would you say, what would you feel?

S: I would be real emotional.

AH: You shouldn't be emotional?

S: Right. That was the definite message: "Don't be real emotional; don't be demonstrative." It was okay to be happy, but don't be real demonstrative.

AH: How do you feel now?

S: Scared.

AH: Scared?

S: And shaky.

Meeting Six 247

AH: Just feel the fear. See where it takes you.
S: It's like there's a sense of vulnerability and emotionalness.
AH: I see.
S: That state would be rejected.
AH: Vulnerability?
S: Yeah. I would feel vulnerable, but I would be rejected if I showed it.
AH: What's the vulnerability like?
S: There's a sense of aliveness and tenderness. And there's a shaking to the gentleness.
AH: So there is a gentleness and tenderness to the vulnerability. So when you feel the vulnerability and let it be there, does it continue to be scary or does it become more of a pleasant thing?
S: There's fear there. I'm not sure if it's vulnerability anymore.
AH: So you are open and expressing yourself. Right? It's not even desperate. You're just open. You must not be believing I am your father now.
S: Yeah. It seems like there's a relief about that.
AH: Yeah. Your mind didn't really believe it until it happened.
S: [*Voice full of tears*] Right.
AH: That vulnerability, which feels scary at the beginning, could be quite a friend in some sense. It's a good way to be, to keep in touch intimately with yourself.
S: Yeah. It feels, you know, kind of alive.
AH: Yes. More alive, more in touch with yourself, more in touch with others.
S: I wanted that so much from my father, and I could never get it.
AH: Um-hmm. To show yourself and feel your feelings makes you vulnerable. So the way you dealt with that was to protect yourself, to isolate yourself, and not feel vulnerable. But you really wanted to be emotionally open with your dad, just as you are now with me.
S: Right. I did that when I was real little. I feel okay now. Thank you.

After a pause, another student wants to work.

AH: Yes, Jennifer?
S: I feel that I have this belief that just because I was born female, I have no Brilliancy. Brilliancy is a male quality; that's what my father taught me.

And so it feels as if I believe he has my Brilliancy, and I want it back. And I've been furious and pissed about that, but I'm really hurt underneath. And it's like I gave up my femininity and my femaleness, being a woman, for him. And I didn't get Brilliancy anyway, and now I'm nothing.

AH: So you're feeling neither male nor female.

S: Yes, sometimes I'm nothing.

AH: How about right now?

S: Right now I'm just real upset, hurt, and angry. It's all a mixture.

AH: So you have a lot of emotions, frustrations. You believe that if you're a woman, you can't have Brilliancy.

S: Right!

AH: Brilliancy belongs only to men?

S: Exactly, and yet I can't be a female either.

AH: Why not?

S: That's nothing. Being a female is nothing.

AH: Oh, I see.

S: Even when a female is what my father told me a female was: like mother, a baby-machine . . . and sex was wrong and dirty. I don't even know how to do that.

AH: Do what? Sex?

S: Yeah. Unless it's wrong and fast.

AH: So how do you feel now in the pelvis?

S: Well, there's some big ball right there that hurts.

AH: Now move your knees. [*Pause*] Okay.

S: It feels like my uterus is contracted. It's just a hard mass, in the area around my kath.

AH: So the uterus is contracted.

S: That's what it feels like.

AH: So it feels hard?

S: Yeah.

AH: When you feel that hardness, what does it make you feel?

S: It hurts, physically.

AH: Is it hard, in a ball, or what?

S: Solid.

AH: Solid ball?

S: Yeah, it's real contracted. Like a block.

AH: How about if you just feel that hardness and don't think of it as contracted or not contracted, or anything. Just feel there's a hard ball there.

S: Feels like I'm stuck or something; I don't know.

AH: Stuck in the way of the ball?

S: No, that's what it feels like. It's just like some blockage, or that something's stuck in the way, in my body, and that it doesn't belong there.

AH: Okay. Just feel it and sense it. If you sense it without saying no or yes to it, what happens?

S: I'm rejecting it.

AH: You're rejecting it. You may do that; but if you reject it, we won't know what it is. You know, it might turn out to be something good. Do you know why you are rejecting it?

S: Yeah [*laughing*], it is bad and dirty—there, I mean. It's like a hard mass.

AH: Some kind of hard mass?

S: Yeah.

AH: Is it the shape of a ball or a different shape?

S: It feels like a circle.

AH: A circle?

S: Yeah, like a ball.

AH: And it's the uterus itself that feels that way?

S: That's what it feels like to me.

AH: And so when you feel that hard ball, that mass, what's the effect on you?

S: It feels like I'm holding it away from the world.

AH: Oh, you are.

S: And protecting it.

S: And protecting it . . . and nobody can get at it.

AH: I see, okay.

S: It's like it's inside of me.

AH: So you're protecting yourself, or your uterus, from contact.

S: Yes, exactly.

AH: You're withdrawing and isolating yourself in some sense.

S: Yeah, that's what it feels like. But it feels like it's wrong or bad. There's something wrong about it.

AH: About what?

S: The uterus.

AH: What do you believe is wrong with it?

S: It's part of being female.

AH: So?

S: That's not okay.

AH: What's not okay about it?

S: I don't know.

AH: So, you're a female. What's bad about that? I mean, the world has males and females.

S: They're no good.

AH: Why do you think they are there then?

S: To have babies, that's all. And to keep the world going, just to be there to be used by men.

AH: Otherwise they're bad?

S: Well, I don't know if they're bad; they're just sort of useless.

AH: Why are they useless? They're only used to make babies. Is that what you mean?

S: Yeah.

AH: So you're saying, "I'm not going to do that; I'm going to hold back my uterus. I'm not going to let any baby get into my uterus." No?

S: Well, obviously not.

AH: "Stop this baby business." Right?

S: Yeah, I think so.

AH: "I'm not going to participate in this conspiracy against women that makes them just breeders."

S: Yeah. I think that's right. It still hurts, but now I'm scared.

AH: Scared of what?

S: Something you said about holding my uterus away from the world so I wouldn't have children.

AH: What's scary about that?

S: I don't know if I want children or not.

AH: Who said you should want children?

S: My father.

AH: Oh, he said you should have children?

S: Yeah. Then I would be useful in this world. That's the only way I can be useful.

AH: Well, let's find out what the uterus wants, not what your daddy says. It seems the uterus should know.

S: When you said that a thought came into my head, like a scream: "Leave me alone!"

AH: Who said it? Who made the scream, "Leave me alone!"?

S: Well, I just had the thought in my head that the uterus was saying, "Leave me alone."

AH: Oh, the uterus is saying that. Maybe. Let's experiment. So say that a few times: "Leave me alone."

S: Leave me alone. Leave me alone. Leave me alone.
That takes away the ball.

AH: Interesting. Maybe that's what the ball is. No? So what happens when the ball is not there?

S: Well, it feels empty, but it feels like a peaceful empty.

AH: Right. So let's feel that emptiness there. See what happens if you feel that emptiness.

S: My legs start shaking, for one. I feel empty in my pelvis.

AH: I think this retreat will be remembered for its shakes. [*Laughter*]

S: My arms and legs are shaking. My pelvis is empty, but it feels good. It feels peaceful, and relaxed, and I'm so clear.

AH: Now move your knees again. Okay.

S: Stopped shaking. That feels better. Peaceful.

AH: Okay, there's more peace. So now how do you feel about being a woman—about feminine and masculine—from this place? What's the feeling?

S: From this place, I love being female.

AH: Okay. Sounds nice.

S: Yeah. What am I doing here? [*Laughter*]

AH: You only had to say, "Leave me alone."

S: "Leave me alone," huh? I don't get it.

AH: "Leave me alone" was the way to protect yourself. "Don't pick on me." When you realized that's what you were feeling, things changed.

S: That part I get. I guess I don't understand about babies, and the function, and what I'm trying to do—having babies / not having babies; getting father / not getting father.

AH: Having or not having babies, that's a whole other question. Who said if you are a woman you have to have babies or not have babies? Who said that? If you are a woman, it means you *can* have babies, no? That's what it means. Who's going to say whether you should or shouldn't?

S: Is that a way of getting father—to have a baby?

AH: Maybe that's what you think. I'm sure that many people think that the way to have father is to have a baby, to get married and have babies.

S: Yeah, that would be a way of having him.

AH: If you believe that Brilliancy means masculinity, and only boys have it, then your option is obviously either have Brilliancy by having a man, or by having a baby boy. How else can you have it?

First, you need to see that there is a deep desire to have your father, and maybe underlying that is the desire for Brilliancy, which then means that you still believe that Brilliancy is a masculine thing. Now that you can say no, it becomes easier to accept being female. The next step for you is to see that being female is not antithetical to being brilliant. This may take time, but it will be one way for you to integrate the aspect of Brilliancy, which is a manifestation of your Being. It is clear how your relation to your father functions as a barrier against you assuming this Brilliancy; you learned from him that Brilliancy is a masculine quality.

This belief is, however, quite universal and is not particular to you. Many people feel that Brilliancy is a masculine thing. It doesn't feel masculine in the way that Will feels masculine, for Brilliancy has a gentleness and softness. But it feels masculine, or people associate masculinity with it, because of its connection with father. And also partly because it is not exactly a fluffy heart quality, which is usually connected with femininity.

In some universal sense, if you divide essential aspects into masculine and feminine, you may make Brilliancy into a masculine quality; but that doesn't mean it belongs only to men. On a universal level, masculine and feminine have nothing to do with men and women, have nothing to do with genitals or gender. They're just different ways of classifying qualities.

In the religious traditions, essential aspects are divided into masculine and feminine in order to go along with the conventional understanding. Because most minds think that the masculine is a particular way and the feminine is another way, the traditions tend to divide qualities into masculine and feminine. But that doesn't mean that masculine qualities are only for men and feminine ones are only for women. Love, for instance, is considered a feminine quality, but it doesn't mean only women can experience Love. Will is a masculine quality, but that doesn't mean only men can experience Will. So each human being, man or woman, can experience equally all the masculine and feminine qualities. From the perspective of this division, Brilliancy has a sense of being masculine.

The way I see Brilliancy as masculine—and this is different from the golden Merging Essence aspect, which is more feminine—is that I see that feminine qualities have to do with beauty. The sense of beauty is connected with the feminine. The masculine qualities have to do with majesty, the sense of majesty. So Brilliancy, when it is present in consciousness, gives a sense of majesty, of royalty, which is not exactly the same thing as beauty. Beauty and majesty are two complementary qualities that are manifestations of the richness of Being.

One of the ways of experiencing Brilliancy is the sense of majesty, regardless of whether you are a man or a woman—gender doesn't matter when it comes to experiencing Brilliancy or its majesty. Both queens and kings have majesty, for example. The sense of majesty has the qualities of expansion and radiance. So some traditions—the Sufi tradition, for example—don't call qualities masculine and feminine; they call them the qualities of majesty and beauty. They don't get into the question of male and female at all.

Brilliancy is the most majestic of all the aspects, regardless of whether they are classified as feminine or masculine. The sense of brilliance and majesty transcends the sexes and sexual differences; Essence is beyond physiological differences—it is as simple as that. Brilliancy can go into the genitals, whether male or female, and give them each a different sense. When Brilliancy engorges the genital region, the woman will become more feminine and the man will become more masculine. Its presence will give the feminine more intensity, more power, more strength, more expansion, more aliveness, and more ecstasy.

In the head and upper part of the body, Brilliancy feels more like majesty. When it gets into the pelvis and genitals, the sense there is more of ecstasy—intense ecstasy, overwhelming ecstasy—regardless of whether you are making love or not. When it gets in that area, it is activated in such a powerful way that the pleasure becomes intense to the point of overwhelming ecstasy. It also makes the genitals feel clean. A lot of the time, people have the sense that the genitals are dirty or not so pure because of all the prohibitions everybody has regarding them. But when Brilliancy enters there, they feel really clean; everything feels immaculately clean and graceful.

Have you seen that movie *Cocoon?* Remember the light and radiance streaming out when those extraterrestrials pulled off part of their artificial skin? Just imagine somebody pulling down their pants and light comes out, just like in the movie. [*Laughter and chuckles*] That is what Brilliancy can do to your experience of your sexual area, regardless of your sex.

12

Meeting Seven

☙

The meeting began with a meditation.

Today we will review and look further at the qualities of the aspect of Brilliancy so that we can get a more complete picture of what we are working with. I have talked about Brilliancy in terms of intelligence. *Brilliancy* is a phenomenologically descriptive term, and *intelligence* is a functionally descriptive one. And then there is the actual experience, the direct and immediate experience of being the Brilliancy. What is that like?

It is true that Brilliancy is a quality that adds brilliance and brightness, which makes all the essential manifestations and capacities shine and expand. But that is not the same thing as actually being this aspect oneself. Brilliancy gives brilliance to everything; and we can say that the brilliance we see anywhere comes from Brilliancy. But Brilliancy is itself concentrated brilliance, brilliance that exists on its own instead of being the brilliance of anything. It is just the existence of pure Brilliancy.

This is very hard to imagine, for nothing in nature exists like that. If you see a color that is brilliant, it is the brilliance of that color, for brilliance in nature is not a color on its own. It is a characteristic of color but not one of the colors. So we see it as a characteristic of something else; we don't see it as an actual existence, as something that exists on its own, as an independent presence. So nowhere in nature do we find Brilliancy on its own, self-existing.

If we remain with the normal view of brilliance, we will not recognize what Brilliancy is. In its pure form, Brilliancy is a presence that not only is brilliant but, more important, is itself the presence of brilliance. That is a very hard thing to imagine when you haven't really experienced it. You may have some perception of what Brilliancy is if you look at a lake or an ocean at a time when the sun is shining on the waves. It can look as though there are pools of liquid brilliance. Notice that sometimes? It's not like something is reflecting brilliantly; it's as if there are drops of brilliance, pure and concentrated liquid brilliance. Pools of it. That's more how Brilliancy actually appears in essential experience.

Brilliancy is. The radiance is substantial. In other words, Brilliancy can be experienced as a substance that is made out of pure concentrated brilliance. It is a powerful, substantial presence; it is a thereness. It has an ontological quality to it, just like any manifestation of Being. It is as much there as your body is there.

Brilliancy can also be seen to be the first manifestation of Being, of consciousness, and of Essence—in fact, of any existence. More accurately, from Brilliancy come all the various qualities of Essence: Love, Compassion, Will, Strength, Peace, and so on—all of these manifestations are differentiations out of that initial Brilliancy. What this means is that this aspect of Being, in its purity, has in its potential all of the differentiated qualities. The different qualities are not explicitly differentiated in Brilliancy itself; they are undifferentiated potentials in its presence. It doesn't look as if green and blue and red and yellow were all mixed together; it's more like white light before it is diffracted into its various colors by a prism.

This means that all the qualities of Essence, all the aspects, are existing in potential in Brilliancy. So if something is blocking the presence of Brilliancy, it will become harder for the aspects to manifest. It's like Brilliancy is the basis—the ground, the source, the original substance, the original manifest consciousness—of all the aspects of Being, and at a deeper level it is the ground and source of everything.

Brilliancy is pure intelligence, before it has become any specific kind of intelligence. It is raw intelligence, intelligence without content. It's not intelligent about this or that, or for this or that; it's just the very substance and existence of intelligence itself. Intelligence can exist as a living force on its own, not yet used for anything or by anything, not yet differentiated into one thing or another, not yet flowing into one capacity or another. So when intelligence is existing on its own, abiding in its own quality, without being used for anything, it is Brilliancy.

Seeing and understanding that Brilliancy is the aspect of intelligence will bring many insights, many understandings. It will reveal to us significances that we haven't seen yet. Because all aspects are potentially present in it and can differentiate out of it, Brilliancy provides us with a specific capacity. And that is the capacity of synthesis.

So Brilliancy is the archetype, or the prototype, of the synthetic force. The presence of Brilliancy in the consciousness will bring about the capacity to synthesize experience. Synthesis is very much needed, as we know, for functioning—for things like integration, wholeness, bringing things together, development, all of that. And this capacity for synthesis that our mind has, that our heart has, that our consciousness has, comes originally from the Brilliancy aspect because this aspect is itself a synthesis, a synthesis even before differentiation. Because it is present before differentiation, and differentiation can come out of it, Brilliancy provides the capacity to synthesize perception, to synthesize experience, to synthesize understanding, in whatever areas synthesis is needed.

Everything is there in Brilliancy without any sign of differentiation, so the synthesis here is absolute, complete; there is no sign of discrimination or of separating one thing from another. The unification is absolute and makes the capacity of synthesis amazing, tremendous.

The capacity of synthesis that arises here is not a function of taking various elements and putting them together but of recognizing how they are not different. It is seeing the unity in the diversity—seeing directly that the various elements in a situation are one—by discovering the place where they are not differentiated. It is a very organic way of synthesizing. That is why when some people ask me, "Isn't the Diamond Approach an integration of the spiritual and the psychological?" I say, "No, I don't see it that way. That doesn't make sense. It's not a putting together of the psychological and the spiritual. The way I see it is that the spiritual isn't separate from the psychological; there is just one thing. And that is reflected in this path." If you look with the eye of Brilliancy, you see that they are really one thing, not two things put together. They are not synthesized in that way. At the core, at the root, they are one.

This fundamental synthesis can happen in any field, in any area, anywhere. For example, when you are exploring your experience of your relationship with your father, Brilliancy makes it easy to see the connections, how things fit and relate to each other, because the tendency of Brilliancy is to take you to the place where the various elements are really one. That has the effect on your consciousness of making it easier for you to see connections and relationships, synthesis and integration, oneness and unity. So the influence of Brilliancy on your consciousness is to bring things together.

So now let's look at the direct and immediate experience of being Brilliancy and what that's like. If at any moment you are experiencing yourself as Brilliancy, we can see that this implies that all the aspects are there, although there is only Brilliancy. You don't see red or green or yellow; the experience is as if they are all there at the same time, simultaneously. They are all there without really being there. And the result is that you do not feel that anything is missing. In other words, to *be* Brilliancy means that absolutely nothing is missing; everything is there. There is absolutely no gap in the experience of Brilliancy. Yet it's not like you could say, "There is this and this and this. No, you can't say that because there isn't this and this and this. There is just the pure immediacy of Brilliancy, and that Brilliancy is you.

So experientially, the state of synthesis means a sense of no gap. Nothing is missing. The way it is recognized in terms of affect is a sense of completeness, absolute completeness, a sense that "I am complete." Usually, we don't know what it means to be complete. We have never felt being complete in a real way. Completeness is a very rare perception. To know it, one has to actually *be* the aspect of intelligence, be the Brilliancy, and be it completely. It is not, "I'm experiencing it, tasting it, feeling it, using it," and so on. No. That kind of experience means there is a sense of incompleteness. The completeness happens when the person totally settles into the actual aspect of Brilliancy. The completeness cannot be described in words.

It can only be contrasted to other kinds of experiences. In completeness, there is no need, no wanting, no desire, and no interest. There is no movement and no impulse toward movement of any kind out of the completeness because nothing is missing. There is not even curiosity; there is no stirring at all in the mind. And completeness is not a collection of parts but a seamless presence. It is a beingness that is a sense of amazing purity and innocence, radiance and brilliance. Its texture is a sense of smoothness, delicacy, exquisiteness, and brightness. A completeness that defies description, really.

So we want to explore this quality of completeness. You realize completeness just like you realize any other aspect: by dealing with its absence, which is incompleteness. The normal human experience is more like that—incomplete. But here by "incomplete" I don't mean "deficient." It's not like I'm feeling, "Oh, I'm castrated" or "I don't have strength; I'm weak." Those particular deficiencies will feel like an incompleteness, but I mean here the more specific state of *being* incomplete, without something in particular being missing. The incompleteness here is not just feeling one of the holes. I am talking about the hole of completeness. Right? If you think of completeness as an actual aspect on it's own, then there's a hole—the absence of completeness—that will feel like incompleteness. It's like what's missing is not strength or this or that. What's missing is completeness. You feel incomplete and you don't know what to do about it.

And that's really the background of everyone's experience, for everybody is feeling in some way incomplete; but usually we don't differentiate that state of incompleteness. For a while at the beginning of our work, we deal with the particular deficiencies of the differentiated aspects: "Oh, I'm weak," "Oh, I am worthless," "Oh, I am unlovable," and so on. And these are true deficient states. However, the sense of incompleteness comes from the deeper state of the absence of completeness itself. Our mind cannot conceive of that at the beginning of our work, so we look for and find something that is missing. But we can deal with the underlying state only by dealing with the root of the problem—which is the sense of incompleteness itself—only by dealing with the incompleteness, without looking for a scapegoat in one of the aspects. We can discover that there is simply an incompleteness there. It might feel like something is missing, a lot is missing, or everything is missing, but usually it's just more a sense of "I'm incomplete; for some reason, I'm incomplete."

Now, as is usual with any deficiency, the mind or the ego makes all kinds of attempts not to experience it. So there is a tendency to fill the hole or cover up the hole of incompleteness. We do that by taking actions within our mind, our feelings, and in the world physically, by doing all kinds of things to try to feel complete, to bring about completeness. Some people may say, "Well, I'm not complete until I have my ideal mate," right? That's one of the beliefs: If I find my ideal mate, I'll be complete. They think that this single aspect will make them feel complete if it's there. But that really won't do it. Or some people say, "Well, if I just have strength, I will be complete; if I'm really smart enough, I'll be complete; if this or that, then I'll have a sense of completeness in my life." People do all kind of things to try to not feel the sense of incompleteness. They do whatever they think will give them the sense of completeness.

So there are basically two ways of avoiding the sense of incompleteness. One is to cover up or avoid the incompleteness. The other is to try to create a sense of completeness, to get a fake sense of completeness. So to really be able to confront the existential depth of incompleteness, we have to see the ways we cover up our incompleteness and the ways we try to get a sense of completeness.

So that's what we will do now. We will do an exploration, an in-depth exploration. You need to be as sincere and as honest and truthful with yourself as you can. You are exploring the strategies—inner and outer—you use to cover up incompleteness or try to gain completeness, regardless of how gross or subtle, direct or indirect. You want to see as many of those ways as possible.

S: I have a question. You said it wasn't like filling up a specific hole of an essential aspect.
AH: Yes.
S: That might still come up, though.
AH: That might still come up, yes. Don't try to differentiate between these two in this exercise. Just see how you cover up the sense of incompleteness, how you try to be complete—all the activity that your ego does.

After the exercise, the students reassemble.

S: I saw real clearly that I've been looking for what I didn't get from my father in these mentor relationships; they're always male, like with a boss. Somehow I work myself into being some kind of apprentice. It came up in our monologue that there's this feeling that it's something behind you. For me, it was especially true. When I had that sense of support and guidance from behind, I had this sense of strength that I could take on almost anything, you know, tackle things I would never attempt to do usually. The last year and a half, there's been an absence of that, and I feel real lost and like there's no energy. I can't summon the part of myself that can perform, achieve, be effective in the world. I saw so clearly that when I have that support, then I have a sense that I can do anything. But when the situation changes, then I lose it. It's so abrupt.

AH: So when no one is backing you up, you don't have support. How do you feel that lack of support in the back at those times?

S: I feel like I don't sit straight. There's a collapsed feeling, and a lot of vulnerability.

AH: You feel that now at the back?

S: I feel like wanting to collapse, and a sort of shakiness inside. It just seems like the core of the incompleteness.

AH: So how does your back feel at this moment?

S: It feels like there's some tension there.

AH: So you don't feel that it's support, or what?

S: No, I don't feel the support.

AH: What's that like, feeling no support at the back?

S: Funny, I feel there's no support in the back, but I feel more jelly-like in the front.

AH: I see, so you feel jelly-like in the front when you have no support in the back.

S: It's in my abdomen.

AH: I see, you become jelly-like when you don't have a firm structure to function.

S: Right.

AH: So feel the jelly-likeness. See what that's like. [*Pause*] What's it like to feel the jelly?

S: It feels all mushy, but in the center I'm holding on, right at my solar plexus.

AH: I see. So you don't want it to be completely mushy.

S: I guess not.

AH: Do you know why? It's scary or what?

S: Yeah. It's a sense that I'll just completely become a puddle—go splat or something.

AH: There will be a big puddle?

S: Yeah.

AH: So let's see what that's like. It might not be as bad as you think. You never know how things happen these days. [*Laughter*] It is hard to tell sometimes what's bad and what's good.

S: I collapse and I want to slump.

AH: Let's experiment. See what happens if you cross your legs; sit cross-legged with a straight back. Yeah, stay like that.

S: I feel that same tightness that goes all the way through.

AH: Goes all the way through?

S: It feels sort of like that, yeah.

AH: All the way to the back, you mean?

S: Yeah, and my lower back too, a lot.

AH: And the general feeling in the belly?

S: It's not there.

AH: It's not there now. Just the tightness. How do you feel in general?

S: I feel dizzy in my head. I still feel tightness in the lower body.

AH: How does your back feel? Does it feel collapsed now? Feel your spine; how does your spine feel?

S: I feel stronger when I lean up against the couch. When it's just me, I feel more like there's tension in the spine.

AH: So you become aware of the spine. What's the sense that you have?

S: It feels like it should be—I mean, my idea is that it should be straight and strong.

AH: And it doesn't feel that way?

S: No, it feels like it could just bend that way.

AH: So feel that, feel that tendency. Let that happen.

S: Now I feel this tightness definitely in my throat.

AH: Uh-huh. Just keep feeling the spine, that tendency in the spine to bend and not be straight.

[*Pause*]

S: I feel a little fear.

AH: Okay, let the feeling come. Let's find out what the fear is about.

[*Pause*]

S: It's like falling.

AH: Uh-huh. Okay, let's see what happens. If you fall, where will that take us?

S: It feels like falling into nothing.

AH: And what happens when you fall into nothing?

[*Pause*]

S: I feel shaking, trembly, definitely not scary anymore.

AH: So it's okay if you fall into nothing?

S: Well, usually it's not; but the way I feel right now, it's more like parachute jumping. I feel like there is a parachute there.

AH: Uh-huh. You're floating down.

S: More than the way I usually experience falling. I have dreams about that.

AH: I see, about falling.

S: But it's fast falling.

AH: Now roll your eyes. [*Pause*] What are you experiencing now, in the solar plexus?

S: A lot of fear and nauseousness right in there.

AH: So it seems that in not holding the solar plexus, you start experiencing fear. Does it open up when you feel the fear?

S: Still feels kind of contracted. I mean, I feel that a lot.

AH: Is it okay to feel that fear?

S: Yeah, sort of. It is still like a knot. And I feel space around my head. But it's still a knot.

AH: So see what happens when you feel the fear. See what the fear will do when you stay with it, when you let that happen.

S: I just start to feel more sick. Fear and sickness in the stomach.

AH: Is that fear about something in particular? You were talking about support and its absence.

S: Well, I think it is about having to be in the world without support. And using false support.

AH: And what is your experience when you feel the false support?

S: That's kind of what I was feeling. The only thing I'm feeling right now is just that knot.

AH: Just the knot.

S: And I feel lighter in the head, with a feeling of emptiness coming down into the head.

AH: So maybe there is a resistance against the emptiness coming down? What will happen, I wonder, if you let it come down?

S: I feel like I'm rejecting this thing.

AH: Ah, I see. Well, just be aware of it. We don't know what it's about yet. Might not even be a knot. [*Pause*] What happens when you just sense it, without doing anything to it? You can be aware of the rejection and all the other reactions to it.

S: It seems to be more on the left, moving to the left and deeper inside.

AH: Interesting. Yeah. It's an interesting knot that moves to the left side and hangs out. Knots usually don't do that, so it might be much more than just a knot. [*Pause*] What's it like?

S: There's kind of a lump in my throat that goes with it.

AH: How do you feel emotionally?

S: Nervous.

AH: Nervous? Not aware of any tears?

S: My eyes feel kind of sad. [*Pause*] And I actually feel kind of sad.

AH: See what the sadness is about. [*Pause*] What does the sadness seem to be about?

S: Has to do with needing my father.

AH: What about needing him?

S: Well, he wasn't around very much, and I was supposed to not have any need for him.

AH: I see, it wasn't okay to feel you needed him.

S: That was being a pain in the ass to him.

AH: So you were supposed to just do it on your own and swallow your need. How do you feel when you let the feeling happen?

S: [*Sighs tearfully*] I feel real hot.

AH: Good. What do you feel besides heat?

S: I had to handle everything on my own. I felt small, so I learned to be in control.

AH: In control?

S: Just for putting so much on me. It was tough.

AH: Expecting you to handle things when you couldn't?

S: He didn't handle what he was supposed to handle. I wasn't supposed to have needs.

AH: I see. You weren't supposed to need him.

S: Right.

AH: How about now?

S: Feel kind of a hungry feeling.

AH: Yeah. There's more than needing here—it's like a hunger. Okay, feel that, that hunger. See where that hunger takes you.

S: It's like just wanting to have him somehow.

AH: Um-hmm, yeah. So strong wanting, strong hunger to have him.

S: I wanted him so much.

AH: Now hunger, what does that mean? When you are feeling the hunger, how do you feel inside you?

S: It feels more physical than emotional. I feel my stomach and esophagus a lot.

AH: Right. It's like physical hunger. So what's happened to the lump now?

S: Relaxed now.

AH: So that lump, maybe, just had hunger inside it. What do you feel inside the stomach?

S: Feels like, ah, I want to fill it.

AH: Right, it's empty. It's like an emptiness wants to take something and put it there, right? Like it's hard to tolerate that emptiness. Need to be filled.

S: Yeah, if it could grab something, it would, you know?

AH: Yeah, your stomach wants to grab things.

S: Yeah.

AH: Um-hum. Those are pretty early needs. Now if you feel the emptiness, the hungry emptiness, and let that expand, see what happens.

S: Um, I feel a little shaky around the knees.

AH: Knees shaky. So if you have your father, you feel full. If you're empty like this, you feel shaky and needy, right?

S: I feel like I can't do it myself. What I would say is, "I can't do it myself."

AH: Yeah. So that's what you were defending against, that you can't do it yourself. Now if you look into that emptiness, what is it like? You're looking outside, wanting to fill it. If you look inside it, what do you experience?

S: Tendency is to go out.

AH: The tendency is to want to go out?

S: Yeah.

AH: How about if you feel the hunger and don't do anything about it? Just continue to be aware of that feeling of hunger.

S: It's a real powerful feeling, you know.

AH: Yeah, powerful. [*Pause*] What's it like now?

S: It just feels real, like I have to have it to live.

AH: Yeah. You have to fill yourself, to be able to do that. Sort of desperate.

S: Yeah. And it kind of feels like a big part of me died.

AH: You say a big part of you died. Which part? What's it like?

S: I was going to say "the alive part."

AH: Yeah. This part seems to be pretty alive, doesn't it? What do you experience now?

S: I'm feeling a little repulsed by my hunger.

AH: I see. So it's not okay to feel needy that way. What's bad about it?

S: It's like exposing that I want something.

AH: What's bad about that?

S: That was the surest way not to get it.

AH: I see, so if you really want it, you are not going to get it.

S: Yeah.

AH: So, better not show that you want anything.

S: Yeah. It's like that exposure makes me feel real vulnerable, like something bad's going to happen.

AH: I see. Well, what kind of bad thing will happen?

[*Pause*]

S: I don't know. It's that whole parental technique of, you know, "If you cry I'll give you something to cry about."

AH: I see. You'll get punished. You'll get punished for wanting and needing. So no wonder you hide that part of you.

[*Pause*]

S: Yeah, this feels real risky.

AH: To want, to need, is real risky—you expose yourself.

S: [*Sighing, crying*] It sort of seems like lots of pain. I feel hurt and hot.

AH: Feels hurt and hot. Good. You are feeling your hurt. So stay with the hurt. See where that will take us.

S: It's sort of a feeling that my needs are way too big. And it takes a lot to cover them up.

AH: Sure, it takes a lot to cover them up. So what will happen if you don't cover them up?

S: I guess I just feel a fear of attack.

AH: So it seems you are afraid of showing that you want and need something from your dad. So was it your father who attacked you? Or was it both parents?

S: My mother was more of the attacker; my father withdrew at such times.

AH: So she'd attack you and he'd leave. Great deal, eh?

S: My dad was pretty absent. [*Laughs*]

AH: How's your back feel now?

S: More normal. I'd like to stop now.

AH: Okay.

After a pause, another student begins to work.

S: I've been experiencing for the past couple of days a feeling that has to do with my genitals. I got to experience myself yesterday as vital, juicy, and full. And it feels to me that that was rejected by my dad. From then on, I took to avoiding him.

AH: Um-hum.

S: How that manifests is through giving up intimate relationships. Being unemotional became a way of dealing with it. It's been difficult for me to feel my feelings of wanting to be as big as him, and as powerful and smart, and compete with him, and so on.

AH: What is it you're experiencing now?

S: I feel fear.

AH: Fear.

S: Part of what I did to be complete is to know. Knowing became a way of being strong, and not needing. To need meant I wasn't strong, not a man.

AH: So for you to ask for help is some kind of castration.

S: Yeah.

AH: So what do you feel in the genitals now?

[*Pause*]

S: I feel like I don't have any juice.

AH: Okay. So what is that like? Is it okay to feel that, or is there a reaction to it or what?

S: It feels really empty.

AH: Empty.

S: I feel scared and lost. Like I need to come up into my head. I feel too afraid to stay in the genitals. But I am feeling them, and there is emptiness there instead of genitals.

AH: So feel the emptiness itself. [*Pause*] What happens when you stay with the emptiness?

S: I feel like I want to be in there because it feels really expansive. But then I get scared away and start going into my head.

AH: What scares you away?

S: It's tied into my very aliveness. It's like if I'm more alive than Dad, then it is dangerous.

AH: So you are scared of being more alive. With that expansion, you are more alive, and then you are scared of daddy? What will happen?

S: He'll reject me, he'll hate me. It's like I'll lose hope of any softness between us.

AH: So for there to be softness between you, you have to push away your aliveness.

S: Yeah, or keep it hidden.

AH: Now roll your eyes. [*Pause*] What about now? What are you experiencing?

S: Well, I'm shaking. And all of me feels empty right now. I feel like a penis-shaped shell; it's real hard, and the rest of me is void, vacant. There's nothing substantial.

AH: Now the shell, is it open at the bottom?

S: Yeah.

AH: How about the top?

S: No.

AH: That's why it's penis shaped. So that shell, you feel it's you?

S: It feels like what I needed to be, for survival.

AH: This is what you needed to be, okay. So that's how you survived with your father. If you are just aware of it, it's an empty shell. So let yourself be aware of the shell and the emptiness at the same time. Not need to make a judgment one way or the other.

[*Pause*]

S: I feel that the emptiness fills up with presence and, ah, the shell breaks apart.

AH: What kind of presence? What does it feel like? [*Pause*] Do you feel it all the way through?

S: Yeah. It feels real whole. Solid.

AH: Um-hum. So now you don't feel you need that shell?

S: I feel flexible.

AH: So the rigidity is gone here. It's more a flexible presence.

S: Full and flexible.

AH: Does that feel more like you than the shell?

S: Oh yes.

AH: Is it okay to be this way?

S: Um, right now it is. From time to time.

AH: [*Chuckles*] From time to time, eh?

S: Not when I need to be in the world and get by, doing what I need to do.

AH: Why not? I mean, does it feel that you can't be there in the world with this?

S: Like I can have it, but I need the shell to be in the world.

AH: I see, you need the shell to be in the world. [*Pause*] So what happens now in the genitals?

S: Relaxed and angry.

AH: Angry. Interesting.

S: I have a feeling like they're inadequate.

AH: Oh, you feel your genitals are inadequate?

S: Yeah, that's why they are angry—because they feel that.

AH: Uh-huh. What are they angry about? Angry because they're inadequate?

S: Because they don't like to believe that.

AH: Oh, they don't like to believe they're inadequate. But do they feel they're inadequate now?

S: Some.

AH: Now, the presence, does it go there or not?

[*Pause*]

S: Yeah, it does, and when it does they feel like what you described last night, about Brilliancy.

AH: Um-huh, I see. Bright genitals.

S: Immaculate. Healthy.

AH: Healthy. So when the flow goes into the genitals, you feel immaculate, healthy. How do you feel in general?

[*Pause*]

S: Like I'm going to explode. Fiery, like lava flow.

AH: Fiery. Things getting hot. Things were clean, now getting hot. Clean and hot. If you look at the lava now, it is bright and fiery; it gets real hot, changes color, right? What color is it when it's real hot?

S: White and bright.

AH: Right. Gets bright. Means more intensity. Very good.

S: Thank you.

AH comments: *This student was afraid to be in his genitals and to feel the fullness and aliveness of his presence there, because of his relation to his father; but he also needed to be strong and masculine for his father. So he developed a character of being strong and masculine but rigid and unfeeling. This structure of his personality is not real but is what he had to be for his father. During his work with me, he experienced this structure as a hard shell in the shape of a penis. His head, which represented knowing, was the tip of the penis shell. By recognizing that it is what he needed to be in his relation to his father, he realized its emptiness: that it is a made-up character, that it is unreal, and is devoid of reality.*

His act of being present with the emptiness of this shell—and his not going along with his judgments of it—transformed it into a clear spaciousness, which then became filled by the alive fullness that his father rejected in him. This fullness, which gave him the feeling of real completeness, was the presence of Brilliancy. His anger and indignation at his father for castrating him made the Brilliancy mix with the aspect of essential Strength. This mix appeared as a flow of lava, in the sense that it is hot, and white-red. The mix of Brilliancy and the red of essential Strength is the bigness and strength that he was trying to be for his father. Now it is real, because these are the true qualities of his own being.

The Brilliancy appeared with the qualities of purity and immaculateness. This is probably because he believed, as a result of his father's disapproval, that his genitals were impure. He did not explore this in his work with me, but it is very likely that these parts of his relation to his father and his sexuality will arise due to the immaculate state of Brilliancy in his genitals.

As happens frequently in the Diamond Approach, work on psychological issues leads to corresponding manifestations of Being; and then those qualities of Being push other issues and conditioned states that are related to them to the surface. It is also instructive to see the beauty and richness of Being as its aspects arise to heal the difficulties of the individual. Aspects and qualities arise to deal with the specific deficiencies and issues that are present, and their mix provides the exact state that the individual needs for the complete transformation of those deficiencies and issues.

13

Meeting Eight

☙

After the sitting meditation, AH asks the students to explore their attachment to the feeling of incompleteness. After the exercise, the students reassemble.

AH: So, any questions or comments?

S: One of the things that occurred to me is that it seems I have a feeling of wanting to protect my father. The more things I uncover about how he really was, the more I feel that I want to protect him. Feeling incomplete is the way I feel protected, I feel secure, which means that I wanted my father—but not the real one. But it feels secure: I feel protected; I feel comfortable. I don't want any change in that.

AH: So you're saying that being incomplete is having your father outside of you.

S: It is a twisted idea, but it seems like he's here, ah, protecting me, keeping me safe. It's like the best facsimile of father.

AH: Right.

[*Long pause*]

S: If I am complete, then I lose this feeling of protection and safety, although it is not all real.

AH: And what happened after you saw that?

S: A big sense of loss, because I realized that I have been protecting myself from seeing how he really was. He had good qualities and he made me feel protected; but he also lacked many things, which underneath made me feel quite unfulfilled and incomplete. Now I feel this incompleteness, but I also feel the loss.

AH: What do you feel you lost?

S: The image of my father. Also the feeling of protection. Now I only feel incomplete.

AH: And what happens when you stay with this feeling?

S: It is difficult. There is sadness, and a hurt, right at the bottom of my chest.

AH: What is the hurt like? Does it feel physical or emotional?

S: Both. It feels like a big wound, a gaping wound that hurts both physically and emotionally. But it is changing. [*Pause*] The wound is expanding, and it is becoming like some kind of a fountain in there.

AH: A fountain of what?

S: Some kind of a wonderful feeling. I feel both bright and whole. Nothing is missing.

AH: I see; you feel complete.

S: Something like that. Yes, complete. I don't need anything. The fullness and presence in the chest feels complete, like the presence of completeness.

AH: And who knows? Maybe as you stay with this presence, you might also feel protected, or whatever. Just stay with it, let it expand and reveal whatever it wants to be.

Another student begins to work.

S: A lot of what's been talked about brings up in me a feeling about the whole world. The whole world is incomplete—that's the way most of us live in it. It seems like it's always going to be that way. My parents were that way. And I'm thinking that if I work on myself, change some little part of the world, that's not enough. [*Pause*] So I'm real scared about that, and feeling that if there is going to be any change, I'm too little to do it. I can't do it. You know, I'm real nervous and scared right now.

AH: What are you nervous, scared about?

S: I guess it's probably a lot of things, but it seems it is such a big world and the forces and the things that can go wrong are so big and so invincible, just like my father.

[*Pause*]

AH: So you are saying you can't change your father?

S: That's true.

AH: So you're saying it doesn't matter how much you change—if your father doesn't change, it will still be scary.

S: Yeah. My father's not living anymore, but it seems that's the way the world is.

AH: Um-hmm. What's your concern about the world?

S: Well, it's partly that I'm scared of it and partly that I want us to make it better.

AH: How do you know that the world wants you to make it better? First you need to ask that. I don't try to make anybody better unless and until they invite me. Maybe you see it differently.

S: I've been wondering a lot in my work lately if what I'm doing is the right thing to do, because a lot of the legal system is like that. It takes a lot in the situation to try to change them or punish them.

AH: What do you think will happen if you don't try to change the world?

S: I guess I have a feeling that nothing will happen, everything will stagnate, everything will get dirty.

AH: In the world, right?

S: Yeah.

AH: What will happen to you then?

S: Well, I would feel useless, maybe.

AH: So you say that if you don't try to help, the world will stagnate, right? So the world is dependent on you helping it; otherwise, it's going to stagnate.

S: In a small part, I think that's true. That's how I feel.

AH: I know how you feel, and that's what I'm saying. We're trying to understand what makes you feel that way. So first we need to see what you feel. You somehow believe that the world is dependent on you for it not to stagnate, at least in a small measure. No? Now regardless of whether this is true objectively or not, we want to understand you here; we want to understand what the true basis of your feeling is. So when you feel that way, where do you think that comes from? How did you get to feel this way?

S: I think it comes from the environment where I grew up, where I felt like I had to be a certain way to keep things going.

AH: I see. That's how it was in your family?

S: That's how I felt it.

AH: So you felt you had to be a certain way to keep things going in the family.

S: Yeah.

AH: In what way?

S: I guess I felt like a peacemaker between my parents and my brothers. And like an organizer, keeping things going.

AH: I see. So that was your role in the family—to be the peacemaker.

S: I don't know how successful I was. Felt like I was under pressure.

AH: Uh-huh, to do this. How are you feeling now?

S: Less scared ... um ... more expanded.

AH: So it sounds from what you're saying that you had to take care of things in the family, in whatever way, so that you could be okay, for you to feel secure. So now you feel you have to do things about the world for you to feel secure. So what did it feel like in your family to have that role, to have the responsibility to keep things going? Do you like that role?

S: No. It's a lot of stress.

AH: How did it feel to you that you were in that position?

S: It's a lot of responsibility. It feels tense.

AH: So what did your father do then? That wasn't part of his job, to keep things going?

S: He didn't do it.

AH: Didn't? Why not?

S: He was a child, you know.

AH: So he was too immature to do that. So what did that make you feel?

S: Um, serious. Growing up before my time. Angry.

AH: What happened to your need for father?

S: In terms of priorities, it was not a high priority; so it never was satisfied.

AH: What do you mean it wasn't a high priority?

S: Well, I felt that some of the other things needed to be done more. It wasn't possible to satisfy all my needs.

AH: What other things needed more to be done?

S: To take care of things, to keep things going.

AH: That is understandable. You needed to survive and feel secure. But that does not change your emotional nature, does it? You were a child anyway. So what happened to the little kid inside? What does that little kid feel?

S: Angry.

AH: Mm-hmm. What else?

S: Hurt.

AH: What is it you feel hurt about?

S: For not having a father. It feels real sad.

AH: For not having a father. What happens when you feel that hurt or sadness? Where does it take you?

[*Pause*]

S: I feel the shakes.

AH: Shakes? Interesting. So what happens when you go along with the shakes?

S: I feel lighter, brighter.

AH: Well, that's important. So, you see, it was important to see the child inside who needed a daddy, because that part felt deprived. Opening to the needs of this child allows you to experience the good father you didn't have, which is this bright presence. Okay.

After a pause, another student begins to work.

S: The last exercise about the incompleteness brought up tremendous sadness for me. The sadness is around this feeling I've had with you. I see now that it's about Father and the whole thing with wanting him and identifying with him, in these issues. And the feeling of sadness and hopelessness is about ever having real completeness. It seems that I've never really had completeness, that most people don't; and when it's there, it's real fleeting.

AH: Mm-hmm. So there's hopelessness and sadness about never having it. What is it you feel now?

S: I feel kind of empty, and I feel the sadness about that. It's tricky. When I really feel emptiness, I feel sad, and then I usually avoid it. But when I am just being in touch with it, like now, I feel overwhelmingly sad.

AH: Sure. So now it seems you are able to feel the sadness and the emptiness, without pushing them away. Let's see now, when you feel those, where will they take us, what will they tell us? What happens when you don't push the feelings away?

S: I feel I'm about four years old now. I feel young and kind of crying, wailing out, and just wanting something. I'm not sure what, but it just feels like a very small child.

AH: Very small, yeah. How are you feeling right now?

S: I feel nervous and there's shaking in the hands.

AH: Um-hmm. What's the four-year-old feeling, what's he crying about?

S: Feels like he wants to be recognized, wants recognition, wants to be seen. He's not seen.

AH: I see, by whom?

S: Mommy and Daddy, especially Daddy.

AH: I see. Daddy isn't seeing you. Where is he?

S: He's around, but he's preoccupied with his own stuff, preoccupied with what he wants, doesn't really see me for who I am.

AH: And how does that feel to you?

S: Makes me feel sad and angry.

AH: Right. So when he doesn't see you for who you are, you start feeling angry and hurt. How about the emptiness? What is the emptiness like?

S: It feels like a dark cave. There's nothing to measure anything; it's just totally empty, black, scary. And there's an incompleteness and a hopelessness about it.

AH: Yeah. If you just feel the emptiness itself, and find out exactly what the emptiness is about, what does it feel like? I mean, not to focus on the reactions about it or to it—like the fear—but to let these be there and to feel the emptiness itself. What does it reveal to us?

S: There's an inadequacy that comes up about emptiness.

AH: I see. So it brings the feeling of inadequacy. What kind of inadequacy is it?

S: Feels like I should fill up the emptiness because it's empty, it's inadequate. Something is not right because it's empty.

AH: I see. So it shouldn't be empty, should be full, right?

S: Yeah, something, not empty.

AH: Not empty. The fact that it's empty is inadequate.
S: Yeah. Exactly.
AH: But when you sense the emptiness itself, does it feel inadequate? Or is that how you feel about it?
S: As I sense it, the emptiness itself does not feel inadequate; it seems it's my mind here that feels it is inadequate.
AH: I see, the mind says it's inadequate.
S: Yeah, just to feel emptiness is actually starting to feel okay.
AH: So the inadequacy is your mind's reaction to it.
S: Yeah.
AH: Very good. So now let's find out what the emptiness is without the mind's reaction. If we are really going to find out what it is, we have to see it on its own, without the mind saying it is this way or that way.
S: The emptiness now just feels like presence. It feels here. It's not black anymore. There's sort of a bluish haze, like a bluish white haze.
AH: Bluish white. Interesting.
S: And it feels present now. It just feels kind of present.
AH: Um-hmm. So more presence now, bluish white presence.
S: Doesn't feel quite like fear or any of that stuff. Just feels sort of here.
AH: It seems that by staying with the emptiness, without your taking the position of the reactions, you start to experience a certain kind of presence. Let's find out more about this sense of presence, the bluish white presence. Do you feel you're here?
S: Yeah.
AH: The question is whether you feel the presence as more like you or like something you feel.
S: No, it feels like me.
AH: Ah-huh. So that presence is more you.
S: Yeah.
AH: Do you like it? Do you like feeling yourself this way?
S: Yeah. Feels great right now.
AH: Mm-hmm. [*Pause*] So let's see what it's like to be that presence.
S: Feels full, feels totally adequate. Feels like a source of energy and power within. It's exhilarating. And feels like I don't have to do anything or go anywhere.

AH: Right. Just being here is fine. Don't have to prove anything, do anything, go anywhere. Just you as you are. Where do you feel it in your body? Feel the body.

S: I feel it especially in the solar plexus and the chest.

AH: And the chest, yeah. So when you open your eyes, how does the room or other people seem to you, while feeling that presence?

S: I feel content to be here with other people. It just feels sort of whole and complete.

AH: Complete, right. And do you feel contact with people?

S: I feel a presence, like a connection.

AH: Presence and connection. Well, that sounds nice. The presence itself becomes a connection, a contact.

AH Comments: *Not having his father in the way he needed him made this student feel empty and inadequate. His work focused on the inadequacy of fathering in early childhood, of not being seen and appreciated for being himself. This deficient state of emptiness and inadequacy was healed when a quality of his being revealed itself as the presence of fullness and adequacy, which is the exact opposite of emptiness and inadequacy. This quality is the aspect of the Personal Essence, which feels like a whole, contented, and adequate sense of well-being.*

This student can continue to explore his relationship with his father, which may take him to Brilliancy, which is the quality that he needed from his father. His work here focused more on what the absence of this quality did to him—how it made him feel inadequate. Beyond that, however, there is an object relation with his father: namely, that he internalized the image of his father, the image of himself, and the emotional tone between the two. He ended up focusing on one part of the object relation—the inadequacy inherent in his self-image—and that led him to the quality of Essence that heals deficiencies. Dealing with the father image will lead him to some manifestation of Brilliancy. He can also work on the totality of the object relation as a unit with his father, and this will take him to yet another quality of Being that is usually related to the emotional tone of the particular object relation unit.

It is important to see here that the resolution is not only a matter of reliving the past and uncovering the unconscious material. Most im-

portant for us, it is also the arising of the qualities of Essence, which are actually the healing and transformative agents. These are the qualities of one's true nature that one lost contact with as a result of these early difficulties and conflicts.*

After a pause, another student starts working.

S: I've been wanting to work, but I've had a lot of difficulty in finding something to work on. It's like all the stuff I want to work on keeps eluding me. It's like trying to grab an eel out of a bucket of eels or something—hundreds of things keep going around all the time. It's like I want it all, you know; I'd like to work on them all. And I also feel a lot of charge about working. And I don't exactly mean fear, although I feel a little fearful right now. I mean it is more of a hopeless attitude that it won't really make any difference. And also that I won't be understood, or be able to communicate—like I'll work and I'll end up after working feeling I didn't really say what I wanted to say, or I didn't really hear it right, or something of that sort. Over the weekend, I felt various charges about the whole thing being worked on with father, and yet I've had a lot of judgments about it. I feel a lot of resistance and I feel a lot of judgments about the resistance.

AH: Um-hmm.

S: And what little things I've got seem like nothing. It's like I'm trying to get something, you know.

AH: So you feel you're not going to be understood?

S: Yeah. And I also have a feeling that I can work better by not even being here, as if my best help comes from myself and not from you or the group anymore.

AH: Mm-hmm.

S: I've been doing that for the last several months. So I feel like withdrawing and just working by myself, which never worked in the past. But that's the feeling.

AH: Well, why not do both? Why not? Why does it have to be one or the other? It seems you feel hopeless about getting help.

---

* See *The Pearl Beyond Price* (1988).

S: Yeah.

AH: Or getting somebody to understand you. So where does that come from? What makes you feel that it's hopeless?

S: The only thing that comes up is that it gets to be a circular thing, and I feel like understanding can't take place, like real communication isn't possible—that somehow I won't be heard for what I'm trying to say, or I'll be misunderstood, or I won't say it. I won't be able to pin it down directly, like with the bucket of eels.

AH: Is that what stops you now?

S: The one right thing to work on won't come up, you know.

AH: Is that because you've had that kind of experience in the past? You were not understood? Like you tried in the past and it didn't work?

S: Well, I suppose it's happened with you once or twice. It felt that way.

AH: I see.

S: I'm not sure about before that.

AH: So you talked to me before and I didn't understand you.

S: Well, maybe you did, but . . .

AH: But you felt I didn't.

S: If you did, it didn't seem like it. It felt like you answered different questions than the ones I asked or something. Happened several times.

AH: Yeah, that is certainly possible. But let's explore it further. First I'd like to know what kind of things you felt at those times when I didn't understand you.

S: I felt misunderstood, hurt, and angry.

AH: I see. I am sorry for causing you hurt. It is possible that I did. We can focus on those instances when I did not understand you, to see what actually happened. Or we can go about it differently, and see whether this kind of situation happens only with me, or whether it has a more general character.

S: Well, I have a basic experience that I'm not understood, in general.

AH: I see. The way you felt with me?

S: Very similar. I usually feel that I'm different or just made different, or something, from other people.

AH: In what way? Maybe it's true, so I want to know in what way.

S: Well, I'll just say what comes to my mind: I come to feel very sensitive, like I'm overly, overly emotionally sensitive. So that feels different, although when I look around, I see other people who are as well. That's how I feel.

AH: So you get easily affected emotionally?

S: Yeah, I guess. Yet I don't feel like a weepy kind of guy or something.

AH: Things touch you easily?

S: It seems that way. I feel like I usually have some kind of emotional charge, anger, or hurt or something.

AH: About things people say, mean, or do?

S: Or about the world, or about things I read in the paper. I read the paper in the morning, and I usually end up getting depressed or something.

AH: And what are you feeling now as we're talking?

S: I feel a lot of energy, mostly in my limbs, like I'd like to strike out—that's sort of what it feels like.

AH: Mm-hmm. You're feeling anger, like some kind of aggression?

S: Doesn't feel like anger, just feels like my arms want to strike out or something.

AH: Okay, let's see. Feel yourself striking out; see what that's like. I mean, you can do it with your arm. That way we'll see what the feeling is.

S: I'm afraid to do it.

AH: Okay. What is the fear about at the moment?

S: Well, I don't know.

AH: Does it have to do with how you feel about me?

S: I think so. I think I am afraid of you, especially that I think I feel angry at you.

AH: You think!

S: I am starting to feel hot. Well, I do feel some anger, and I want to strike out; but I get real scared. It's always been real difficult for me to work with anger.

AH: What's scary about feeling angry?

S: I feel like striking out, then I am scared I'll get struck back.

AH: Did that happen in the past?

S: Um-hmm.

AH: Who struck you back?

S: Oh, my father. I always felt wimpy around him. He was overbearing with me, and a couple of times I struck out at him; and one time he pounded me right back.

AH: So that really scared you? And now you are scared the same thing will happen with me.

S: This happened when I was about thirteen. I was getting to feel a little bit stronger. He unjustly struck me.

AH: How do you feel now when you remember that?

S: I feel a little stronger, you know, as if I could actually do something. In that incident, he chased me out of the house and I jumped, climbed up on the roof, and I was cursing at him and swearing at him. And what happened afterward was that I was made to apologize that I hurt him so bad. So I felt kind of guilty about hurting my father, you know, and I felt kind of enraged about it because I didn't feel it was an honest or just thing. No one ever listened to my side of the story. The overall feeling is of being a confined person.

AH: Part of the effect of that guilt is to feel you are being confined. It holds you back, probably. It's one of the things that hold you back.

S: Yeah—I can't act a lot of times. I'm frozen.

AH: Right. You are going to hurt somebody, and they're going to hit you back. There's guilt, and there's fear, right? Both feelings hold back the rage. Let's connect this with what you started working with. Did you feel your father understood you or not?

S: No, not at all. Utterly not.

AH: How do you feel about that?

S: Feel angry about it. I feel quite angry at him about it.

AH: Right.

S: Kind of vicious toward him actually.

AH: Yeah. So there's a lot of anger about not being understood. Sure makes a lot of sense. From the sound of what you are saying, he didn't understand you at all. It's not like sometimes he understood, sometimes he didn't.

S: Nothing, nothing.

AH: Nothing.

S: It's like he had a whole idea about something that didn't have anything to do with me, and that idea feels deadly to me. It feels like it kills me, killed me or something.

AH: When you feel the anger—and let it happen—what more does it reveal? Where does it take you?

S: In terms of concepts, or . . . ?

AH: Whatever—just feel the feeling. Does the feeling get more intense, does it change, does something else happen? What? We want to follow the unfoldment of your process.

S: Well, I've got the disease of the room—the shakes. [*Laughter*]

AH: Mm-hmm. It must be this house. [*Laughter*]

S: Feel hot, I feel hot in my clothes.

AH: Yeah, good.

S: You know, my chest is sweaty.

AH: Let's see what happens when you allow the heat. The more you allow the anger, the more there'll be heat. Shaking in the hand, that's fine. Seems to be a tremendous amount of anger that's been held for a long time, for many reasons.

S: Yeah. It's like I don't have any idea what to do with it. That's what I feel like.

AH: Let's see . . . what can you do with it right now? Just imagine yourself punching him, the way you wanted to. [*Pause*] Imagine yourself doing whatever you want to do, whatever comes.

S: I just feel sad now.

AH: So sadness arises after a while. Okay. Do you know what the sadness is about?

S: I feel very alone, real abandoned. Um, it's almost a feeling like there was an act of viciousness directed my way, like he actually wanted to kill me or harm me brutally or something.

AH: You are saying he hated you. Right? Is that what you feel, it was a hateful action? Sounds like you're saying he directed hatred toward you. Maybe that's how it feels. That probably would make you feel very lonely. Not to be understood, to be treated harshly like that would make you feel alone. I mean, your father is someone you usually go to for protection. He does the opposite of that. How do you feel now?

S: I'm shaking and sad and angry.

AH: Very good; you're letting your feelings be. So as the feelings emerge, the shaking starts, because it is just the release of all the holdings.

S: I think it was because he hated me that way, or it seemed like he did, that I felt weird around other people.

AH: I see. [*Pause*] What's happening now?

S: Same thing.

AH: Same thing continues. What do you feel in the chest?

S: Well, it feels shaky and hot and angry at the hurt.

AH: Now roll your eyes. [*Pause*] How about now—what are you experiencing?

S: Feels like everything kind of slowed down.

AH: Yeah. What does it feel inside?

S: Slower. It's like I can stay with it a little more.

AH: Stay with the feelings. Let's see how they unfold.

S: Like I can relax into it a little bit.

AH: So there's less shaking?

S: There's still shaking.

AH: Still?

S: Less. You know, I feel that kind of a shout inside of me said, "I don't need you."

AH: Right. Say that a few times.

S: I don't need you.

AH: Good. Again.

S: I don't need you.

AH: Good. Let the feeling come.

S: **I DON'T NEED YOU! I DON'T NEED YOU!**

AH: What's the feeling that goes with it?

S: Like I need you. [*Laughter*]

AH: That's interesting. Let's find out what that feeling is about.

S: I feel like I try to substitute it into myself, like being my own dad or something.

AH: Mm-hmm. But underneath that, there is still the need for Dad.

S: Oh, a lot, very much the need, just a real desire to melt into his arms and love him and have him love me.

AH: Um-hmm, right.

S: And have everything be forgiven and understood.

AH: Right. Understanding.

S: Talk to each other and stuff.

AH: Mm-hmm. Sure. So is it okay to feel that need, that wanting?

S: It's okay. I don't feel it real strongly. It's okay. In fact, that was one of my criticisms of my own work this weekend: that I didn't feel that need as much as I wanted to feel it.

AH: Do you feel any resistance against it now?

S: I think I'm resistant to it somewhat. I don't exactly feel it. What I'm starting to think is: This is hopeless; it's like getting ensnared in a thicket and I'll never work out of it. You know, like you'll just have to go on to somebody else or something.

AH: I don't get it. What's the problem? Sounds like everything is going fine.

S: Well, if you want to call it a problem, I feel a restlessly incomplete kind of feeling.

AH: Oh, I see. So you feel restlessly incomplete. Well, fine, let's investigate that; let's find out what that is about.

S: I bet it has to do a lot with my father because now it feels like I want something.

AH: So let's find out. If you let yourself feel the wanting, maybe the wanting will tell you what it is about. You said a minute ago that you feel hopeless about getting what you want, and that that was stopping you from feeling the wanting.

S: I also feel like I'm too demanding about what I want. Like what I'm asking for is too unreasonable or impossible, or something of that sort.

AH: Maybe it is and maybe not—we'll find out; we're willing to see. So you feel the wanting. What does the wanting say? What does it want?

S: I guess I still want my dad, or I want him to love me. That's what comes to my mind.

AH: Makes sense. Is it okay to feel that?

S: Yeah, it's okay. It feels empty in a way.

AH: Uh-huh. I see.

S: It doesn't get me anything.

AH: Well, maybe you are feeling the emptiness that's behind the wanting. If there was no emptiness, you wouldn't feel you want anything. So what does the emptiness feel like?

[*Pause*]

S: It's kind of faint, but it feels disorienting.

AH: Disorienting, I see.

S: Confusion.

AH: Confusion, okay. So disorientation, confusion, emptiness. What else?

S: Loss, sinking, falling away.

AH: Loss.

S: Alone.

AH: Alone.

S: Alone in the blackness.

AH: Yes, uh-huh.

S: There's an angry voice that comes down from above. It's like, "Fuck you, I don't want it anyway" or something like that. I want to be here.

AH: What is the here, the emptiness?

S: I don't really necessarily like it. It's just like the rebellious part of me is saying that so that I don't feel empty.

AH: So there's still anger.

S: Yeah. Still holding on to some outside object.

AH: That way you don't have to feel completely alone.

S: Yes.

AH: If you are angry at somebody, you can think of them, so there is an interaction going on, at least in your mind. You say there is an emptiness, feeling lost, alone. If that happens and you go with that, where does that take us? Can you stay with that state and not do anything about it?

S: Feels like I start to lose my mind—not in the sense of going crazy, just no mind.

AH: Right. I understand. So what does that feel like?

S: It's a relief. My mind feels like it let go of a burden.

AH: Uh-huh. It has.

S: My mind is always working and moving in crazy ways that don't mean much of anything. Feels like a relief so I can get some peace for a change.

AH: Yeah. So it's peaceful to lose the mind. And what happens to the emptiness now?

S: It's still empty.

AH: Yeah?

S: It's still empty and lacking.

AH: Does it still have those feelings of being lost and disoriented, and all that?

S: No.
AH: So those feelings are gone now?
S: Feels like a resting place, final rest.
AH: Yeah. So the emptiness is restful now. It doesn't have all these feelings that first came with it.
S: Yeah. No feelings. It's nice because it doesn't do anything. You get to just sort of hang out or something.
AH: Mm-hmm. It feels like a vacation.
S: Yeah. A well-needed vacation.
AH: The best vacation is the vacation from the mind. If your mind stops for a while that's the best vacation around—better than going anywhere.
S: Really is. It's just like being in the Caribbean.
AH: Yeah.
[*Pause*]
S: It almost feels like there's another little part of me, like a bubble that wants to pop and just kind of evaporate into the emptiness. Something left for me, you know. Would like to do that.
AH: Right. What happens when it does that?
S: Well, it feels like I have all the support that I ever wanted.
AH: Oh, interesting. So you start feeling support now.
S: Yes.
AH: Mm-hmm. Inner support.
S: Strange . . . you can't tell where it's coming from.
AH: Yeah. You just feel support. When you feel support, do you still feel the emptiness, or is it more a sense of presence?
[*Pause*]
S: Well, it's a funny thing. It's like an empty presence or something.
AH: Okay. Presence that is empty.
S: Yeah.
AH: Emptiness and presence are the same thing here, then.
S: Yes. That's what it feels like. It's a funny kind of emptiness because it's empty, and yet it's something.
AH: Yeah. Interesting, right? Empty but something.
S: There are no thoughts or emotions or efforts. There's no effort of any kind, yet something seems to be occurring, like support that supports the core of myself.

AH: Yeah, that's how Being usually functions. That's how Being is—nothing needs to be done, there's just a "thereness" there that makes things possible.

You usually think of support as doing something, but real support has nothing to do with that. It is an inner sense of solidity, of a solid ground within you that feels like support for being truly yourself. True support is our contact with a certain quality of our Being, which is an authentic sense of presence, which is beingness.

When this inherent inner support is not present in our experience of ourselves, we start to effort. Efforting becomes the ego's way of acquiring support or of supporting ourselves. The fact is that this efforting cuts us off from our true and essential support, which is complete effortlessness. Essential support is an aspect of Essence, so it is Being, but in a solid, firm, and strong way, the way a mountain is present.

It seems that you wanted support from your father; but due to the kind of relationship you had with him, you did not get it. And you also felt that you were not supposed to want it from him. But you knew you wanted to be seen and understood, implying the need for his support. The fact that you did not get him to support you to be yourself—by seeing, understanding, and loving you—means you became disconnected from your own innate support. So you had to go back, understand this part of your relationship to him, and feel the fear, anger, and hurt until you got to the need itself, the wanting. This then connected you to the lack of support itself, which revealed itself to be an emptiness.

The arising of a deficient emptiness indicates the lack of a quality of Being, of an essential aspect. Since this absent quality is essential support, Being first manifested in the peaceful and restful state. This is because you usually try to support yourself through effort—mostly mental and active effort—while real support is an effortless state of presence. So Being manifested in a quality that puts the mind to rest, that quiets the mind and empties the mind. This made it possible for you to recognize the quality of the true support that you needed from your father.

It is so wonderful to see the exquisite intelligence of the functioning of Being. Since what was needed was support—and your fake support is effort, and a mental effort at that—Being manifested in a state of peace and restfulness to eliminate the efforting. More specifically, it manifested in a state of mental peace that eliminated mental effort and activity. This made it possible for you recognize true support and for you to see how it is not an activity, and not an effort. It is presence, which at deeper dimensions of Essence is inseparable from emptiness.

It is important for all of us to appreciate here how his work started with a psychological constellation—the relationship with father—and that it unfolded naturally and spontaneously into the realm of Being, into the dimension of Essence. The resolution was essential, spiritual, and it happened after going through the deficient emptiness. The importance of the end result is not just the resolution of the particular issue—that of father's support—but is primarily the reconnection with our Being and the reowning of the essential and spiritual dimension of our humanity.

After a pause, another student starts to work.

S: I feel like with this weekend's work, I saw some huge possibilities of something. Aside from what we learned from this weekend, I feel right now that I've had enough; I've heard enough people follow the story with father. If anybody else says, "I feel hurt and rejected," or whatever all those things are, I am going to burst. I feel guilt because I relate to those things myself, and it's always been hard for me to work on my father because of the absence of the relationship. I feel the weekend is incomplete if I'm not heard personally, by you.

AH: Mm-hmm. Sounds good, go on.

S: Um, let me tell you *my* story. [*Much laughter*] I feel like puking; I've had enough of this. [*Laughter*] I feel, um, a real sharp—it wasn't a pain, but like a long, sharp needle went through my solar plexus.

AH: Um-hmm.

S: During the last exercise, about incompleteness—and also now—I feel a lot of tingling along the top of my head. And also a pulsating feeling right in here [*points to top of head*].

AH: How do you feel emotionally?

S: Emotionally, that part feels more mature. I said I've had enough of people's issues and my own issues about my father. It is true that it is very painful, all this rejection and abandonment. I feel I always felt that I had an enormous amount of responsibility—a burden was put upon me, of having a father who was absent. On top of that, he was very sick and never present. There's a sense of having to take care of him before anything else.

AH: Before you?

S: I traded my aliveness for his state. I never really consciously felt this, but I think it happened when he died. I felt the responsibility of his death very personally. That's why I could never deal with it.

AH: What do you mean, "the responsibility"?

S: Like maybe his death was caused by me, that I did something wrong.

AH: Oh, I see. So you believe it was your fault.

S: Mm-hmm. Yeah.

AH: I see. So you felt guilty about him dying.

S: I guess so. I really felt that way.

AH: Yeah.

S: I'm bad and wrong.

AH: So why do you think it was your fault? What did you do?

S: Well, it has to do with the way it was around the house; we had to be very careful and quiet.

AH: Mm-hmm.

S: And if anybody stood up to him, he would either get angry or strike them, usually my mother. There was a sense of it being a very dangerous place to be, a dark and heavy place. I felt I had to be that way, so quiet. So how can you be happy, nice, alive, and childlike when you have to be so quiet all the time? Then he died. I'm sure he never said that, but he may have.

AH: I see. So you felt because you were alive and all of that, you caused him to die.

S: Right.

AH: So your aliveness caused his death.

S: Yeah. I might have been too alive and too excited.

AH: I see, too excited.

S: Maybe I was too excited, but he was dying—kind of, anyway.

AH: So how do you feel now that you think of it?

S: Just a lot of that pain. Lots of tingling too, as I feel the pain.

AH: Pain and tingling, very good. Let the tingling happen—tingle, tingle.

S: [*Giggles*]

AH: What else do you feel?

S: Well, I feel warm in my head. Outside of that, I feel almost sorry for being different from heaviness. I feel like my head is getting taller and bigger.

AH: Now roll your eyes. [*Pause*] How about now, what do you experience?

S: Feels like boundless expansion and lightness.

AH: What happened to the tingling in your head?

S: It's still there. Still tingling.

AH: Yeah. Sense that tingling. See how it feels.

S: At once a lot of twinkling and a lot of sparkle. A lot of sparkle.

AH: Right.

S: White Christmas–like twinkling.

AH: White Christmas, interesting. How do they feel, these sparkles? How do they make you feel?

S: Feels good.

AH: Sparkles, huh? Does the sparkle come down to the head? Or is it just over the head?

S: It's around the head, like a ring, like an angel.

AH: Oh, like a ring. I see, like a halo. A halo of sparkles.

S: And also on the top of the head.

AH: See what happens if that tingling flows down into the head.

S: It sparkles.

AH: Um-hmm, sparkles.

S: Sparkles are coming out of my mouth.

AH: Mm-hmm [*chuckles*], sparkles. A sparkling head, a sparkling mouth.

S: My brain is all sparkles. [*Laughter*]

AH: So what's it like when your brain is sparkling?

[*Pause*]

S: Feel a contentment, and sort of drawing a conclusion to a story. There is a feeling of newness, a fresh start.

AH: Newness and freshness. That sounds wonderful. No wonder you felt you had had enough of all the stories. Something new is happening to you.

S: Freshness and brightness, not heaviness and sickness.

AH: I see. So let's see what happens when you stay with the freshness, the newness and brightness.

S: Sparkles.

AH: Sparkles. Good. What happens to your perception?

S: Everybody's eyes start to sparkle.

AH: Ah-ha. So what happens now when the sparkle goes down into the chest?

S: A great big hole first, then the heart starts sparkling.

AH: So when the heart is sparkling, what is the feeling?

S: Exciting. Very happy, full of joy. Full of love.

AH: Right. Happy, light, sparkling, loving, sweet.

S: Just like I was when I was two and three years old.

AH: Oh, I see. So that's what you blamed for your father's death: that you were alive and sparkly at that time.

S: Uh-huh.

AH: So you had to block that part. Very good. Interesting. So you think this should be the end of the chapter?

S: No, there is no end of the chapter. It's the beginning of the chapter.

AH: Oh, it's the beginning of this chapter. Wonderful, that is even better, fresher.

S: Ah-huh, right. The end of the chapter for what is old and dead and decaying.

AH: And you are now beginning a new life.

S: Beginning of a new life for me and a new life for him too. That old relationship is dead. And I feel like I can give him a new life, also. A different life. Because there is a side that I know of him that I didn't see much. It's just the circumstances that made him that way.

AH: It's the other side of him. So you understand him in a different way now.

S: Mm-hmm. I feel more compassionate about him, instead of the ordinary feeling of protecting him. I had to protect him. I had to take care of other people first before I could do things for myself. So that's also important now: that I feel good toward him, but at the same time I can take care of myself.

AH: Sounds nice.

S: I feel happy and bright.

AH: Sparkly and happy and bright. It's a good beginning and a good end. Right? Sounds like a good time to have music.
S: Do you think so?
AH: Don't you think so? [*Laughter*]
S: And champagne. [*Laughter*]
AH: Very good. In a minute. We'll have to get ready. [*Pause*]

That can be the next subject. We can talk about champagne. Why not? That sounds like a good ending for the party. No? Sparkling champagne.

AH comments: *The state of Essence that Yvonne ended up experiencing, that of sparkly and fresh brightness, is one of the ways that Brilliancy manifests. It is interesting to see that here she got connected to a state that is not only light and new—the way she felt as a child—but that this state of lightness and newness is a manifestation of Brilliancy. This indicates that she wanted her father to be light and sparkly and happy, instead of the way he was usually: serious, heavy, and sick. Being manifested not only in the lightness and newness of childhood, but in the lightness and newness of sparkling Brilliancy, which was exactly what she needed her father to be. It is when Essence manifests with such precision that we see the amazing intelligence of Being, which can fulfill us in ways that we can hardly imagine.*

This student might have continued working to see how this manifestation of Essence gives her the father she wanted. I didn't go further, however, because she was in such an exalted state of ecstasy that I didn't want to disturb her state of Essence by bringing in psychological considerations, especially since she was feeling the Brilliancy state as the beginning of a new chapter. In order for her to integrate this essential state, it will be important for her to understand that she is in fact getting the father she wanted. Under normal circumstances, such an insight will arise spontaneously on its own. It would not be surprising if it were to arise later the same day, but in some instances, the process takes much longer to unfold. However, this piece of work did initiate a new chapter in her life. Soon afterward, she separated from a long and conflictual relationship with a man, and met a new man whom she ended up marrying.

That might seem to be a great result, and it is. But from the perspective of our work, the essential value is the fact that she regained contact with the sparkling intelligence of her Being. More accurately, Being functions in such a complete way that its manifestations not only heal our psychological suffering but also become our realization of our spiritual dimension. Being is the true integration and healing of all dimensions, and not only what is called the spiritual. In fact, Being shows that "spiritual" experience is basically the wholeness of our reality.

We've talked about and worked with Brilliancy in many ways. However, we haven't discussed the most obvious thing about Brilliancy, which is the fact of brilliance—the fact of luminosity, of radiance, of brightness, and what that means. What is the feeling of that bright luminosity—the actual radiance, luminescence, and bright brilliance—when it is experienced?

Brilliance means light, and light means more clarity. Light, brilliance, and clarity indicate a certain inner experience, which is the experience of awakeness. The more there is light and brightness, the more you wake up; the more there is dullness, the more you go to sleep. The presence of Brilliancy has an awakening effect, and especially if it is in the head, the experience is of being awakened, of being awake.

This experience of awakening operates on two dimensions simultaneously: the psychological and the phenomenological. Psychologically, to be awake means you are literally awake—like having awakened from long sleep, or from illusions, from dreams, from all the sufferings of ignorance. This is the psychological awakening: Now you see the truth and wake up from the lies and the ignorance that you have been living in. It also means you wake up to your true nature: You now see what and who you are, instead of what you thought you were.

The second sense of awakening is phenomenological. It is the sense of being awake, clear, and bright, as if you just woke up. Suddenly your head is above the clouds, and you start seeing. So this awakening is not only a matter of awakening to some truth; it is a particular state of Being. It is being awake—you actually and literally experience yourself as a bright and brilliant presence. You have not only awakened, but you are the awakeness; you are the awake and brilliant presence.

That is what Brilliancy does when it explodes in the brain. When it explodes in the perceptual centers, it is a sense of waking up in Essence. We've seen Brilliancy in many ways—as intelligence, as synthesis, as completeness, and so on—but now we are seeing it in terms of actual enlightenment. You are awake not only because you have an insight about something, but also by the fact of being the state of awakeness. You feel as if you were a light bulb. You are actually awake, and everything is awake. All your senses are bright and open and clear. You are an awakeness that is awake to everything. This awakeness is also you, your very beingness, the very substance of your soul. Awakeness has to do with a certain manifestation of Brilliancy that I call the state of the brilliant champagne drink. And that's what we want to do an exercise on.

Brilliancy attains more qualities here. It is not just a luminescent, radiant, brilliant, and shining presence, but that fluid, flowing, and shining presence is now the flow of brilliant diamonds. The luminosity attains a crystalline quality, a diamond quality, which gives it a sense of clarity and awakeness.

What do you become clear and awakened to? Your nature, to what is you. You become a light, but the light—by becoming light—becomes awakened to itself as a light. You become a light unto yourself. What you awaken to, which is a specific effect of the brilliant drink, is that your nature itself is pure preciousness itself, the utmost preciousness that there can be. So you realize that your nature is not only luminous and brilliant intelligence, but that it is precious. You see and appreciate now the sense of preciousness of Being, which is your essence and the substance of your consciousness. It is this preciousness that awakens, it is this preciousness that wakes you up, and it is this preciousness that you awaken to. This is the preciousness of Being, of Essence, and the preciousness of what a human being is.

But it is not like you are seeing something that is precious. This is only the Brilliancy itself when it is diamondized, when it is in the diamond or crystalline form. In other words, this presence of diamond Brilliancy is the essential prototype of the quality of preciousness. It is Being manifesting its preciousness, or manifesting as preciousness. That by itself feels like the presence of preciousness.

And that preciousness, that luminous crystalline diamond Brilliancy, or brilliant diamondness, as it flows into the head, is experienced the way Yvonne described in her experience a few minutes ago. As it flows into the head, it gives you not only the experience of awakening, but of awakening with a joyous sense to it. You are so awake, the mind is so awake, your Being is so awake, the soul is so awake, the awakeness is so extreme, that you experience yourself drunk. You are actually drunk on awakeness. You are so awake that you are drunk. You are drunk, but you are drunk on clarity. You are so clear that the clarity is making you drunk. You are drunk on the brilliant diamond drink. You may feel that you have no control, like you've had two bottles of champagne. But what is making you get drunk is how clear you are, not the dullness that we associate with drunkenness. Here it is essential drunkenness. [*Laughter*] You are drunk on the preciousness of your nature, of who you are. And the more you get drunk on this brilliant champagne, the more awake you are. And the more awake you are, the more you are drunk.

This brilliant and luminous drink, this liquid brilliant crystalline presence, gets you drunk with awakeness as it flows into the head. But what happens when it flows into the heart? The crystalline brilliance awakens the heart. Brilliancy becomes like diamonds flowing out of the heart, very teeny little diamonds, like granulated, colored sugar. They are rainbow-colored little diamonds flowing out of the heart from the source that is Brilliancy. When the brilliant drink descends into the heart, it turns into the rainbow-colored, granulated kind of sugar. It attains sweetness, happiness, love, and light, and all the contentments of the heart, but with brilliance to them. The heart feels so happy now that it feels lighter than antigravity; you feel as if you were going to levitate. It's not like you're not heavy, but rather that you have lightness, the opposite of heaviness. Your heart is so light that it's going to fly away. Fly away on what? On happiness, happiness and joy and celebration. So that's really what awakens in the heart.

It's hard to imagine how you can be drunk on clarity, that the clarity, the brightness, the awakeness can become so extreme that you become really and literally drunk.

So, we are going to do a meditation, what we call the brilliant drink meditation. The meditation will be a visualization with music. The visualization has to be what we call an embodied visualization, in the sense that as you visualize, in some sense, you create the presence. It is a creative visualization. You're not just seeing a picture, you're seeing an embodied picture.

You're experiencing, and you're visualizing, a fountain on the top of the head that is brilliant white, so bright that it is difficult for you to look at. You see and experience it flowing down, down, and into the head. As it flows down, it comes down sparkly, like a crystalline kind of brilliant fluid or drink that's so brilliant, white, and clear and bright. And as it flows into and through the head, your head wakes up and becomes bright. You experience yourself bright and brilliant, with the sense of intelligence, completeness, and preciousness. All with the clarity and precision of diamondness. You become a lighted bulb, but the bulb is lighted with some kind of unusual fuel—fuel that is much more powerful than nuclear energy. This power gives it clarity, awakeness, and brightness. But it is a fluid, a fluid that is filling up; and as it fills up, it goes into the heart. And as it goes into the heart, it becomes sweeter and more colorful—all kind of colors. As it permeates all of the body, it becomes a sense of rest, fullness, and contentment.

So there will be a contentment, a rest, and a presence of fullness, but with an unusual kind of lightness that makes you feel that you can't contain it. You feel that you have to get up and dance or sing or something. It feels that it is too light for you to be sitting; sitting somehow doesn't go with that lightness.

So there's the lightness, there's the awakeness, and at the same time there's the very contented and calm kind of presence. As the presence of the Brilliancy weaves through your body and consciousness, and comes down sparkling, it attains different qualities: Here in the head it is an awakeness, a brightness, and a clarity. Here in the heart it is more of a lightness and a happiness and joy. And here in the belly, it is more a sense of presence that's full and contented.

So we will do this meditation, this creative visualization, as if it were a matter of allowing the visualization to happen and take over—spontaneously and on its own—as we listen to the music. You can have your eyes closed.

After the meditation.

S: It is amazing how it is like the sensation of champagne. And the preciousness!

AH: That's what it's like: tasting the brilliant champagne drink. It's like waking up has to do with waking up to the preciousness of what exists.

When you wake up to the preciousness of what exists, the feeling is that of celebration and uplift. You feel amazingly uplifted. You feel celebration in a joyous way—celebration of Being, Essence, Truth. You can even hear the celebration, the preciousness, as it expands the head. The brilliant champagne drink has a music of its own, similar to the music we just heard; but it sounds more like the tinkling of diamonds together. Ever hear that sound, how diamonds tinkle? A very delicate and subtle sound. But the inner sound has a musical tone as well. As it twinkles it tinkles. [*Chuckles*] And the tinkling has an effect on the brain: It relaxes it, expands it, and opens it up from within, as if the cells themselves open up. The more there's the tinkling and the relaxation, the more there's brilliance and intelligence; and the more there is an awakening, the more there is an awareness of the preciousness that lies within us. It's our Being.

The way I see this retreat is that it is not supposed to be complete in the sense that you feel that's it, you've done it, and now you can forget about Brilliancy and its issues. I'm sure it's not going to be like that. It is going to bring up many things about Brilliancy for you so that we can learn about it more, integrate it in our experience. That is everybody's continuing work—in the group, by yourself, in private sessions. Just as when we work with any manifestation of Being, this retreat merely introduces you to this particular one. Your work now has started on Brilliancy and its issues, but you will continue it, on your own, to be able to integrate it as much as possible.

S: When you said, "Well now we're going to go on to the next part; we're going to talk about celebration," I'd been sitting on the chair, you know, feeling real scared about reaching out and telling my story. "Oh, no! I missed my chance . . . maybe next retreat." Then you started talking about the celebration and the diamonds. In some way, I started feeling kind of what Yvonne was talking about—little sparkles all around.

AH: Sparkles, um-hmm.

S: And you started talking about exactly what I was feeling, and I was thinking, "How do you know what I'm feeling? [*Laughter*] Are you like this all the time? That's impossible." And I realized that part of it was that in the first day of the retreat, I didn't have anything unfold at all. And it wasn't until we did one of the first exercises that I realized that I'd been holding on to not wanting my father. And out of that acknowledgment, and feeling all this wanting, things somehow turned inside out. And now I'm in this place where my fingers are tingling. I did feel drunk, but the room is starting to expand and everything is real crystal clear.

AH: The wanting, obviously, is the biggest thing that people had to feel. One of the big things that people were resisting was actually feeling the wanting for father. Allowing that wanting, as you can see, really started the process. What you said about turning inside out is then exactly what happens. The soul first wants by directing itself outward for the father. But the resolution is a turning inside out, turning to its inside for the father. First you feel the pain as you turn inside out, or outside in. But continue to turn inward, and you realize that the completeness and the preciousness are there. But in order to be able to make the turn, to even allow yourself to want it, you first have to deal with the issues of father. I am glad you shared your story with us. Great!

S: Yeah, it's wonderful. For a moment I thought I was going to lose it. I thought, "Oh no!" And when you started talking about these images and the rainbow, and letting it go down to the heart, I thought, "Okay let's go down to my heart." Then I thought, "No, no, don't push it; it might go away, might not come back again." [*Laughter*]

AH: [*Chuckles*] I understand.

Another student speaks.

S: It was interesting what you said about wanting the inside of your body because I've had this feeling all day about wanting to dig in, just to scratch it out and get inside, yeah.

AH: Yeah, the wanting can get really powerful when we really feel an all-out kind of wanting, a wholehearted, instinctual everything.

S: And just being able to recognize it seems to do a lot.

AH: Yeah. It's important to feel the wanting because what we're wanting, what we're missing, is much more than our physical father. Father represents it, is a symbol for it. All that we have talked about stands behind that symbol. So the wanting, obviously, is very deep, very powerful.

S: Yeah, feels really powerful, almost instinctual.

AH: Um-hmm, everything.

S: Oh yeah, it's like you can't say what it is because it's so much.

AH: Yes. [*Pause*]

It is interesting to see what the presence of Brilliancy does, the various ways that it functions as the intelligence of Being. I was planning for this meditation to be the end of the retreat. But then Yvonne's work brought her to the sparkling presence before I said anything about it. At that point, we had only thirty minutes left. So in a sense, she reminded me of what we were going to do, without knowing what she was doing. [*Laughter*]

Okay, see you next time.

About the Diamond Approach

The Diamond Approach is taught by Ridhwan teachers who are ordained by the Ridhwan Foundation. Once ordained, Ridhwan teachers are also ministers of the Ridhwan Foundation. They are trained by DHAT Institute, the educational arm of the Ridhwan Foundation, through an extensive seven-year program, which is in addition to their work and participation as students of the Diamond Approach. The ordination process ensures that each person has a good working understanding of the Diamond Approach and a sufficient capacity to teach it before being authorized to be a Ridhwan teacher.

The Diamond Approach described in this book is taught in group and private settings in California and Colorado by Ridhwan teachers. For information, contact:

Ridhwan
P.O. Box 2747
Berkeley, CA 94702-0747

Ridhwan School
P.O. Box 18166
Boulder, CO 80308-8166

Satellite groups operate in other national and international locations. For information about these groups, or to explore starting a group in your area, taught by certified Ridhwan teachers, write to the Berkeley address above or visit www.ridhwan.org.

Diamond Approach is a registered service mark of the Ridhwan Foundation.

Index

abandonment, 146
Absolute, the, 32–33, 65–66
action
    intelligence and, 103
    right/correct, 93–94
    thinking and, 39
aloneness, 146, 195, 198, 241.
    See also emptiness
analysis, 70–72
    capacity for, 96–97
anxiety, 29, 77. *See also* fear
attachment, 208
    to people, 212
attunement, 81
awakening, 296–99
    psychological and phenomenological, 296
awareness, 42. *See also* consciousness; self-awareness and self-reflection

balance, 84–85
beauty, 12, 97

Being, 9–10, 42, 59, 290–91, 296
    aspects of, associated with parents, 173
    brilliance of, 66–68
    intelligence of, 70
    qualities of, 31, 32, 65
    as the truth of reality, 41
beingness, 290
belly center, 242–44, 248–52
blackness/black space, 66, 67, 205–6.
    See also colors; darkness
bliss, 28–29, 35, 56, 57
brain and intelligence, 22, 96
brightness, 117–18, 125, 130, 132. *See also* luminescence/luminosity
brilliance, 15–16, 255, 256, 296. *See also specific topics*
    of Being, 66–68
    meaning of, 296
Brilliancy, xi, xiii, xiv, 16–18, 88, 182.
    See also specific topics
    Almaas's first experience of, 130
    applying and integrating it into one's life, 113

Brilliancy *(continued)*
   brilliance and, 15–16, 255–56
   capacity to tolerate and embody, 22–23, 105, 179, 180
   as catalyst, 29
   diamondized, 297
   diamonds compared with, 298
   experience of, 28–29, 34, 54, 67, 105, 112–13
   experiential qualities of, 39
   vs. exquisiteness, 20
   fear of other people's seeing one's, 106–7
   intelligence and, 17, 53, 255–57
   intensity of, 31
   is who we are, 125
   as masculine, 247–48, 252, 253
   most people never experience, 23
   vs. other aspects of Being, 31
   presence of, 18, 34, 47–48, 59, 124. *See also* presence
   prevalence of, 23
   projected onto one's father, 133–36, 168, 178
   pure, 255–56
   qualities of persons embodying, 23–24, 296–97
   resistances and blockages against, 108, 128
   as threatening, 118
   true quality of, 183
   ways it is experienced and recognized, 53
   yearning for, 49
Brilliancy diamond, 69, 75–78
Buddha, Four Noble Truths of, 208

castration, 125–26, 191, 221
Catholic Church, 187, 188
change, 208–9
children, 108–12. *See also* parent(s); sexual reproduction
   discouraged from and punished for being brilliant, 118–21, 126
Cocoon (film), 254
colors. *See also* blackness/black space
   brilliance of, 16, 18–19, 66–67
   of essential aspects, 53
   of fire/flames, 243, 244
   of heart aspects of essence, 57
compassion, 209–10, 214–16
completeness, 54–60, 273–74. *See also* unity
   and the Absolute, 32–33, 65
   Brilliancy and, 33, 83, 258
   characteristics associated with, 55–56
   contrasted with other kinds of experiences, 258–59. *See also* incompleteness
   intelligence as the functioning of, 58
   longing for, 58
   meaning of, 55, 56
   nature of, 258–59
   perfection and, 65–67
   sense of, 55
   as universal, 60
consciousness, 101, 125, 257, 258
   awareness, presence, and, 42–43
   stream of, 50
contentment, 53–54, 56. *See also* completeness
control, emotional, 152–53
creative thinking, 95

darkness. *See also* blackness/black space
   feeling/experience of, 195, 198–99. *See also* emptiness

Index 307

defense mechanisms. *See* projection; splitting
deficiency. *See also* holes and gaps in psyche; incompleteness
   sense of, 54–55, 57, 162–63, 207
   soul, 22–23
delusions, 143
development, 182
dialectic, Hegel's. *See* synthesis: thesis, antithesis, and
Diamond Approach, vii–x, 49, 176, 303
   methodology of, ix, x
   synthesis and, 26
   theory of holes in, 117, 118. *See also* emptiness
   universal message of, x
Diamond Guidance, 69–75, 82
   Brilliancy and, 68–69, 81, 83
   faculties used by, 70–71
   nature of, 34, 65, 115
   ways it functions intelligently, 68–70
Diamond Vehicle, 34
diamondness
   brilliant, 297
   of Guidance, 71
   of love, 231
diamonds, Brilliancy compared with, 298
differentiation, Brilliancy prior to, 257
discriminating capacity, 74–76, 96–97
discrimination, 13
disorganization, feeling of, 157
doubting oneself, 110, 198

ecstasy, 57, 253. *See also* bliss
ego, 43–44
   vs. presence, 43

Einstein, Albert, 97–98
elegance and intelligence, 12
emotional deficiency, 162–63. *See also* deficiency
empathic capacity, 106, 114
emptiness, feeling of, 116–18. *See also* darkness
   allowing oneself to experience the, 140, 147–48, 205–7, 222, 265–66, 278
   behind wanting, 287
   fear, object relations, and, 149, 212–13
   indicates lack of a quality of Being, 290
   presence and, 291
   transformed into feeling of fullness, 278–80
enlightenment, 46
   turning point on path to, 41
equality, 84–85
equanimity, 84–85
Essence, 9–11, 45, 76, 106, 215
   aspects of, 10, 31–35, 53, 54, 116, 124. *See also specific aspects*
   is who we are, 124
   manifesting, 2, 34, 100–101, 106, 208, 295
   openness to, 106
   as presence, 42, 43, 76
   presence of, 42, 47, 233
   qualities of, 2, 31, 256
   spiritual dimension of, 232
   teaching, 106
   transforms, 231
Essence-of-the-Essence, 31
Essential Identity, 82. *See also* Point
evolution, xiv, 182
existing, 141. *See also* Being
   and feeling like one doesn't exist, 140, 141

expansion, experience of, 128, 129, 132, 155, 168
experience, 200. *See also specific topics*
   understanding the truth of present, 127
exquisiteness, 20, 21
external orientation, 105
eyes, 183

fake brilliancy, 36
falsehoods, 63–64, 85–86
father-child relationships, 132–36, 144–45, 244. *See also* Oedipus complex; parent(s)
   internalized, preventing the experience of Brilliancy, 245
   mothers and, 174, 175, 201
   what lies beneath, 160
father image
   projecting onto, 133–36, 154, 168, 178
   split into "good father" and "bad father," 137, 139, 179, 181
Father of the Point, 181–82
father(s), 201. *See also under* longing; love
   anger at, 168–70
   Brilliancy and, 179–81, 204, 244, 245
   functions of, 178–79, 201, 202
   God and, 177–78
   idealization of, 193. *See also* father image
   identification with, 165, 167–69, 179–80
   loss of, 205–7. *See also* longing: for one's father; separating from one's parents
   roles of, 174–76, 201

fear, 149, 153. *See also* anxiety
   dealing with, 146, 156
   of father, 209–11
   misunderstanding as root of, 148
   recognition of self and, 209
   of seeing, 217–18
femininity. *See* gender and gender differences
fire and flames, 243, 244
flexibility, 108–9
Four Noble Truths, 208
Freud, Sigmund, 189

gender and gender differences, xiii, 190, 247–48, 252–53
genitals, 253–54, 267–71. *See also* belly center; castration
Gestalt therapy, 49
God
   Brilliancy and, 39
   as father, 177
   intelligence and thinking of, 39
   relationship with, 177–78
   will of, 182
gold, 243
grief. 132, 203, 205. *See also* longing
groundedness, 242–43
group field, 8
guidance, 175. *See also* Diamond Guidance
   intelligent, 72–75, 103
guilt, 184–86, 188–89. *See also* superego attacks

hallucinations, 143
happiness. *See* pleasure
hara (energetic center), 242, 244. *See also* belly center

hate and love, 170–71, 239. *See also* splitting
Hegel, Georg Wilhelm Friedrich, 37
holes and gaps in psyche, 54–55, 57, 117, 149, 213, 217. *See also* deficiency; emptiness; incompleteness
homosexuality, 191

identification, 142, 143, 179. *See also* self; self-image
  with one's self-image, 64
  with parents, 176, 177, 185, 190–91. *See also under* father(s)
identity, 85, 142, 152. *See also* Point; self; self-image
illumination, 14, 15, 66, 73, 100. *See also* luminescence/luminosity
incest, 189–90
incompleteness, 54–60, 273–74
  barriers to feeling, 59
  completeness contrasted with, 258–59
  confronting and tolerating, 60
  feeling vs. being incomplete, 60
  as path toward completeness, 60
  ways of avoiding the sense of, 259–60
innocence, 108, 113
inquiry, 74, 83, 84, 92, 196–97
  intelligence in, 69–70
  open-ended, 91–92
insight, 26–28, 36, 73, 74, 85
  as continuous process, 82
integration, 29, 32. *See also* synthesis
intellect
  intelligence and, 115
  synthesis and, 30

intelligence, xi–xii. *See also specific topics*
  analytic, 70–71
  applying one's, 97, 101, 102
  being, 124–25
  cannot be taught, 95
  direct experience of, xii
  essence of, 2–3, 17
  facets of, 67–69
  as the functioning of completeness, 58
  functions of, 94–95, 99–103
  inherited/innate, 22
  in inquiry, 69–70
  longing for, 58
  vs. mental capacity, 102–4
  nature of, xi–xiii, 10–12, 95–96, 98–101, 103, 124, 255
  as organic, 13–15, 38–39, 95–96
  penetrating, 86–88, 99–100
  question of, 101
  signs of the presence of, 99
  smoothness of, 99–100
  source/origin of, xii
  synthetic, 71–72
  unconscious beliefs about, 102–4
  of universe, 38–39
intelligent guidance, 72–75, 103
internalization, 179. *See also* identification
IQ, xi, 11, 17, 22

joy. *See* bliss; pleasure
judgments, 59, 112, 185, 187, 196. *See also* superego attacks

kath (energetic center), 242, 244. *See also* belly center

learning, 94, 148
letting go, 144, 150, 184–85, 208–9. *See also* separating from one's parents; surrender
liberation
  prerequisites for, 63
  understanding and, 63–66
light, 66–67, 125, 296. *See also* brilliance; colors; illumination; luminescence/luminosity
lightness and light-headedness, feelings of, 171, 172, 299
logos, viii
longing, 145–46
  for completeness, 58
  emptiness and, 287
  for intelligence, 58
  for love, 145, 195–98, 235
  for one's father, 164–65, 167, 169, 177, 180, 187, 202–4. *See also* father-child relationships; separating from one's parents
  for one's mother, 195
  sexual, 187–89
Love, 57, 231–33
  diamond quality, 231
  experience of essential, 233
  gender and, 253
love, 12, 95, 145, 197, 219. *See also under* longing
  from fathers, 227–32
  hate and, 170–71, 239. *See also* splitting
  identification and, 185
Loving-kindness, 10
luminescence/luminosity, 18, 20–21, 68–69, 86, 117, 297. *See also* illumination
luminous fluid of Brilliancy, compared with cerebrospinal fluid, 21–22

Mahler, Margaret, 173
manifestation and the manifest, 33, 34
masculinity. *See* gender and gender differences
mathematics, 97
meditation, 298–99
mental realm and synthesis, 30
Merging Essence, 173–75
methodology, viii
mother-child relationships, 173–74, 184, 186. *See also* parent(s)
mother(s). *See also* parent(s)
  longing for, 195
  roles of, 173–76

nondual presence, 77
  stages of realizing, 77–78

object relations, 211–15, 280
objects and presence, 45
Oedipus complex, 189–91, 216, 220–21
oneness, 26, 78. *See also* synthesis
"organic," 13–14. *See also under* intelligence

parent(s). *See also* father(s); mother(s)
  aspects of Being associated with, 173
  discouraging children from being brilliant, 118–21, 125–26
  lack of love from, 145
  and parent-child relationships, 109–12, 130–32. *See also* father-child relationships
  separating from, 128–29, 132, 144, 158

split into "good parent" and "bad parent," 137, 139, 140. *See also under* father image
penetrating capacity, 86–88, 99–100
perfection(s), 65–66
Personal Essence, 32, 35, 215, 219
personality, 83
planning, 39
Platonic forms, 31, 32
pleasure, 28–29, 35, 56, 253. *See also* bliss
Point, the, 82, 83, 181–82. *See also* Father of the Point
potency, 125, 132
presence, 41–51, 279–80. *See also under* Brilliancy; Essence
   all-inclusive experience of, 47–48
   awareness of one's, 42
   of Brilliancy, 18, 47–48, 59
   consciousness, awareness, and, 42–43
   vs. ego, 43
   emptiness and, 291
   Essence as, 42, 43, 76
   experience of, 45, 46, 76, 147, 159
   invoking, 8
   meaning of, 41–42
   nondual, 77–78
   objects and, 45
   realization of oneself as, 41
   teaching and, 6–7
   time and, 44–48
projection, onto one's father, 133–36, 154, 168, 178
psychological realm. *See* spiritual and psychological realms

purity, 271
   presence of, 21, 175

radiance, 20, 33, 47, 48
realization, 35–36, 41, 158
   prerequisites for, 63
Red essence, 71, 77
relativity, Einstein's general theory of, 98
resistance, 197, 200
responsibility, 175, 176
Ridhwan Foundation, 303
Ridhwan School, ix
rigidity, 108–9
role models. *See* father(s): identification with; identification: with parents

sacrum, 222–23
sadness, 195–96. *See also* emptiness
self, 141. *See also* Point; true self
   sense of, 116, 205–7
self-awareness and self-reflection, 42–45, 48
self-centering, 50
self-doubt, 110, 198
self-image. *See also* identification; identity; Point
   identification with one's, 64
separating from one's parents, 128–29, 132, 168, 169, 192. *See also* longing: for one's father
separation anxiety, 77
separation-individuation, 173, 189
sexual abuse, 189–90
sexual reproduction, 248–52
sexuality, 187–88, 248–52. *See also* gender and gender differences; genitals; Oedipus complex

shame and disgust, 152–54
simplicity, 97
small-group format, 90–91
solar plexus, 223
soul, 176–77
    holes and gaps in, 54–55. *See also* deficiency; emptiness; incompleteness
    truth and the, 63–64
Soul Child, 204
space and spaciousness, 214, 215
Spacecruiser Inquiry: True Guidance for the Inner Journey (Almaas), 61
spinal cord, 224
spine, 262
spiritual and psychological realms
    as inseparable, 232, 257–58
    synthesis of, 26, 257
spiritual immaturity, 35–36
spiritual realization, 35–36. *See also* realization
splitting, 137, 139, 140, 143, 170, 172, 179, 181
    way to resolve, 143
"strangeness," 85
stream of consciousness, 50
Strength, 31, 32, 71, 270
subject/object dichotomy, 42–43. *See also* objects and presence
suffering, 208
superego attacks, 59–60, 83, 185, 187. *See also* judgments
support, 290–91
surrender, 150–51. *See also* letting go
symbiotic phase (separation-individuation), 112–13
synthesis, 25–33, 36–38, 74–75
    of all aspects, Brilliancy as, 33–34, 54, 55
    analysis and, 25, 30, 70–72, 74, 75, 77
    meaning of, 25, 33
    mental, 30
    nature of, 25–26, 31
    prerequisites for, 30
    presence of Brilliancy as prototype of, 71
    thesis, antithesis, and, 37–38
    and understanding, 27–28
synthetic capacity, 28, 29, 39–40, 74, 76, 82
    of Brilliancy, 36, 58, 257–58
synthetic intelligence, 70–72

tan-t'ien (energetic center), 242. *See also* belly center
teachers, 126–27
    embodying Brilliancy, 106
teaching, viii. *See also* inquiry
    presence and, 6–7
    and timing of presentations, 90
    unfolding of, 7
teaching formats, 5–6
    small and large-group formats, 90–91
thereness, 290
thinking and action, 39
time and presence, 44–48
timelessness, 48, 49
    yearning to merge with, 49
transformation, 148
true self, 182. *See also* self
    being vs. not being one's, 123
truth, 85, 121–23, 127
    being cut off from the, 120–24
    intelligence and finding the, 98
    intention to see the, 196
    and the soul, 63–64

understanding, 27–28, 148, 196. *See also* inquiry
   liberation and, 63–66
   one's present experience, 49–50
unification, 29, 74–75. *See also* synthesis
unity, 26, 29–30, 54, 72, 74. *See also* synthesis
   discriminating the underlying, 78–86
universe, intelligence of, 38–39

visualization, creative, 298–99
void. *See* emptiness
vulnerability, 247

wanting. *See* longing
"weirdness," 85
wholeness. *See* completeness
Will, 75

yearning. *See* longing